ALONE TOGETHER

ALONE TOGETHER

by ELENA BONNER

Translated from the Russian
by Alexander Cook

Alfred A. Knopf   *New York*   1986

To Andrei, Mother, the children,
and to all those who helped to make my journey
from Gorky to the West possible

THIS IS A BORZOI BOOK
PUBLISHED BY ALFRED A. KNOPF, INC.

ISBN: 0-394-55835-9

LC number: 86-82152

Manufactured in the United States of America
FIRST EDITION

Illustrations

following page 148

Elena Bonner in uniform, 1943.

Bonner as a medical student in Leningrad, 1949. (Arieh Levran)

Bonner and Yuri Shikhanovich visit friends in exile in Uvat, Siberia, 1971.

Sakharov in Gorky, 1982.

First photograph of Sakharov in Gorky, allegedly taken June 15, 1984, the fourteenth day of a hunger strike. *(Bild Zeitung)*

Bonner in Gorky. *(Bild Zeitung)*

Two photographs of Sakharov in the Gorky apartment, November 1985.

Sakharov in Gorky, December 1983.

A policeman on duty outside the Sakharovs' Gorky apartment.

The yard behind the Sakharovs' apartment building.

Sakharov and Bonner on the balcony of their apartment, March 1985.

Portrait of Sakharov and Bonner taken in a state photographic studio, October 1985.

A forged postcard from Bonner to the family in Massachusetts.

Sakharov undergoing a physical examination. *(Bild Zeitung)*

Bonner with grandson Matvei on arrival in Boston, December 1985. (Boston *Globe*)

Bonner talking to her mother, Ruth. (Richard Sobol/SIPA)

Christmas in Newton, with grandchildren Matvei and Anya. (Richard Sobol/SIPA)

A family portrait. (Richard Sobol/SIPA)

Bonner and her son, Alexei Semyonov, visiting Washington, April 1986.

At Disney World with grandchildren. (Richard Sobol/SIPA)

Bonner writing *Alone Together* in Newton. (Richard Sobol/SIPA)

After her meeting with French Prime Minister Jacques Chirac in Paris, May 1986. (Richard Sobol/SIPA)

The view from Bonner's Moscow apartment. (Richard Sobol/SIPA)

Bonner with British Prime Minister Margaret Thatcher at 10 Downing Street, May 1986. (Richard Sobol/SIPA)

A meal with friends Emil Shinberg and Galya Yevtushenko, June 1986. (Richard Sobol/SIPA)

Bonner in the train station, and on the train to Gorky. (Richard Sobol/SIPA)

Publisher's Note

Elena Bonner wrote this book while on six months' leave of absence from her Gorky exile. In that time, she had multiple coronary bypass surgery and surgical procedures to relieve atherosclerosis in her right leg and to remove a benign tumor from her lip.

Since her return to the USSR on June 2, 1986, her family has been able to communicate with her only by means of censored mail and telephone calls, and she has been unable to review the proofs of this book.

Minor changes have been made in the manuscript by the translator. Footnotes, unless otherwise indicated, have been added by the translator or by the author's son-in-law, Efrem Yankelevich.

Foreword

Why did I write this book? I could say briefly: I wanted to. I wanted to tell about what has happened during the last three years. Doing it the way many people do it—using a tape recorder—did not work for me: It's one thing to chat with friends and quite another to dictate a book. I had to sit down in a traditional fashion at a typewriter and think. And it became clear that "wanting to" wasn't enough—I had to recall and write, not the way things seemed, but the way they were. All of this will be of help to Andrei, so I consider it my duty. No one else was with him, and Andrei himself is so efficiently isolated in Gorky that he cannot tell this story.

This book was supposed to be about Andrei, but it turned out to be about me. However, every word was written for him.

In two days a TWA jet will carry me from the New World to the Old, and in another week I will have returned to the old world of unfreedom, familiar and joyless. At least I will leave these pages in freedom.

Elena Bonner
Newton, Massachusetts
May 21, 1986

ALONE TOGETHER

I

The plane hangs suspended in midair somewhere over the middle of America. Everything below moves so slowly it seems to be standing still. The sky of absolute blue seems to be standing, too—the illusion of tranquillity comes from the complete absence of clouds. I have never flown in such clear weather, with such total visibility. There are mountains, tongues of snow and glaciers; dark landslides of forest; taut-stretched threads of roads; shining saucers of lakes; little houses suitable for dolls. Occasionally, I see large expanses without dwellings—like Russia, America is not totally inhabited.

Midway in my path from San Francisco to Boston, I am returning. People come home, but I, where am I going? Halfway between sky and earth. How do you find a point of reference, if it is all "sky"? This is also the midpoint of my trip to Italy and the United States —not in space, but in time. Moscow allowed me ninety days, and now—incredible generosity—it has added another three months. Thus, I have one hundred eighty days of freedom, and I am right in the middle. The middle of freedom. I don't think I ever met anyone who knew exactly how much he was allowed and when, while for me it was all written down and sealed on my passport.

Of course I do not know what I am, and therefore, I do not know what to expect upon my return (to where? home?). What will I receive in exchange for my foreign-travel passport—documents of an exile or an ordinary internal passport? If I am an exile, I should have been given a travel document indicating that I was being released for medical treatment with a temporary suspension of my sentence; we have such a provision in our laws. But perhaps I have been pardoned? After all, I did apply to "the Highest Name," as they used to say in the olden days. Wherever I look—it's the middle. Beginning—middle—end.

The middle of my trip. But it's only according to Western concepts that a trip begins with a person setting off—getting into a car, train, plane, or walking. (Incidentally, do people walk here? I keep seeing running Americans. I have the feeling that the whole country is an adolescent running to school.) In our country you start on a long journey with OVIR, the Division of Visas and Permissions. There are regional, city, oblast, republic, and all-union offices, and they fall under the auspices of the MVD, the Ministry of Internal Affairs. It has existed, I think, as long as the government, and in San Francisco I just met one of its clients from long ago. She was born in the United States. In the twenties her parents brought her with them to the USSR to build communism. She applied to leave in 1937. She received permission in 1941, just before the war. Now she teaches at Berkeley.

So, I went to the regional OVIR on September 25, 1982. The date is connected to a man, about whom my seatmate on the plane is reading right now. This is not a literary device—it's really true; everyone is reading about Anatoly Shcharansky* now. I had made a special trip from Gorky, so that his mother, Ida Milgrom,† could meet with foreign correspondents at my house. We were going to announce that Shcharansky would begin a hunger strike on September 27. At that time, it was difficult for Tolya's family to find a place in Moscow where they could make the announcement.

I came early, and I had two free days, just enough time to get and fill out the forms, two copies, on a typewriter, without mistakes or corrections. I had the photos ready (oh, how horrible-looking I'd become!). The need to think about the trip had arisen in the spring, when the flu led to a worsening of uveitis in my left eye, and the pressure in my right one began jumping around.

Everything went smoothly at OVIR, since I had a copy of my

---

*Anatoly Shcharansky (1948–   ). Refusenik and member of Moscow Helsinki Group. Arrested March 1977 and sentenced in July 1978 to three years prison and 10 years labor camp for espionage. Released in a publicized spy swap and emigrated to Israel in February 1986.

†Ida Milgrom (1908–   ). Anatoly Shcharansky's mother.

father's death certificate. I had learned in years past that leaving blank the space for the place of death always upset the lower ranks of the Ministry of Internal Affairs (MVD) who accepted the documents. They did not notice the other discrepancies in the death certificate, which listed the date of death as 1939 while the entry of death was made in 1955—whose job was it to remember that?*

I was glad I had applied—it was a step taken. But even though I knew there would be difficulties ahead before we obtained permission, I could not imagine what the path would be like. And now in a plane over the middle of America, my seatmate is reading a newspaper. I see the photograph: a smiling Anatoly (who doesn't look bad —they fattened him up before the exchange) and, leaning against his shoulder, a serious Avital, his wife.† My seatmate to the left is napping, in his lap a copy of *U.S. News and World Report*‡ with a cover photo of a man with a thin, exhausted face and lowered eyelids —there it is, Andrei's path to obtaining my trip to America. What he describes in his letter to the president** of the Soviet Academy of Sciences is only part of what happened to us over the three years since the day I applied at OVIR. Everything that he did not tell, I must tell now.

I have very little time, and I do not have very much strength. I do not want to remember. I want to forget, because the life we live there is so different from normal life in general and life here. The story is not a happy one, and it is hard to make it entertaining. These are not memoirs—everything is too near and too painful for that to be the case. A diary would be good here, but in our life it is impossible to write a diary; it is bound to end up in the wrong hands. More than anything else, this is a chronicle. Since I do not have the time to turn it into what could be called a book, let those who want to read it treat it accordingly. I will try to be maximally accurate in the presentation.

---

*See Appendix I for a copy of the death certificate.
†Avital Shcharansky (born: Natalia Shtiglits, 1950–   ). Wife of Anatoly Shcharansky. Emigrated to Israel in 1974.
‡*U.S. News & World Report*, February 24, 1986. A second feature article on Sakharov was published in the March 3 issue.
**Anatoly Alexandrov (1903–   ). Atomic physicist, president of the USSR Academy of Sciences since 1975.

For me this is also a postscript to Andrei's memoirs. I was their initiator, and later typist, editor, and nursemaid. I had to do everything as the nursemaid—to make sure the manuscript survived and became a book and reached its readers—and to tell that story alone would call for another volume of memoirs, or perhaps a mystery book (should we change genres?); but the time for that has not come.

As the completion date for his book Andrei chose February 15, 1983—my birthday. We celebrated that day alone: we were both dressed up, there were flowers, Andryusha had drawn posters, and I cooked with inspiration, as if we were expecting the whole family. There were many telegrams from Moscow, Leningrad, from the children and Mother. It took us three days to eat what I cooked. But the time came to restock our larder and I went to the market—by Gorky standards the day was warm and clear. When I got back and Andrei opened the door for me, I did not recognize him. He was freshly shaven, wearing a gray suit, pink shirt, gray tie, and even the pearl stickpin I had given him during our first Gorky winter on the tenth anniversary of our life together.

"What happened?"

In response he silently handed me a telegram. It was from Newton, Massachusetts. "LITTLE GIRL SASHA BORN. LIZA* FEELS FINE. EVERYONE SENDS KISSES." When I had read the telegram, Andrei said: "That's not a baby, it's a hunger strike."† And whenever we get new pictures of the children from Newton, he calls Sasha "our hunger strike."

The previous fall I had begun to be aware of my heart; of course, it had hurt occasionally before, but only in passing somehow. I was aware of it, but I never thought much about it, I really didn't have time to think. By the fall of 1982, I had made over one hundred

---

*Elizaveta (Liza) Alexeyeva (1955–   ). Computer scientist. Married Elena Bonner's son Alexei in a proxy wedding ceremony at Butte, Montana, in June 1981. Was permitted to emigrate and join her husband in December 1981, after the Sakharovs conducted a seventeen-day hunger strike. Now lives in Westwood, Massachusetts, with her husband and their daughter, Sasha.

†In the fall of 1981, Sakharov and Bonner went on a seventeen-day hunger strike demanding permission for Liza Alexeyeva, the wife of Alexei Semyonov, Bonner's son, to leave the USSR.

Gorky-Moscow round trips. Of our friends, Vladimir Tolts* had already left, Yura Shikhanovich'st apartment had been searched, Alyosha Smirnov‡ and before him Vanya Kovalyov** had been arrested. I would bring two large chiller bags with perishable foods and all sorts of other things from Moscow, necessary and not too necessary, while Andryusha worked on his memoirs, periodically rewriting sections. Not because of the author's severity, nor because of the grumblings of his first reader, first editor, and first typist (all of them me)—no! Because of another's will and another's hand. Sections kept vanishing. Once from the apartment in Moscow; once stolen along with his bag at the dental clinic in Gorky; once that same autumn from our parked car, which had been broken into, with Andrei knocked out by some drug. Each time he rewrote his book. Each time there was something new—sometimes better written, sometimes not.

The day after his bag was stolen at the dental clinic, Andrei met me at the train station. He looked haggard, as if he were suffering from insomnia, a serious disease, or prolonged pain. His lips were trembling and his voice broke: "Lusia, they stole it." I realized right away that he meant his bag, but he spoke with such acute pain that I thought he meant it had happened right there at the railroad station.

The time when the bag was taken from our car, Andrei walked toward me with the expression of a man who has just learned of the death of someone close to him. But after a few days—all he needed was for us to be together—he would sit down at his desk again. Andrei has a talent, I call it his "main talent," to finish what he starts.

---

*Vladimir Tolts. Historian, worked on samizdat news bulletins. Emigrated in 1982 and now lives in Munich.

†Yuri Shikhanovich (Shikh) (1933–   ). Mathematician. Arrested in November 1983 for editing *A Chronicle of Current Events* and sentenced in September 1984 to five years labor camp and five years exile.

‡Alexei (Alyosha) Smirnov (1951–   ). Computer engineer, arrested in September 1982 for working on *A Chronicle of Current Events*, and sentenced in May 1983 to six years labor camp and four years exile.

**Ivan (Vanya) Kovalyov (1954–   ). Engineer, member of Moscow Helsinki Group, worked on samizdat news bulletins. Arrested August 1981 and sentenced April 1982 to five years labor camp and five years exile.

What I had to do was to develop a talent "to save," and I developed it, God knows. I tried to make sure that "manuscripts don't burn."* And to make sure that Andrei's writing would not rot in the cellars of Lubyanka or some other prison.

So there. In September Tolya Shcharansky's mother and I announced his hunger strike, in October I commemorated Political Prisoners Day† by myself (a press conference), and in November I was no longer simply aware of my heart in Gorky, but could feel it burning in flames.

I spent almost a week in bed; I couldn't do anything. I didn't want to do anything, even read, and certainly not type on the Erika typewriter, which, as Galich's‡ song has it, "takes four copies."

In December, on the eighth, I went to Moscow. I was searched on the train, which was shunted onto a siding far beyond the city. As the train moved, I looked out the window while the investigator read me the search warrant, and a song kept going through my head: "We are peaceful people, but our armored train is on a siding." I tried to remember who had written the words, whose they were. Andrei writes at length about that search in his memoirs, so I won't go into it here. They took away a large chunk of his manuscript— burned again!

About my heart. As I walked beside the tracks, I had to drag myself along. And then there was a staircase, which seemed insurmountable to me, to the bridge over the railroad tracks. I felt ill on the bridge, and then with the return of consciousness came another line: "And our girl walks by in her greatcoat, walking along burning Kakhovka Street." Lord, it's by Mikhail Arkadyevich Svetlov.** We used to dance to that song, playing it on the gramophone; we had to turn the handle. And Svetlov would walk by and say, "Come on,

---

*From Mikhail Bulgakov's *The Master and Margarita.*

†October 30. An unofficial event established in 1974. The press conference was usually held in the Sakharov apartment, but by 1983 almost none of the customary participants remained in Moscow.

‡Alexander Galich (Ginzburg) (1919–1977). Actor, playwright, and poet, Galich was best known as a balladeer. Expelled from the Writers Union in 1971 after signing a number of protest documents, he emigrated in 1974 and settled in Paris.

**Mikhail Svetlov (1903–1964). Russian poet and playwright.

kids, pick a different song, why don't you dance to Altauzen* instead; his name is more appropriate—it's American, his name is Jack." We were dancing the foxtrot. And back then that spelled America for sure. And probably an American name was a disparagement—a foreign influence. However, I don't know about influences; I did dance the foxtrot, but I wasn't aware of any influences—I wasn't interested.

What they confiscated on the train was the fourth loss. And there were others to come. So don't be surprised that I call myself a talent. The book will come, it already exists.

After the search I managed to get back to the city and to send Andrei a telegram about it. And then I hurried home to Chkalov Street. I was in a hurry, because Ida Petrovna was due. I had promised to call in the foreign press corps, so that she could tell them what was happening to Tolya. No sooner had I washed than I heard noise on the stairs. When I opened the door two policemen were trying to push Tolya's brother Leonid back into the elevator. I shouted, "Wait for me on the street. I'll come down to you." But I didn't know if I had the strength to go out. And what if they didn't let me out? But they did, and I went down and we decided to meet with the press on the street. We walked in the direction of the train station. The road was uphill. I felt I could not walk; I was nauseated, my legs were rubbery, and I was embarrassed in front of Ida Petrovna and Lenya. We reached the trolley bus stop and rode to Tsvetnoi Boulevard. There, with the puppet theater in the background, we telephoned the press and waited, and then talked with them on the boulevard about Tolya, about my search, and about many other things.

The next day I decided that I had to think about my heart. From the telephone booth near our house, which still worked then, I called for a doctor. An unfamiliar doctor came and made an appointment for an examination at the Academy of Sciences Hospital. The electrocardiogram revealed no changes. I believed the results, thinking that all my discomfort was caused by nerves, and that I had to go

---

*Yakov (Jack) Altauzen (1907–1942). Poet, killed in action during World War II.

on living as I had been, even if my heart made me constantly aware of itself.

"Unfortunately, birthdays come but once a year," but in 1983 I celebrated mine twice—once in Moscow and once in Gorky. To the first celebration Shikh (Shikhanovich) brought Nikolai Yakovlev's* book *CIA Target—The USSR*. Belka† was very upset that he brought it, she had read it but hadn't said anything to me. That is her usual way —not to upset people. I took the book to Gorky with me. I did not read it for a long time; I didn't want to—the very thought of reading it was repugnant, and I couldn't get over my fastidiousness.

Andrei read it almost immediately, and said he would definitely write about it, but not just then. He had just finished the article "The Danger of Thermonuclear War," and was still in the throes of agitation from writing it and of making sure it would be published. It took a lot out of me, too. Once again, Andrei scolded me for the time I hadn't allowed him to sue the newspaper *Russkii golos (Russian Voice)*, printed in the United States, which back in 1976 began a press campaign against me, continued by the Sicilian *Sette Giorno*. Yakovlev merely expanded and organized the material, so to speak.

I will not deal with Yakovlev's writing, nor with the many other things that Sakharov's memoirs touch upon, but later, I will describe my first attempt to get court protection from slander. Naturally enough, though, we were distressed. At first, Andrei was more upset, then I was upset, and living in the aura of such literature is harmful, not only psychologically, but physically.

Andrei at least had an outlet. On July 15, 1983, Yakovlev came to see him—the man wanted an interview, or something like that. What he received was a slap in the face. (Andrei writes of this incident in his book.) After the slap, Andrei calmed down and was very pleased with himself. As a physician, I felt that this was a necessary release of stress for him; as a wife, I was delighted, even though such actions are not in my husband's nature.

---

*Nikolai Yakovlev. A historian and lawyer, he is considered an expert on the USA and has written about twenty books on aspects of American history and politics. *CIA Target—The USSR*, Progress Publishers, 2nd revised edition, Moscow 1984 (Russian edition: Molodaya gvardia, Moscow, 1983.)

†Bela (Belka) Koval, a Moscow friend.

Our lives went on in the same way and at the same pace as before, even though my heart kept hurting. I spent a third of the time in Moscow, where I was besieged with people and with piles of work: in order to do the work, I had to chase away the people, who took offense even though the work was primarily theirs, not mine.

Now, here in the States, there are God knows how many people who are insulted that I do not socialize. I am trying to carry on as few conversations and discussions as possible about which émigré has turned into what here and how different he had been there. I do not want to explain, and it's impossible to explain, that here too I have work; there are lunches I must attend (why, why is everything done over meals?), and I want to spend time with my grandchildren and children. Not to mention that for six weeks before the surgery I was taking as many as twenty nitroglycerine pills a day, and for six weeks after the operation things were very hard, too.

But people don't understand; they take offense. Politeness be damned! I just want to scream, "There are so many of you and only one of me!" I barely have time to write these lines or to see friends. I can't predict when the day will come, the hour, for spending time alone with each of the children. And that each child will be ready for that day or hour, to be alone with me, to open up with me. And who of those who will read these words can know what awaits me there, beyond the line, beyond the border, and how everything inside me turns to stone with fear? Am I made of stone? Listen to this strange-sounding and contrary concept: *abroad is there, not here.* But more about that at the end of the book.

Things were very bad in Moscow. Sergei Khodorovich* was arrested and a stupid trial was coming up for Vera Lashkova;†

---

*Sergei Khodorovich (1941–   ). Engineer, programmer. Arrested in 1983 when serving as chief administrator of Solzhenitsyn's Prisoners Aid Fund, he was sentenced in December 1983 to three years labor camp. He was tried again in 1986 for infractions of camp discipline and sentenced to an additional three years.

†Vera Lashkova (1944–   ). Laboratory assistant. Tried in 1968 on charges of typing samizdat and sentenced to one year labor camp. In April 1983 a Moscow District Court ruled that she could be evicted from her apartment (and therefore from Moscow) since she did not live in it regularly—this was retaliation for her continued human rights activity.

it was not clear why or how they could throw her out of Moscow. But in Gorky spring was coming. I love spring and so does Andrei. And even though things were bad, my soul was gradually relaxing, melting.

We were overjoyed by the fact that the days were getting longer and we could go for walks by the side of the road. We were still allowed to travel to the Zelyony Gorod (a district of Gorky), where there are woods with several sanitoriums and children's camps and dachas. We could listen to the radio there. But now that region is also forbidden to us.

I felt poorly almost all the time. On April 25, after breakfast, I was cleaning up in the bedroom while Andrei was in his room working. Suddenly I felt something sharp pierce me, and I could say nothing, or move, or cry out. I stopped to inhale and stood there; then slowly, almost creeping, I reached Andrei's nitroglycerine pills by the side of his bed. (I didn't have my own then.) The pain subsided after a moment, and I could call Andrei, and lie down. That was the start of constant nitroglycerine, salves, validol, analgin, noshpa, papaverine, several injections of atropine, and one of promedol; I had bouts of nausea and incredible weakness. My blood pressure was low.

I did everything for myself—patient and doctor at the same time. Frightened Andrei helped as best he could. I seemed to be falling into nonexistence. On the third day I developed a low-grade fever that lasted two days. I knew it was a heart attack. But even though I knew it, I tried to deny it subconsciously. The first week I got up only to go to the bathroom. During the second week I began creeping farther and generally getting back my strength.

It came in waves—sometimes better, sometimes worse. Then we received a telegram that Alyosha Smirnov's trial was beginning. On May 12 I went to Moscow and Shikh met me. It was hard walking to the taxi, but we made it. In the evening Masha Podyapolskaya,* Elena Kosterina† (Alyosha's mother), and Lyubanya (Alyosha's

---

*Maria (Masha) Podyapolskaya (born Maria Petrenko, 1923–   ). Geologist, human rights activist and widow of Grigory Podyapolsky (1926–1976), a geophysicist and associate of Andrei Sakharov on the Moscow Human Rights Committee.

†Elena Kosterina. Human rights activist and mother of Alexei Smirnov.

wife) came to see me and told me that the trial would be held the next morning at ten in Lublino. I pictured the stairs to the bridge over the tracks—it had to be crossed to reach the courthouse. So many had been tried there: Bukovsky, Krasnov-Levitin, Tverdokhlebov, Orlov, Tanya Velikanova, Tanya Osipova, among others. And I felt sick—not in my mind, but actually sick: my head spun, my heart contracted, my nails turned blue.

Masha asked, "What's the matter with you?"

"I'm sick." And then: "Forgive me, but I won't go to the courthouse. Have someone come after the recess and tell me. And I'll inform the press. And do the same thing in the evening."

I was embarrassed before Lena—her son was going to be tried the next day. But I felt I would not be able to last otherwise.

Ever since the time I came to Moscow and was searched, there were policemen posted at my door, and a police car was parked in front of the house. The press would not be able to get through to me. I could not use the telephone near the house to call them because it had been disconnected. I would have to go toward the Kursk railroad station or past the bridge to get to a phone. But I would manage somehow, slowly, without witnesses, alone, on my own. Just as I would manage to sit down and type what they told me. My heart hurt when I typed. But I would be alone. I don't know how to be sick in public; I don't like sympathy or even help. I'm like an animal—I need to be alone, to hide, to get into my hole.

The trial lasted two days. What a brave man Alyosha is. He survived the beatings and the investigator's pressure. I was filled with pity for him, for Lena, for Lyuba.

The next day—it was a Saturday—my friends Ira* and Lesik Galperin† came from Leningrad. We had a long and delicious coffee. As usual, when friends visit, morning coffee is transformed into a kind of ritual, perhaps the best part of our socializing.

And then I went to the Academy of Sciences Hospital. My heart kept hurting; it hadn't stopped hurting for a minute since April 25.

*Irina Galperin. Wife of Leonid Galperin.
†Leonid Galperin: Chemist, emigrated in 1985 with his wife, Ira. Close friend of Elena Bonner.

They performed an EKG. The doctors sat me down in an office. The head doctor began to tell me she could not let me go home; I had to be hospitalized immediately—myocardial changes, an infarct. It had happened, they said, over three weeks before.

I was stunned, and even though I had known since April 25 that I had had a heart attack, I didn't believe it. I didn't want to believe it. Or else I was too afraid to believe it. It would scare you; it would scare anyone, but especially me, with our life. The doctor was very worried, and while she worried, I thought and came up with an idea. I said that I agreed to hospitalization if they would bring my husband from Gorky and hospitalize him with me—he was long overdue.

I must explain the basis for my request. Academicians enjoy the privilege of having their wives stay with them in the hospital while they undergo (once a year on average) a physical examination lasting two or three weeks. From the moment of his exile, Andrei had received no help from the Academy's medical service. Therefore my request (if you accept that everything was the way Academy functionaries said it was, that Sakharov was fine and lived like all other academicians) was fully justified. If you consider Sakharov an exile, then my request for him to come (or be brought) to Moscow was still justified, since the law provides for temporary suspension of exile if the person or someone in his immediate family is gravely ill. This moment in our lives was glaring proof that Sakharov's situation is totally illegal and that he cannot appeal to the law.

Marina Petrovna, the doctor, said it was not up to her, that she would pass my request along to the administration, but she could not allow me to leave alone—she was responsible for my life now. I was taken home in an ambulance with a nurse at my side. My return with such an escort shocked—even scared—Lesik and Ira Galperin.

I began a telegraphic correspondence with Andrei. The physicists from the Lebedev Institute who visited him on May 19 tried very hard to calm him down; apparently they had been misled by the Academy Hospital physicians. The concern of those doctors for my condition was intense only on the day I first turned to them. Later it fell sharply, not without outside influence, I think—another example of what Andrei calls "controlled medicine." Someone probably told the physicists that I was exaggerating.

Academician Skriabin* (as one of his colleagues told Andrei) simply announced: "We will not let her blackmail us with her infarct." In this case he appears to have identified with the KGB, otherwise what does the "we" mean? After all, it wasn't the presidium of the Academy of Sciences that was holding Sakharov in Gorky.

But during our telephone conversation (he was in his office, and I with my heart condition in a telephone booth on the street), Skriabin spoke with marked respect and didn't forget to mention that we were of the same generation and had both been in the army. That's why I was so interested to learn that this same Skriabin discussed me with an American scientific delegation in a way rarely heard in a communal flat kitchen. Even our fishmongers sound more cultured, in their speech at least.

On May 19, realizing that without pressure and help I would never manage hospitalization for the two of us, I decided to call a press conference the next day. Policemen stood at my door and a police car was outside. But I went out anyway, phoned several news agencies, and asked them to come. Quite a few reporters showed up.

Standing by the window of a bookstore, holding my nitroglycerine, I told them of our situation. The Western press ran stories about this meeting, but apparently my condition was not appreciated fully; if I was out on the street, perhaps I had not had a heart attack. One newspaper called it a microinfarct; the others avoided any diagnosis at all. Sometimes I think that if the press—for the only real defense for us and for everyone fighting for human rights is publicity —had treated my request for aid more seriously, if our friends throughout the world had understood how tragic our situation was in those days, then we might have avoided much of what followed.

On May 26 there was a medical consultation at my house. There were two women—Dr. Bormotova, the head of the department where academicians and their families are treated; and the same physician, Marina Petrovna (surname unknown), I had seen earlier. The two men with them were introduced to me as cardiologists,

*Georgi Skriabin (1917–   ). Biochemist, secretary of the Academy of Sciences since 1980.

consultants to the Academy, but one of them did not strike me as a physician. Judging by Andrei's description, these were Doctors Grigoriev and Pylaev, who later came to see him.

They once again offered me hospitalization alone. They felt that until the heart process evened out—the EKG of May 24 showed deterioration—it was life-threatening for me to be home. I refused, repeating my conditions. They wanted to record only my refusal in the case history, but I did not let them do that and wrote, in my own hand: "I not only do not refuse hospitalization, I insist upon it, but I agree to be hospitalized only together with my husband, Academician Andrei Dmitrievich Sakharov—who may require hospitalization even more than I do—and only in the hospital of the Academy of Sciences of the USSR." After I wrote this Dr. Bormotova began to cry, but not out of fear for my life (as Evgeny Feinberg* interpreted it), but because she had failed in her assignment to hospitalize me alone. Later she would offer me a car with a doctor and nurse to take me to Gorky, where I would allegedly be treated. That was pure KGB planning—to lock both of us up in Gorky even back then.

Skriabin told me in late May that Academy doctors would go to see Andrei, to determine whether or not he needed hospitalization. They actually did visit him on June 2 and concluded that he ought to be hospitalized for tests and treatment. You would think the problem was solved. Such a simple matter in essence—to hospitalize two sick people in a medical establishment within the system to which they belong. In the Soviet Union medicine is bureaucratic and compartmentalized by profession—for drivers, railroad workers, people from the Ministry of Internal Affairs, the Kremlin, the Academy. But the ball rolled off in a completely different direction.

In the first days after the doctors' visit, both of us—Andryusha in Gorky and I in Moscow—expected to be hospitalized, but time passed, and I gradually began to feel a little better. They kept offering me first hospitalization and later a sanitorium stay, but alone, without my husband. I wrote an appeal to American and European scientists and handed it to correspondents on the street.

---

*Evgeny Feinberg (1912–   ). Theoretical physicist, corresponding member of the USSR Academy of Sciences. Sakharov's colleague from the Lebedev Institute.

To American and European Scientists

I appeal to you for help. Today our highly tragic situation has been intensified by my illness and the deterioration of the health of my husband. On April 25 in Gorky I had a heart attack. I treated myself. Why we cannot be treated in Gorky, you will see from my letter to President Alexandrov of the Academy of Sciences of the USSR and from my statement to the press on May 20. On May 11 I managed to come to Moscow and since then have been trying to get permission for both of us to be treated at the hospital of the Academy of Sciences in Moscow. The only thing I have managed to achieve so far is that consultants from the medical department of the Academy were sent to see my husband in Gorky for the first time in three years. They concluded that he needed hospitalization, tests, and treatment. I am afraid that without your help from abroad even that minimal demand—treatment by doctors whom we can trust at least to some degree —will not come to pass. We will not receive the treatment necessary to save our lives—the Sakharov question will be resolved by the death of one or both of us.

As to our future. Even if we obtain treatment, after a myocardial infarct I will no longer be able to carry the load that fell on my shoulders after the illegal deportation and isolation of Sakharov. That in turn will mean that Sakharov will completely lose contact with the outside world. This will be tragic not only in terms of our personal safety and fate, but in social terms. Sakharov's uniqueness—he is the only competent and independent voice among Soviet scientists—will be lost to the whole world. This will affect those who seek a resolution of the most acute problems of our times—disarmament and maintaining peace.

Today Soviet leaders and Soviet scientists ask you to act with them in defense of mankind's future. It is up to you to judge whether that call is sincere, if at the same time they are keeping Sakharov isolated, denying him the right to make public statements or to participate in intellectual activity, are stealing his papers, and are killing him by leaving him without medical help. Sakharov's life, his right to scientific and public activity, his right to live freely where he chooses, depend most of all on the activity of the world community of scientists.

In the hope that you will understand our situation, I am writing this letter and asking you to make an effort to use your authority to defend Andrei Sakharov, his life, and his free voice.

June 12, 1983   Elena Bonner

On June 20 *Newsweek*'s Atlantic Edition carried an interview with the president of the Academy of Sciences, Anatoly Alexandrov. I will quote the part of the interview that deals with my husband.

Q. *You mentioned the desirability of more scientific cooperation. American scientists say that one barrier to more cooperation is KGB harassment of the exiled Andrei Sakharov. What is your reaction?*

A. He was involved with the same things that [America's] Edward Teller was involved in [development of the hydrogen bomb]. I think that if, around Teller, our people organized some kind of system of constant contact, the U.S. government would not have a very sympathetic attitude. Nor would the American scientific community. Probably, in some way, they would try to liquidate such a situation. I think our government acted very humanely with Sakharov, because Gorky, where he lives, is a lovely city, a big city, with the whole range of academic institutions. The academics who live there don't want to move.

Q. *It is fifteen years since Sakharov left secret research. Why can't he leave Russia?*

A. In that area, fifteen years isn't such a long interval. The systems he took part in developing still exist and will exist. If, God forbid, there were a military confrontation, the Americans could know whether they were good or bad.

Q. *Why is he still an Academy member if you consider him, as Pravda said, a helper of American imperialism?*

A. We hope that Sakharov will think things over and change his behavior. Unfortunately, I think that in the latter period of his life, the fault lay more than anything with a rather serious psychic shift in him.

I believe this was the first response to Sakharov's "The Danger of Thermonuclear War," even though the interview took place before the essay appeared in *Foreign Affairs* that month.* But such things are known ahead of time to those who need to know them, sometimes long before publication. (This bears thinking about.) I feel that the hesitation about putting us in the hospital was a reaction to the article by the people who decide such matters.

The entire tone of Alexandrov's interview was so hostile, so aggressive, that I cannot understand why it passed practically unnoticed by Western scientists involved in nongovernmental disarmament discussions and by the press. I am not aware of a single response from a colleague of Andrei's to Alexandrov's words. I could not keep silent and I sent a letter to him as soon as I read the interview.

Academician A. P. Alexandrov
President of the Academy of Sciences of the USSR

Anatoly Petrovich!

I am writing to you because of the interview you gave to *Newsweek* (number 25, June 20, 1983). In it you say (and I quote): "in the latter period of his life . . . [he underwent] a rather serious psychic shift."

What gave you the right to say those words—Sakharov's principled statements on important contemporary issues, which do not always correspond with the opinions of the government of the USSR? his uncompromising honesty, known to you personally?

*"The Danger of Thermonuclear War," *Foreign Affairs*, Summer 1983.

You know that forcibly removing Sakharov to Gorky and holding him there is flagrantly illegal, and that the Academy of Sciences has done nothing to correct this illegality. You know that today Sakharov is in acute need of hospitalization and treatment for his diseased heart and that continued postponement may result in his death. However, instead of helping, you make your unprecedented statement.

As far as I know this is the first time in the history of the Russian-Soviet Academy that its president has accused a member of the Academy of mental incapacity.

This statement of yours, Anatoly Petrovich, will go down in history.

June 14, 1983   Elena Bonner-Sakharov

P.S. I am addressing this letter not only to you, but to all foreign academies and scientific societies of which Academician Andrei Dmitrievich Sakharov is a member.

II

When we began our life in Gorky, both Evgeny Feinberg and Lydia Korneyevna Chukovskaya* were concerned about Andryusha's heart and recommended a Dr. Matusova. I think they were angry with me for making light of their suggestion and claiming that no one but KGB-approved and -assigned doctors would be allowed to treat us. Well, it's understandable that Feinberg would be angry: the Academy has labeled me an extremist. And even though Yakovlev lies about me—still and all, there might be some truth in it. But as for Lydia Korneyevna? That must come from a lack of understanding of the uniqueness of our situation.

And what happened? When things got very bad with my heart, we tried to get help from Dr. Matusova through Maya Krasavin (at that point three people were still allowed to see us: Mark Kovner† and sometimes Felix and Maya Krasavin‡) and we received a reply —on paper, so that no words were spoken aloud: she can do nothing openly, but will look at my cardiograms through Maya as long as no one knows. And later our contacts with Maya ceased. In Moscow, Yura Shikhanovich secretly brought my cardiogram to a doctor who was a mutual friend of his and of Lydia Korneyevna's. Lydia Korneyevna thought it possible to ask this doctor to come see me. This was in the "good days," that is, when the police posted guards at my door in Moscow only from eight in the morning until midnight, and not around the clock. Shikh told me he was coming.

*Lydia Korneyevna Chukovskaya (1907–   ). Writer and editor, expelled from the Writers Union for human rights activities.
†Mark Kovner. Physicist and refusenik living in Gorky.
‡Felix Krasavin. Skilled metalworker living in Gorky. Maya Krasavin. Physician, wife of Felix Krasavin.

The doctor arrived at twenty after twelve, but the police were still at the door, apparently expecting him. He was let in. I saw he was very worried by the fact that his documents had been checked. After the examination and a brief chat he told me with embarrassment that if I were to need him again, I would have to apply to the Academy, and if they officially asked him for a consultation, he would be glad to help me. Our relationship ended with that; he even stopped looking at my cardiograms. Yet no one had actually threatened him. It was fear. That doctor freely treats Lydia Korneyevna; it has not complicated his work situation and he is not afraid of doing it. But we are another matter.

The same thing happened when this first doctor stopped checking my electrocardiograms and another doctor took over, at the request of a friend. He went even further—he examined me twice at the home of this friend. I never mentioned his name. But TASS did.*

Incidents with doctors started soon after Sakharov became part of our family. Once an uninvited psychiatrist came to see my mother for what he called a consultation, but what was actually an attempt to frighten her. Then my own problems began. In 1974 I needed surgery for thyrotoxicosis. On Natasha Gesse's† recommendation, we turned to a doctor she knew. Dr. B. set a date for the operation, asking us to get an official referral to the hospital where he worked. Andrei applied to the Leningrad City Health Department and to the Ministry of Health, and we received the referral.

But when I arrived for surgery, he told us through Natasha that he could not operate on me, since he would not be allowed to defend his dissertation if he did.

We were very angry with Natasha for not telling this story, to which she was the main witness, when she testified before the U.S. Congress about our life.

After I did have thyrotoxicosis surgery, I developed acute com-

*See Appendix II.
†Natalia (Natasha) Gesse. Editor and author of children's books, a friend of Elena Bonner's for more than thirty years, she emigrated from Leningrad in February 1984 and now lives in the United States.

plications in my eyes. Andrei and I went to Professor Krasnov, who had performed my first eye operation in 1965, before I was Sakharov's wife. The operation had been successful. For many years before that I had been his father's patient. But this time, Krasnov refused to operate on me.

I went into the Moscow Eye Hospital to await surgery, but doctor friends told me to leave, since they did not know "who would do what to me." It was after that incident that I got the idea of going for surgery to Italy, where my friends Maria Olsufieva* and Dr. Nina Harkevich† were living.

I have always been amazed and upset by how quickly our friends manage to forget all this. They are often the first to wonder, why did I have to travel to faraway places to get my medical treatment? I have always said that I could have been treated in a Soviet hospital if I were not Sakharov's wife, except, of course, for the record-setting sextuple bypass.

On July 3, 1983, *Izvestia* ran a letter from four academicians, a reply to Andrei's "The Dangers of Thermonuclear War." The letter was signed by A. A. Dorodnitsyn,‡ A. N. Prokhorov,** G. K. Skriabin, and A. N. Tikhonov†† (they say that Prokhorov regrets signing, because he is not well received abroad now; I don't think Skriabin cares how he is received as long as he is sent abroad; and I do not know whether the other two learned men travel or not). Their letter created a furor. Soviet people believe academicians, especially since in this case one of them, Prokhorov, is a Nobel Prize laureate. But Soviet people don't know that these academicians were too embarrassed to give the name of Sakharov's article in their text, since it would have undercut the argument that Sakharov is a warmonger.

A flood of letters began—twenty a day, fifty, seventy, one hun-

---

*Maria Olsufieva. Friend of Elena Bonner, living in Italy, and translator of Andrei Sakharov's books into Italian.

†Nina Harkevich. Physician, friend of Elena Bonner living in Florence, Italy.

‡Anatoly Dorodnitsyn (1910–   ). Mathematician.

**Alexander Prokhorov (1916–   ). Physicist. Shared the 1964 Nobel Physics Prize for his work on masers.

††Andrei Tikhonov (1906–   ). Mathematician.

dred, it peaked at one hundred thirty-two one day, then gradually diminished but did not end. Sakharov was berated and calumnied in individual and collective letters. When friends tell me that they were written under official prodding I cannot prove otherwise, but I am totally convinced that they were written spontaneously by our Soviet people themselves. They are sometimes awakened to social activity, if only to this kind of letter-writing.

Among the letters is one from Volodya Chavchanidze. I call him "Volodya" familiarly instead of Vladimir because he was in graduate school with Andrei, and Andryusha refers to him that way when he recalls stories from those days. There was a letter from a classmate of my daughter's. And from a colleague of Andrei's, whom he mentions kindly in his memoirs. There were many clergymen, many pensioners, but the majority of letter writers were war veterans, and as far as they were concerned Andrei was calling for thermonuclear war. That was the impression they received from the letter of the four academicians.

In July, to support the academicians the magazine *Smena* (with a circulation of over a million) published an article by Yakovlev, which repeats and expands on what he had written in his book *CIA Target—The USSR*. The flood of letters changed direction, and many became openly anti-Semitic. Threats increased, particularly against me.

In August, it was no longer the president of the Academy but the head of state (Andropov then) who announced in a conversation with U.S. senators that Sakharov was crazy.

We were threatened at the market, when we went to sit out on our balcony, or when we were in the street. I think the only thing we were spared was beatings. The climax was the pogrom I suffered on the train on September 4, when I was leaving Gorky.

The day train leaves Gorky at 6:20 A.M. and arrives in Moscow at 1:40 P.M. There were two middle-aged women and a man in the compartment with me.

One of the women asked, "Where do you live in Gorky?"

"On Gagarin Street."

"In house two hundred fourteen?"

"Yes."

"Are you Sakharov's wife?"

"Yes, I am the wife of Academician Andrei Dmitrievich Sakharov."

Here the man butted in. "He's no academician. He should have been kicked out a long time ago. And as for you . . ."

He didn't say what. Then one of the women announced that she was a Soviet teacher and could not ride in the same compartment with me. The other woman and the man agreed with her. One of them called the conductor. Everyone was talking loudly, shouting. The conductor said that if I had a ticket she could not throw me out.

The shouting intensified and passengers from other compartments joined in. They filled the corridor, demanding that the train be stopped and I be thrown off. They shouted things about the war and about Jews. For some reason I stayed absolutely calm, as clear as the windowpane against which I rested my left hand.

Then the conductor disappeared. People kept squeezing past the compartment in the corridor, peeking in, yelling. Anger and curiosity must have been equally strong. Eventually the conductor returned and she took me out into the corridor. We pushed past the others, and I could physically feel their hatred. She put me in her own compartment, and I stayed in there until we reached Moscow.

From Sakharov's diary:

> For Lusia with her sensitive emotions, daily contact with hostility and hatred from people around her is difficult (for me too). An old woman brandishing her fist, and more like that. The confrontation in the train on September 4 was provoked by KGB agents, of course, but the majority of the passengers, some willingly, others out of fear, took part in the general brouhaha. . . . Lusia sent me a telegram: "It was very frightening and therefore I was completely calm . . ." Shikh and Belka, who met her, could tell from her face that something horrible had occurred. After Lusia told them, Belka wept.

The crowd, pogrom, fascism—it all comes down to the same thing in our world. All during the shouting, while they threatened me, and until the moment when I saw Shikh and Belka on the platform, I kept wishing I had a yellow star to sew onto my dress.

The evening of September 22 was balmy for that time of year, and Andryusha and I stood on the Gorky platform for a long time. We were worried about a possible repetition of the pogrom, but the night train is less suitable for that sort of thing, and for the first time in 3½ years I had managed to get a first-class ticket. When we got on the train we saw several people laughing, drinking champagne—clearly not KGB—near my compartment. They let us pass, Andrei put my things in, and we went back out into the corridor. One of them asked which of us was traveling. I replied. Then another one, standing nearby, called into the compartment: "An attractive woman is riding with you." After my previous trip, with the pogrom, this exclamation seemed strange, and I said to Andrei, "If they only knew."

We stood at the end of the car a bit. Every parting is sad for us, even for a few days. We always recall the lines "Who can know at the word 'separation'/Just what kind of separation is in store."* Andrei got off and the train started as in the song from the movie *Irony of Fate*. That is our life, Andryusha's and mine: the irony of fate.

Inexplicably, I remembered early 1971. I was doing something for Andrei at his place, and somehow the conversation turned to fame. Andrei said: "Well, all of those valences have been filled up a long time ago for me." I think he meant: "It won't grow any greater. Please God, spare me any greater fame." However, now we have the thousands of letters filling up the house, letters we're in no shape to read. It would take a state archive to organize them and save them.

The fame he has now is a wife who is recognized on the street and in the train, and whom the mob is ready to lynch.

I went into the compartment. My companion was older than

*From "Tristia," by Osip Mandelstam:
        Who can know at the word "separation"
        Just what kind of separation is in store
        What the cock's crowing portends
        When the fire burns in the Acropolis?

Andrei and I, with a good gaze and eyes, and a large smile—perhaps a shade professional. What's called an open face. There was something familiar about him. He spoke like a host, though a genial host. "Let's get acquainted," he said. "Zhzhenov, Georgii Stepanovich."* He seemed to expect a reaction from me, either to his name or to his friendliness.

I later realized that he was used to being recognized, to getting a stormy reaction to his name—he's an Honored Artist or has some even higher award. But except for a few, I don't know actors by name.

I was as amicable as I could be in reply, even though I wasn't feeling very friendly at first: "Bonner, Elena Georgievna." I saw his hand reaching not for mine but for the door, which he shut, and then he said in a low voice, "The very one?"

"Yes, that one."

"I wouldn't have thought so."

"I'm not as scary-looking as the one you read about?"

"I guess."

"Will you be able to bear my company, or would you like me to ask the conductor to move me to another compartment?"

He said nothing.

"Well, if you're not saying anything, I'll stay, and you do as you like."

A half-empty bottle of vodka and an open bottle of champagne stood on the table. He poured two glasses and offered me one.

"I don't drink."

"At all?"

"At all."

"Strange!"

"Why? Did someone tell you a tale that I'm a drinker on top of everything else? Yakovlev doesn't write about that."

"Yes. Well, how about some tea?"

"I drink tea."

He took a tin of tea from his briefcase. He liked good tea. He

*Georgii Stepanovich Zhzhenov (1915–   ). Actor, People's Artist of the USSR.

went out and came back with the conductor, who brought everything necessary for tea.

A very long conversation ensued until four in the morning. He was alternating tea and vodka, and by the end of our talk he was very drunk, to put it mildly. I would like to recount the essence of our conversation, which is an answer to a question I am often asked: "How do people feel about you and your husband; do they believe what Yakovlev wrote?"

When I asked Zhzhenov how he could believe Yakovlev's lies, he replied with a question: "Why shouldn't I believe it, on what basis shouldn't I?"

"On the basis of your own life experience. How old are you?"

"Sixty-seven."

"Do you remember the Doctors' Plot? The magazine *Zvezda*, Akhmatova, Zoshchenko, the cosmopolites?"*

He was silent and then, after yet another shot of vodka, he began talking about his own experiences.

He had studied in Leningrad at a theater institute and begun his career there. In the thirties he was arrested. He only returned to normal life in the fifties. And he started all over—this time in the provinces. He got into a film by accident, playing a not-very-young soldier. After that he returned to the stage in Moscow. He achieved success late, but that made it all the more precious.

So this was his life. And yet I had to convince him, although he knew Soviet reality. He said what he believed, that things had changed in our country. But when he spoke, I could see he was convincing himself, not me. During our conversation I kept feeling that after just a little bit more, a tiny bit, he would burst out, and stop feeding himself lies. But it didn't happen.

---

*In 1946, Stalin's deputy Andrei Zhdanov launched a purge of liberal and non-Bolshevik elements in the Soviet literary world with speeches attacking the literary journal *Zvezda*, the poet Anna Akhmatova, and the satirist Mikhail Zoshchenko.

Nine Kremlin doctors, seven of them Jews, were arrested in January 1953 and charged with plotting to kill Soviet leaders under orders from Zionist organizations and the CIA. The survivors were released after Stalin's death. The postwar campaign against "cosmopolitanism" took on a clearly anti-Semitic character after the murder of the actor Solomon Mikhoels in 1948.

I even tried to get him to come to my flat for coffee when we left the train, so he could see with his own eyes the apartment from which I allegedly chased Sakharov's children, or, rather, my mother's two-room apartment. And I would show him the lease, which states that the apartment was given to my mother in 1955. I told him that the police were on guard only after eight in the morning (that's the way it was back then), that he would have his coffee and go, and that no one would ever hold it against him.

"No."

"But why, why not?"

"I'm afraid."

"Of what?"

"I'm afraid, that's all."

At four in the morning, having finished off the bottle of vodka, he kissed my hand and said that he bowed to Andrei and to me. But he was afraid. *Afraid.* Later in the morning he tried not to look at me. Hurriedly, without meeting my eyes, he shook my hand and left with a quick, dry goodbye.

Yura Shikh was waiting for me at the platform. The first thing he said was "Zhzhenov was in the same car with you. He's a good actor; I like him." Shikh is a theater and film buff, and had recognized Zhzhenov immediately. I told him the whole story. Shikh was angry with me for some reason; he thought I hadn't been eloquent enough. I could have convinced him and certainly persuaded him to come for coffee. He was wrong, though. You cannot convince fear of anything or with anything. Not by word or by deed. You can only overcome your own fear.

III

We decided to sue Yakovlev. The idea was not mine; Andrei thought it necessary, and many friends agreed with him. I realized it would require a lot of work on my part. I had to write out a complaint, and gather documents. Then apply, petition, probably several trips to court, explanations. Where would I find the strength, when it was difficult for me to walk even a hundred yards, when even sitting at the typewriter made me break out in a cold sweat. If Andrei's statement had to be notarized, would I find a notary willing to do it? I had to get Yakovlev's address somehow. And finally, I would have to read his stuff carefully, something I had not done yet. First of all, it made me sick, and second, whenever I thought about what he had written about Seva* I felt a heart attack coming on.

But all the ifs were overcome. I even got Yakovlev's address from an acquaintance. She lives not far from him and when she gave me the number, she added a rather long tale about his personality and his past and present private life. Thus, if I subscribed to Yakovlev's own methods, I could throw in several dozen spicy pages.

After two or three weeks of nonstop writing alternating with heart attacks, nitroglycerine always in hand, I felt ready for court. I had:

1. A complaint.
2. My autobiography and deposition
3. The deposition of Andrei Dmitrievich Sakharov
4. A copy of the magazine *Smena*, number 14, July 1983.

*Vsevolod (Seva) Bagritsky (1922–1942). Poet, son of the well-known poet Eduard Bagritsky (Dziubin), and childhood sweetheart of Elena Bonner; he was killed at the front.

To the regional People's Court of the Kiev District of Moscow from Bonner, Elena Georgievna, residing at Moscow, B-120, Chkalov Street, 48 b, apt. 68, against Yakovlev, Nikolai Nikolayevich, residing at Moscow, Smolensk Embankment, 5/13, apt. 135. Codefendant, *Smena* magazine, address 101457 GSP, Moscow, Bumazhnyi Alley, 14

In the defense of honor and dignity (based on article 7 of the Civil Code of the RSFSR).

COMPLAINT

N. N. Yakovlev's article, "The Downward Path," is printed in the magazine *Smena* (number 14, July 1983). This article defames me. In my complaint I do not concern myself with the general tenor of this article, the distorted and defaming information on my husband, my children, and people who were close to me in the past. I direct the court's attention only to several of the author's claims. I move to the text of the article (all citations are from *Smena*, number 14, July 1983).

1. It was a timeworn story: a stepmother kicking out the children of her widower husband. . . . Bonner swore everlasting love and began with ousting Sakharov's three children, Tanya, Lyuba, and Dima,* from his home and installing her own instead—Tatyana and Alexei."†
2. "Bonner got her hands on all of Sakharov's money in the USSR a long time ago . . ."
3. ". . . armed with forged references, she managed to get into the medical institute in Moscow . . ." "leading a wanton life . . ."
4. "In her dissolute youth she had developed an almost professional knack for seducing and subsequently sponging off older men of considerable stature. The time-honored technique had

---

*Tatiana (Tanya) (born 1945), Lyubov (Lyuba) (born 1949), and Dmitri (Dima) (1957) are the children of Andrei Sakharov and his first wife, Klavdia Vikhereva, who died of cancer in 1969.

†Tatyana Yankelevich (born 1950) and Alexei Semyonov (born 1956) are the children of Elena Bonner and her first husband, Ivan Semyonov (they were divorced).

only one hitch—an older man usually has a woman who is close to him, as a rule, his wife. The hitch is removed by removing the woman. The lady in question began by taking the husband of her sick friend away from her—blackmail and obscene phone calls drove his wife to her death. The enterprising lady was on the point of marrying the poet Vsevolod Bagritsky, but he was killed in the war. Disappointment. However, the lady had a different man to fall back on: she was having a stormy affair with Moisei Zlotnik, a well-known engineer.

"The hitch was his wife. Zlotnik killed her—and was sentenced to a long prison term. It was a famous case which prompted Lev Sheinin,* a popular Soviet criminologist and author, to write a short story entitled 'The Disappearance': Zlotnik's lover was referred to as Lusia B. The crime was committed in wartime: out of fear, Lusia B. joined a hospital train as a nurse."

5. "Bonner had a habit of persuading her husband to do this or that by hitting him with anything at hand."

All these citations come under article 7 of the Civil Code of the RSFSR, since they defame my honor and dignity. They are all fabrications by the article's author, with no basis in fact.

I ask the court to determine the true circumstances—the law provides that the burden of proof rests completely on the defendant —and to return a verdict ordering that Citizen N. N. Yakovlev and *Smena* publish an appropriate retraction.

September 26, 1983   Bonner, E. G.

In his article Yakovlev presents my biography in a tendentious way. I therefore feel obliged to give a brief autobiography.

I was born in 1923. My father, Gevork Alikhanov,† head of the

---

*Lev Sheinin (1906–   ). From 1923 until 1950 worked as a criminal investigator for the procurator's office. Then began a career as an author and playwright, published *Notes of an Investigator.*

†Gevork Alikhanov (1897–1939?). Prominent Armenian Communist, father of Elena Bonner, arrested in 1937 and executed.

personnel department of the Comintern, member of the All-Russian Communist Party (Bolshevik) since 1917, was arrested in May 1937 as a traitor to the homeland, and posthumously rehabilitated in 1954. My mother, Ruth Grigorievna Bonner,* a member of the CPSU since 1924, was also arrested in 1937, as a member of the family of a traitor. She was rehabilitated in 1954 and granted a special pension.

I had completed seventh grade in Moscow when my parents were arrested.† My younger brother‡ and I moved to Leningrad to live with my grandmother and uncle. My uncle was arrested in late October 1937, his wife was exiled, and my grandmother brought up the three of us, my brother and myself and my uncle's two-year-old daughter. My brother and I were in Leningrad without documents (we did not have our birth certificates) and were sent by the regional education department for a medical examination, which determined my age as 16, not 15, and in February 1938, in accordance with the medical commission's findings, I was issued a passport giving my year of birth as 1922. I finished high school in Leningrad in 1940; while at school I worked as a cleaning woman, and during summer vacations after eighth and ninth grades I was a file clerk at the Telman Factory in Moscow.

In 1940 I entered night school at the Herzen Teachers Institute in the Russian Language and Literature Department and worked as a Pioneer leader at school. Never did I believe—either as a child or as an adult—that my parents could have been enemies of the state. Their ideals and their internationalism had been lofty models for me, which was why I joined the army when war broke out (as a nurse, in the Red Cross courses). I volunteered, following my heart's desire, if you take those words seriously and don't use them lightly.

On October 26, 1941, I was concussed and badly wounded near the Valya Station (on the Volkhov front), and I spent time hospitalized in both Vologda and Sverdlovsk. In late 1941 I was discharged

---

*Ruth Bonner (1900–   ). Mother of Elena Bonner. Arrested in 1937, she was rehabilitated in 1954. Now lives in Newton, Massachusetts, with her grandchildren.

†Most Soviet students begin school at seven and complete ten grades, through high school.

‡Igor Alikhanov (1927–1976). A merchant marine officer and brother of Elena Bonner.

into a reassignment unit in Sverdlovsk and from there sent as a nurse to hospital train number 122. In 1943 I became a senior nurse, and was given the rank of junior lieutenant of the medical corps.

In 1945 I was promoted to lieutenant.

In May 1945 I was sent to the Belomorsk Military District as deputy chief of the medical unit attached to a battalion of engineers, from which I was demobilized in August 1945, as a group 2 invalid —almost total loss of vision in the right eye and progressive blindness in the left (results of the concussion).

For the next two years I struggled stubbornly to save my sight, and with gratitude list here the physicians who helped me: Dr. Fridlyanskaya (the polyclinic on Trud Square, Medical Academy), Professor Chirkovsky (First Leningrad Medical Institute), Dr. Sukonshchikova (Institute of Eye Diseases)—these were in Leningrad; then I was twice hospitalized at the Institute of Eye Diseases in Odessa, where my treating physicians were Professor Vladimir Petrovich Filatov and his wife, Dr. Skorodinskaya.

In 1947 my condition stabilized, but I have been classified ever since as either mildly (group 3) or moderately (group 2) disabled, depending on the condition of my eyes. In 1970 I was designated a moderately disabled lifetime invalid of the Great Patriotic War.*

In 1947 I enrolled in the First Leningrad Medical Institute, where I completed a six-year course in 1953. From that time until I reached retirement age, I always worked, except for an interval of little more than a year in 1961–62, when my son was severely ill. I was a district doctor, a pediatrician in a maternity home, and I worked in Iraq on assignment for the Ministry of Health of the USSR.

I often combined my professional medical work with literature. I was published in the magazines *Neva* and *Yunost;* I wrote for All-Union Radio; I was published in *Literaturnaya Gazeta (Literary Gazette)* and the newspaper *Medrabotnik (Medical Worker);* I contributed to the anthology *Actors Who Died at the Front During the Great Patriotic War,* was an editor-compiler of the book *Vsevolod Bagritsky: Diaries, Letters, Poems,* worked as a

---

*A photocopy of Bonner's service record is reproduced as Appendix III.

free-lance literary consultant at the Writers' Union, and at one time was an editor in the Leningrad division of Medgiz, the medical publishing house.

I received recognition for my contributions to health care. I joined the Komsomol in 1938, and through all my years of service in medical trains I was the Komsomol organizer and, at the institute, the union organizer of the course. Neither while in the army nor in subsequent years did I feel a psychological right to join the Party as long as my parents were listed as traitors to the homeland or, in the more frequent parlance of the times, "enemies of the people." After the criticism of Stalin at the Twentieth Congress and especially the Twenty-second, I decided to join the CPSU, and in 1964 became a candidate and in 1965, a member. After the invasion of Czechoslovakia in 1968 I considered this step a mistake and in 1972, in accordance with my convictions, I left the Communist Party.

I have two children: a daughter, Tatyana (born 1950), and a son, Alexei (born 1956). Their father, Ivan Vasilevich Semyonov,* had been at the First Leningrad Medical Institute with me and still works there. We separated in 1965. In 1967 Tatyana entered Moscow University, and was expelled in the fall of 1972 for participating in a protest demonstration in front of the Lebanese Embassy against a terrorist act—the killing of Israeli athletes at the Munich Olympics. She was reinstated in 1974 and graduated successfully in 1975, with an "excellent" in her diploma defense. Alexei graduated with an "excellent" from high school and was also a top student at Moscow's Lenin Pedagogical Institute in the mathematics department. He was expelled in his final year—officially, for not completing his military training (a subject that is not part of the institute's curriculum). My son-in-law, Efrem Yankelevich,† graduated from the Moscow Institute of Telecommunications.

---

*Ivan Semyonov (1924–   ). Physician, classmate of Elena Bonner at the Leningrad Medical Institute and her first husband. Now head of the department of forensic medicine at the Leningrad Medical Institute.

†Efrem Yankelevich (1950–   ). Electronics engineer, Elena Bonner's son-in-law, emigrated in 1977 and now lives in Newton, Massachusetts.

My complaint lists five points. My husband, Andrei Dmitrievich Sakharov, deals with three of them in his deposition. I shall cover the remaining two—point 3 and point 4.

3. "... armed with forged references, she managed to get into the medical institute in Moscow. . . ."; "leading a wanton life. . . ." (*Smena*, No. 14.) I never attended any institute in Moscow. In 1947 I entered the First Leningrad Medical Institute, with a certificate of graduation from Leningrad Middle School No. 11 (now No. 239), took the general admissions examinations, and was enrolled upon passing them. I did not use any forged references. I do not wish to discuss the epithet "wanton" in relation to my life; my brief autobiography is given above.

4. "In her dissolute youth she had developed an almost professional knack for seducing and subsequently sponging off older men of considerable stature. . . . she was having a stormy affair with Moisei Zlotnik, a well-known engineer.

"The hitch was his wife. Zlotnik killed her—and was sentenced to a long prison term. It was a famous case which prompted Lev Sheinin . . . to write a short story entitled 'The Disappearance': Zlotnik's lover was referred to as Lusia B."

The tragic murder of my school friend Elena Dolenko by her husband, Moisei Zlotnik (cousin of another school friend, Regina Ettinger), took place in October 1944. The last time I saw Elena Dolenko was in late 1942, when she returned to Moscow from evacuation in Ashkhabad. I also saw Moisei Zlotnik then at the house of Regina's older sister, Evgeniya Ettinger. Zlotnik and Dolenko were married much later, in the fall of 1943. I never saw them once they were husband and wife. I learned of Dolenko's disappearance just before New Year's of 1945, when I was once again in Moscow with the hospital train for several days. In late April 1945 I was called from the hospital train to the procurator's office in Moscow for questioning, and learned then that Zlotnik had been arrested and that he had killed Dolenko. My own involvement in the case was confined to that single interrogation, when I was asked about the character of the victim and the killer and my relationship with them (I had known Dolenko since grade school, Zlotnik since 1938). I was never recalled for more questioning or to the trial.

Lev Sheinin wrote a story based on that tragic crime. In the fictional version, Glotnik/Zlotnik is a sex maniac (according to the evidence in the official trial, Zlotnik killed her out of jealousy) who had three mistresses, one of them "Lusia B." But in Sheinin's story, to which Yakovlev refers, "Lusia B." does not in any way instigate the murder, but is, to the contrary, herself a victim. And Yakovlev could just as easily have chosen to accuse either of the other two women, "Nelli G.," living in Leningrad, or "Shurochka," living in Moscow, of responsibility in the murder (following the fictional story).

Now I must digress a bit to mention someone who could be described as Yakovlev's predecessor. In 1976 I received two letters, signed by Semyon Zlotnik, claiming to be a nephew of Moisei Zlotnik and demanding "6,000 rubles and a certain sum abroad," from me, since he had decided to emigrate from the USSR. The letter writer reinforced his "request" with the threat "to reveal my relationship with his uncle" and "my dark past" in general. I did not respond to those letters. A while later, people who knew Sakharov or me (academicians, writers, doctors, political and public figures, our friends) in Moscow, Leningrad, and many countries began receiving standard manila envelopes from Vienna with a photocopy of Sheinin's story and a letter signed by Semyon Zlotnik, which described my "dark past."

We know of at least one thousand such packages. The return address was "Adambergergasse 10/8, 1020, Vienna, Austria, sender, Sandler." Austrian reporters determined that there is no such address nor any such person in Vienna. But the story does not end there.

In 1980 the newspaper *Sette Giorno* printed an article referring to a story by "a poor émigré from Russia, Semyon Zlotnik," giving my "biography"—which includes not only two murders and all the slanderous material in Yakovlev, but also quotes from my letters to and from a relative in France who died in 1972. (These letters went through the ordinary mails, but by some miracle ended up in the hands of Zlotnik.) The article said that Zlotnik was living in France. It all looks plausible, but . . . no one from the Zlotnik family ever left the USSR, and there is no Semyon Zlotnik, nephew of Moisei Zlotnik, in the family. And there never was. This whole story smacks of Lieutenant Kije.* . . . It is not my job to determine who made it up.

Returning to point 4, Vsevolod Bagritsky, son of the poet Eduard Bagritsky, was neither elderly nor wealthy. He was born on April 19, 1922, in Odessa and died on February 26, 1942, near Lyuban, not yet twenty years old. We were in the same class at school and shared a desk, walked to school together, and he used to read poetry to me. His father used to joke and call me "our legitimate fiancée," and Vsevolod's mother, Lydia Gustavovna Bagritskaya, and his aunt, Olga Gustavovna Cuok-Olesha,† called me that until their deaths. Seva and I were childhood friends, and we were each other's first love. We also had a shared destiny: we were together when my parents were arrested, when his mother was arrested, when his brother died. He accompanied my aunt into exile and took care of her two-year-old daughter. Then we stood in line all night together to hand in monthly food parcels for our mothers in Butyrki Prison. Parcels were accepted alphabetically, one letter per day, and we were in luck, our mothers' names started with the same letter.

We were separated, and I lived with my grandmother in Leningrad. I would visit him in Moscow, and he spent his school vacation with us in Leningrad. Then came the war and Seva's death. Lydia

---

*An officer who was created by Tsar Paul's misreading of an army promotion list, and who continued to be promoted until he suddenly "died" when the tsar wanted to meet this outstanding officer. The subject of a novel by Yuri Tynyanov and a suite by Sergei Prokofiev.

†Olga Cuok (1901–1978). Sister of Lydia Bagritskaya and wife of author Yuri Olesha.

Gustavovna Bagritskaya* wrote to me from the women's camp in Karaganda: "Lusia dear, how will we live without Seva . . ."

But the living go on living. Lydia Gustavovna was rehabilitated and returned to Moscow. And until her death in 1969, my family consisted of my mother, my children, my husband Ivan Semyonov (until our divorce), and Lydia Gustavovna. The children knew that they had Grandma and "Lydia." When Lydia Gustavovna was ill I nursed her, and we put together Seva's book, at first not for publication but for ourselves.

Many of the poems in the collection existed only in my memory, other material I gathered piece by piece from friends, some from Kornelii Zelinsky. Then Lydia Gustavovna was given Seva's field bag, pierced by a shell fragment, with his notebook and documents.

In his lifetime, only a few poems by Vsevolod Bagritsky were published (see the collection *Line, Interrupted by a Bullet*, Moskovsky Rabochy, 1976, page 82). In 1964 the publishing house Sovetksy pisatel' published *Vsevolod Bagritsky: Diaries, Letters, Poems*, compiled by L. G. Bagritskaya and E. G. Bonner. The book received the Lenin Komsomol Prize and has long been a bibliographical rarity. Readers of *Smena* should find it and read it. This book is a historical document, without a single line made up by anyone. Everything was written by Vsevolod. Yakovlev readily cites Sheinin's detective story, but he cannot cite Bagritsky's book. The detective story by the main investigator of Stalinist times and Yakovlev's "detective story" have internal similarities. Bagritsky's book is entirely different. Yakovlev cannot draw the reader into the complex, pure world of the tragically lonely youth in the years 1937–1942; he has to "enmesh" (forgive the criminal jargon) the reader with himself in the murk of his story instead.

I turn to Bagritsky's book, a letter to his mother in labor camp, written October 14, 1940: "While we were working on the first act of *The Duel*, I managed to fall in love with a sickly girl (she has heart trouble), overcome the objections of her family, and marry her. We lived together for a month and realized that we could not go on. Our

*Lydia Bagritskaya (?–1969). Wife of Eduard Bagritsky and mother of Vsevolod Bagritsky.

family life did not work out. She moved out. And now once again I am alone with my old Masha [Seva's nanny—E.B.]. Once again I can lie with my feet up on the bed and smoke in my room. But I feel that the hard and complicated part is still ahead—I must go to the registration office for a divorce. My wife was Marina Vladimirovna Filatova, a very sweet girl.* We still are on excellent terms. I can't understand why I married her. Everyone tried to talk me out of it, including her. But I married her anyway—that was stupid! Thoughtlessness must predominate in me."

And here is another letter—from Masha, the nanny, to Seva's mother, written in December 1940. "Hello, dear, sweet, Lydia Gustavovna! I'd like to see you like I would the sun. How long do I have left to live with Seva? My health is bad. I wash, sew, and gather some food for him. I collect some clothes too. I bought him three pairs of shoes and three shirts. He wore yours out, and gave some to his friends. And I darn his socks as best I can, but he doesn't ask much. . . . In the fall Seva got bored, and got married out of boredom, but he quickly divorced. The girl was good and modest, but very sickly. Our legitimate fiancée, Lusia, is in Leningrad. Well, we're waiting impatiently for you to come home. I kiss you, be well, Masha."

That is the whole story of Vsevolod Bagritsky's marriage and divorce, in his own words. If the book is not sufficient to establish the truth, then I am informing you that the entire Vsevolod Bagritsky archive is in the Central State Archive for Literature and Art, the originals of these letters and his passport pierced by a bombshell. The passport has stamps for his marriage and his divorce, in the fall of 1940. I never saw Filatova or spoke with her on the telephone.

Referring to Vsevolod with the words "Disappointment—he died in the war," Yakovlev insulted not only me, but everyone who lost relatives in the war and the memory of all the boys who did not come home. I did everything I could in memory of my boy who did not come back: I gathered up everything that remained of him, was the closest friend to his mother until the day she died, almost a

---

*According to Vsevolod's friends, her real name was Margarita, but she called herself Marina. She died in Moscow in late 1943.

daughter to her, and taught my children to love her and to honor Seva's memory.

It always hurt that because of their own busy lives Seva's friends did not show proper attention to his mother, except for two meetings set up on my initiative. They never came to visit her. Perhaps now they will defend Vsevolod's memory? I ask that Seva's comrades at the film studio be called to court, as well as the directors of the studio, Alexei Arbuzov and Valentin Pluchek, the writer Isaya Kuznetsov, other studio members, and the writer Alexander Svobodin—they were eyewitnesses to Seva's marriage and divorce. I was living in Leningrad at that time.

I could conclude the factual side of my statement to the court here. But what does Yakovlev need with my biography, especially told the way he tells it? Because in our tragic life someone hopes to use this filthy "literary" concoction to drive two elderly and very sick people to death, because he can confuse the minds of millions of trusting readers—and creativity à la Goebbels is suitable for this. This is confirmed by the thousands of angry, ugly letters that we receive, suggesting that Sakharov "repent," "divorce the Jewess," and "live by his own mind, not Bonner's." It is confirmed by the pogrom against me on the Gorky-Moscow train, the scenes directed at Sakharov and me in the streets of Gorky, the innumerable threats to deal with us and to kill us.

In 1983, one of the most widely read Soviet magazines (circulation 8,700,000), *Man and the Law,* ran a series of articles by Yakovlev, *The CIA Against the Land of the Soviets.* While the Jewish-Zionist theme is rather muted in his book *CIA Target—The USSR* and in *Smena,* limited to an emphasis on Jewish names and references to anonymous, mythical students of Sakharov, in *Man and the Law* (number 10, 1983), it becomes absolutely clear and open. Here is a quote from a section of the article "The Firm of E. Bonner and Children":

> In its attempts to undermine Soviet order from within, the CIA has turned to the services of international Zionism. . . . It uses not only the network of American, Israeli, and Zionist services and the Jewish Masonic organ B'nai Brith,

which has ties to them, but also elements subjected to the influence of Zionist propaganda. One of the victims of the CIA's Zionist agents is Academician A. D. Sakharov. Whatever angry words (however well earned) are spoken about Sakharov, from a human point of view one takes pity on him ... using the peculiarities of his personal life of the last fifteen years (more on this below), provocateurs from subversive agencies pushed him and keep pushing this spiritually unbalanced man to actions that contradict the image of Sakharov the scientist. It's as old as the hills: After the death of his wife, a stepmother entered Sakharov's house. . . . . A horrible woman forced herself on the widower Sakharov.

Forgive the very long quotation, which repeats some of the material in *Smena,* but in context it maintains that I am the *agent provocateur* for the "subversive" Masonic, Zionist, and CIA services, and that I bear responsibility for Sakharov's public activities, while he is a victim, a mentally unbalanced man. The anti-Semitic nature of Yakovlev's article in a popular legal magazine is essentially the incitement of national hatred. In this connection I must recall the case of the "killer doctors" and Lydia Timashuk,* one of the most shameful pages of the history of our country. Yakovlev's readers, perhaps, have forgotten about this, but he—a professor and historian —should remember.

What does Yakovlev want from me? For me to betray my husband? I have never betrayed anyone. To frighten me with the prospect of being tried for treason under Article 64 of the Criminal Code of the RSFSR (right up to the death penalty)? I never belonged to the services of any intelligence organization—American, Masonic, Zionist. All of Yakovlev's writings stem from the fact that I am Sakharov's wife, and also a Jew, which simplifies his task. But I hope to live my life to the end worthy of the Russian culture and milieu in which my life has passed, and my Jewish and my Armenian nationalities. I am proud that it is my difficult lot and happy fate to

*Lydia Timashuk. A physician whose letter helped to instigate the arrests in the 1953 "Doctors' Plot."

be the wife and friend of Academician Andrei Dmitrievich Sakharov.

September 26, 1983   Elena Bonner

DEPOSITION

I wish to make the following deposition in connection with my wife Elena G. Bonner's complaint concerning the injury to her honor and dignity caused by Nikolai N. Yakovlev's book *CIA Target —The USSR* and article "The Road Down" (*Smena*, number 14, July 1983).

1. It is a total falsehood when Yakovlev asserts (*Smena*, page 27) that "in the late 1960s Bonner finally spotted big game—Andrei Sakharov, a widower, a member of the Academy of Sciences. True, he had two daughters, Tatiana and Lyubov, and a son, Dmitri. Bonner swore everlasting love and began with ousting Tanya, Lyuba, and Dima from his home and installing her own instead— Tatyana and Alexei . . ." No one has the right to write about someone else's personal life in such a vulgar tone and so falsely, as does Yakovlev in the cited excerpts and in many other places in his articles and books. In a recently published article in the journal *Man and the Law* (number 10, 1983), Yakovlev intensifies his insinuations: "A horrible woman forced herself on the widower Sakharov." Elena Georgievna Bonner did not "force herself" on me, she did not "swear eternal love." I asked her to become my wife. Since then she has selflessly borne that difficult lot, that tragic fate. It is *our* fate— *our* happiness and tragedy. I ask that you protect us from Yakovlev's mean and vulgar interference.

In fact, my two younger children from my first marriage— Lyubov Andreyevna Sakharova (born 1949) and Dmitri Andreyevich Sakharov (born 1957)—who lived with me until my second marriage in a three-room apartment at the address, Moscow, Marshal Novikov Street (previously, First Shchukinsky Alley), house 1, apartment 16, with a living area of 610 square feet, continue to live there now, without any interruptions. My wife, E. G. Bonner, and her children, Tatyana (born 1950) and Alexei (born 1956)

[Yakovlev incorrectly says 1955], did not live a single day in that apartment. After our marriage I moved to the two-room apartment of my wife's mother, where in 365 square feet there lived five people (besides me).

My elder daughter, Tatiana Andreyevna Sakharova (born 1945), got married in 1967, when my deceased wife, K. A. Vikhireva,* was still alive, and has lived on her own since then. I made a down payment on a cooperative apartment for Tatiana through the Academy of Sciences, and in 1972 she moved into a three-room apartment in central Moscow (Rostovskaya Embankment, house 1, apartment 26), where she lives with her husband and daughter. Everything I have said on this point can be confirmed by housing registers and depositions of witnesses. As witnesses, I ask that you call: Bobylev, Alexander Akimovich;† Zeldovich, Yakov Borisovich;‡ Romanov, Yuri Alexandrovich;** Feinberg, Evgeny Lvovich.

Yakovlev intentionally uses diminutives for the names of my children and the full name for my wife's children to give his readers the impression that small children were "thrown" out onto the street.

2. It is a lie that my wife "got her hands" on my savings. In 1969 I turned over 139,000 rubles to the State Fund (for the Red Cross and for the construction of an Oncology Center). During the period 1971 to 1973 I gave my children from my first marriage and my brother, Georgii Dmitrievich Sakharov,†† over 500 rubles a month. In 1973 I transferred to the account of my children from my first marriage half of my remaining savings, in the amount of 14,400 rubles. In 1972 I gave my elder daughter, Tatiana, my ZIM car. From 1973 to 1977 I paid my son, Dmitri, a monthly allowance, and have given him money on occasion since then. I have also continued to assist my brother financially. All this since 1971 was

*Klavdia Vikhireva (1919–1969). Andrei Sakharov's first wife.
†Alexander Bobylev. A relative of Sakharov's first wife, Klavdia.
‡Yakov Zeldovich (1914–   ). Nuclear physicist, Academician and colleague of Andrei Sakharov.
**Yuri Romanov. Nuclear physicist.
††Georgii (Yura) Sakharov (1925–   ). Andrei Sakharov's brother. A chemist, but unable to work owing to illness.

done with the knowledge and approval of my second wife and sometimes at her initiative.

3. Yakovlev writes a patent lie when he calls my son-in-law, Efrem Yankelevich, half-educated and a loafer. Yankelevich successfully graduated from the Moscow Institute of Telecommunications in 1972. He now lives in the United States, where he is performing complicated and responsible duties as my representative abroad, with power of attorney. Yakovlev calls Alexei Semyonov and Tatyana Semyonova-Yankelevich loafers and idlers. This is deliberate slander, which can easily be refuted by documents.

4. Yakovlev writes: "With the change in his family situation, the focus of Sakharov's interests changed. The theoretician took up politics, began meeting with those who came to be called 'human rights activists.' " Yakovlev's implication is false. I met my future wife, Elena Bonner, in the autumn of 1970. (Yakovlev has deliberately altered the date to the late 1960's.) I had become seriously interested in social and political issues by the mid-1950's. I played a role in the conclusion of the 1963 Moscow Limited Test Ban Treaty. This can be confirmed by calling as a witness Efim Slavsky, Minister of Medium Machine Building, and a member of the Central Committee.* My essay *Reflections on Progress, Peaceful Coexistence and Intellectual Freedom* was published in 1968, more than two years before I met Elena Bonner. My later statements have primarily elaborated the ideas on society which were outlined in that essay. I made the acquaintance of many noted human rights activists during the first half of 1970 before meeting Elena Bonner.

5. Yakovlev misrepresents the circumstances of the hunger strike my wife and I underwent with the aim of obtaining permission for our daughter-in-law, Liza Alexeyeva, who had become a hostage of my public activities, to emigrate to the United States to be with her husband. I state that the decision to go on the hunger strike was made by both of us; we both realized the absolute necessity and seriousness of that step. We both fasted (see *Izvestia* of December 4, 1981). On the thirteenth day of the hunger strike we were removed

---

*Efim Slavsky (1898–   ). Engineer, Minister of Medium Machine Building (responsible for the testing and production of nuclear weapons) 1957–63 and 1965–85.

by force from our apartment, separated, and confined in different hospitals. We stopped the hunger strike on the seventeenth day, when the authorities assured us that our demand would be satisfied.

6. Yakovlev writes: "Bonner had a habit of persuading her husband to do this or that by hitting him with anything at hand." Approvingly, Yakovlev quotes an article printed in the New York newspaper *Russkii golos:* "It looks like Academician Sakharov is now a hostage of the Zionists who dictate their terms to him through Bonner, a cantankerous and unstable woman." Yakovlev writes: "This is the testimonial given Sakharov by those who managed objectively to set him working for the interests of imperialism. How? For that we will have to look into Sakharov's personal life. It was a timeworn story—a stepmother came into Sakharov's house. . . . People have noticed that his emotional state undergoes regular changes. Calm periods, when Bonner leaves Gorky for Moscow, alternate with periods of depression, when she comes back. Then follows a spell of joint work on some anti-Soviet squib, interspersed with rows; with Sakharov on the receiving end. Keep this in mind when studying the frequent 'revelations' broadcast in Sakharov's name by Western radio voices."

I assert that all the statements I have quoted from Yakovlev are deliberate, malicious, and provocative lies. Yakovlev does not cite nor can he cite any proof that my wife, E. G. Bonner, beats me and thus gets me to act and write what she wants. Yakovlev's allegation, which defames the honor and dignity of my wife and of myself, is absolutely false. Also false and unfounded are Yakovlev's assertions about the fluctuations in my moods, allegedly depressive in the presence of my wife. I assert that all my articles, books, and appeals published in the West or disseminated in the USSR express my personal convictions, which were formed throughout the course of my life. Yakovlev depicts me as a bewildered, overgrown child, in subjugation to an imperious, treacherous, and mercenary woman. He also writes that I am mentally unwell. Recently this insinuation was repeated by A. P. Alexandrov, president of the Academy of Sciences of the USSR. In this manner they are trying to discredit my public statements by implying that they are not my own ideas, but are instead instigated by others. They are also pursuing a second and possibly more important aim: they want to paralyze my public activity by placing my wife in a dangerous, unbearable situation and by damaging her health. Insinuations about my wife's personal life and imaginary past crimes and slurs on her moral qualities reinforce the attacks. Her nationality is emphasized, pandering to popular prejudice.

I am deeply grateful to my wife for her selflessness and steadfastness in our tragic life, and for her reinforcement of its humanistic direction, for which I am indebted to her. But I firmly state that I bear sole responsibility—I alone—for my public activity and for the form and content of my statements. I categorically deny Yakovlev's contention that my statements have been distorted by pressure from my wife, E. G. Bonner, or anyone else. I believe my statements serve the interests of peace, progress, freedom, human rights, of a humane and open society, and I reject Yakovlev's accusation that they are of an anti-national or pro-imperialist nature.

I am the author of every one of the statements attributed to me (provided the texts have been authenticated by my wife or by Efrem Yankelevich, my representative abroad). Yakovlev's use of the phrase "revelations broadcast *in Sakharov's name*" is tantamount to a malicious lie. It seems advisable in this connection, however, to declare formally that I cannot be held responsible for any statements made in my name which may be published in the Soviet Union or abroad unless the texts have been personally confirmed by me, by my wife, Elena Bonner, or by Efrem Yankelevich. (I am not aware of any counterfeit statements in circulation at this time.) My declaration covers articles, books, memoirs, statements, appeals, interviews, and all publications, including scientific articles.

My current circumstances oblige me to announce that, in the event of my death, I have bequeathed to my wife, Elena Bonner, my author's rights in all my written works, published and unpublished. I appoint her the sole executor and heir of my literary estate. In the event of my wife's death, I appoint Tatyana Yankelevich the sole executor and heir of my literary estate. My wishes in this regard as well as a number of other dispositions have been recorded in a notarized will. The original will has been deposited at the Prioksky District Notary's Office in Gorky.

November 19, 1983   Sakharov, A. D.
Gorky, Gagarin Avenue, 214, apt. 3

. . .

The courthouse of the Kiev District of Moscow. There is a long line to see the judge and there is no sign anywhere about letting war veterans in first. I've never experienced receiving hours like this. Everyone is in a large room that resembles a classroom. There is a door leading into another room. A pretty young woman comes out and asks each person, in front of everyone else, what his or her business is. As a result, some get certificates, others blank forms, still others are told they must pay fees, and some are simply sent to another institution. The number diminishes rapidly, and the remaining people go into the judge's chambers one at a time. Some are in there three to five minutes, others longer. It's my turn. I explain why I am there and hand over my packet of documents and a copy of *Smena*. The judge begins reading. Her secretary comes in and hands her a note. The judge excuses herself and leaves. The secretary remains with me.

The judge returns in a few moments and says, "I cannot accept your complaint without permission of the chairman. Go and see him."

I had already walked up three flights to see the judge. Ever since my heart attack, I counted floors—every floor was an event for me. Now there was one more flight, and then I was at the chairman's door. He had a line, too. Not long, about four people. But they spent more time with him. Right after me, three people came in together. From their conversation, I realized that they had been at a trial. I didn't know what the full story was, but apparently the son of the two elderly people had been found guilty. The mother was tearful and kept talking; the father was rather silent. The young girl with them must have been the wife, but her face did not show any great grief or concern.

This judge had a large, tired face. He was heavyset and had on a gray, worn suit, with ribbons and medals on his chest. When he got up from his desk to go over to his cabinet his prosthesis creaked —he was missing a leg (must have been a disabled veteran). He took my papers and sat down comfortably. Maybe he was going to read them. Yes, he was reading them. Almost a half hour. Then: "So, Elena Georgievna, go see the judge again, I'll make sure she accepts your suit." He offered me his hand. I shook it and in a state of bewilderment, for I had expected another refusal, went to see the judge. Now, thank God, I was going downstairs.

As soon as a visitor came out of the judge's office, the secretary called me in. The judge entered my name in a large notebook and glued in the tax stamp which I had bought before coming to the courthouse. I signed, and the secretary put all my papers in a file with the word CASE written in large letters. Beneath she added my name, address, and the date.

The judge said, "We will let you know within the month when your case will be heard."

As I went down the stairs, it seemed to me that everything had gone well. It looked as if there would really be a trial and that maybe I should warn the girls (they're my age, but still girls to me) in Leningrad that I'd be calling them as witnesses. I had graduated from school with some of them and from the medical institute with others.

Outside, in a vain attempt to find a taxi, I wandered through narrow streets around the courthouse. Slowly (it was very slippery and my heart ached from the stairs) I headed toward Kutuzov Avenue. Then I began losing my first rush of enthusiasm. The fresh October wind quickly managed to cool my optimism.

Back in Moscow, the suit was often discussed among my friends. They were divided pro and con. Interestingly, most of those who were against suing I had considered friends; in our everyday lives we saw one another frequently, and we helped one another, and there were other characteristics of friendship in our relationships. Yet they could still say, "She's better off not going to court; after all, not everything in her life is crystal clear." I know for a fact that many of our so-called friends said just that. The ones in favor of a suit would never say or even think anything like that. They would never discuss, in a semi-Yakovlev manner, hypothetical possibilities. If they had any doubts, they would simply ask.

Those in favor of suing, Andrei, of course, among them, won the day on going to court. Many of our friends felt there would be a trial, but that Yakovlev would be neither found guilty nor acquitted: the verdict would be vague. Others thought he would be found guilty, but no retraction would be printed. But ever since I had been cooled off by that October wind, I had had a very definite view of the matter: nothing would happen.

October passed. On my next visit to Moscow, Shikhanovich urged that I go see the judge. We agreed he would take me the next day after work, and then he ascertained that both the judge and the chairman would be receiving at that time. However, after we got to the courthouse and made it up the three flights of stairs, we learned that my judge was ill and the office closed. We went up yet another flight: office closed, the chairman of the court had been called to a party committee meeting. He would be there the following week.

A week later I went with Emil.* (The reception hours were during the day and Shikh could not leave work.) The district judge was still out sick. But her secretary, who seemed to have been expecting me, said that the chairman would see me. We went up to his office. He asked Emil to leave, even though I had wanted to have our conversation in his presence. I guess he didn't want a witness. When we were alone, he took my file from his cabinet and placed it on his desk. With his hand resting on the file he said, "I cannot accept your case for examination."

"Why not?"

He shrugged and tucked his head into his shoulders.

"I can't."

"Then give me a written explanation. That's standard; it's in the Code of Criminal Procedure."

"It's standard, but I won't give you an explanation. I can't."

"Well, where do I file a complaint that the law is being broken?"

"File a complaint? Elena Georgievna, you are a clever woman. If you have the time and the energy to spare, then you can complain, but I don't recommend it."

Then I asked, "Tell me, were you given orders from a high level not to accept my case?"

He gave me a sharp look, not with the dead eyes he had had during our conversation, and said, "High enough."

"I understand. But I've written the truth and Yakovlev is lying."

"I know." He went on. "I checked a few things. For instance,

---

*Emil Shinberg. Physician and friend of Elena Bonner.

you never lived in Sakharov's apartment. And I read Vsevolod Bagritsky's book."

We both fell silent. Then I got up to leave, and I wanted to shake his hand. He came out from behind his desk, prosthesis creaking, with my file in his hands. I extended my hand, he extended my file, then understood my gesture, switched the file to his left hand, and shook my hand.

"Would you like me to hold onto your file? I'll put it in my safe. You must have copies. Maybe it will lie here long enough. Maybe they'll start rehabilitating again."

"Keep it."

We shook hands. I came out with a strange, mixed feeling of respect for this man because he had told me a lot; and surprise that he understood; and regret that he could work within that system. And compassion: "What can you do?"

I told the story to Emil, and then at home to our friends, and then in Gorky to Andrei. And to this day I keep thinking, "Maybe there really will be a new wave of rehabilitation. I doubt it somehow." But even if there isn't, perhaps my case against Yakovlev might still go from that safe into the category of cases that are stamped in the upper right corner: "To Be Preserved Forever."

IV

That winter Natasha Gesse was searched in Leningrad. I did not treat it seriously. I feel the same now. They weren't looking very hard for anything, or they would have found it. The thing they were after was to push her into leaving the USSR. They did not want me to have a friend whom I could trust completely. The search was made as soon as Natasha came from the train which had brought her from me in Moscow. They wanted to see if I was hiding anything in Leningrad.

Soon after the search, Zoya* died. The house in Leningrad had been emptying while we lived in Gorky. It began with Regina (Inna) Ettinger's† death in October 1980. Natasha decided to emigrate and soon thereafter received an invitation. Shikh sent us a phototelegram with an immortal quatrain:

> Natasha got her invitation
> alas, farewells are to be.
> And our coming Communism,
> alas, she won't see.

I went to Moscow on my usual train, which leaves at eleven P.M. and arrives at seven-fifteen the next morning (in the unlikely event the train isn't late: it isn't the Moscow-Leningrad Red Arrow Express). I don't remember any special details of that trip, or how I felt. I do remember that it was cold in Moscow and that it was a long walk

---

*Zoya Zadunaiskaya. Editor of children's books and friend of Elena Bonner.
†Regina (Inna) Ettinger (1922–1980). School friend of Elena Bonner.

along the platform. Shikhanovich, who met me, was telling me various camp and other unpleasant news while we walked. When we got to the house, we had coffee and . . . Actually, that was one reason for my visit. Shikhanovich insisted that we celebrate the birthdays of my daughter-in-law, Liza, and Sasha, my grandchild in Massachusetts. He said that Liza's departure to join my son, Alexei, and Sasha's birthday were our common victory. When she was born, people in Moscow drank this toast: "To Sasha and to our freedom!" And so it was decided to mark those two birthdays, especially since I had been in Gorky rather than Moscow for Mother's birthday, Andrei's, and my own the last few years.

Over coffee, I gave Shikhanovich money for various purchases for Gorky and for Liza's birthday. He was supposed to divide up and assign the cooking chores, and buy the wine and vodka. On his lunch hour Shikhanovich came by with some of the purchases—I remember that he brought the wine. Crouching by the refrigerator, putting things away, he told me more Moscow news which was not very encouraging. I had the feeling that he sensed the hours of his freedom were numbered. He left around two.

That evening he returned and took me by taxi to Galya Yevtushenko's.* We had a long talk sitting on the bench near her courtyard entrance. Snowflakes swirled gently under the streetlights. A strange dog became attached to Shikh. Actually, "strange" is the wrong word—all dogs belonged to Shikh.

The next day I learned that Shikhanovich had been arrested. Thus, we celebrated Liza's birthday without him. "Celebrate" is not the right word. Alya, Shikh's wife, was in a mood blacker than night, and everyone else felt terrible too. We were accustomed to having Shikh at every celebration; even when no one had the strength to be festive, he pushed us. His motto was "We don't have enough holidays, and we need them too!" It was obeyed strictly when he was on the outside, thanks to his persistence.

Natasha was in fact leaving and was in the phase of awaiting permission. Andrei and I were sure that she would get it quickly. In

---

*Galina (Galya) Yevtushenko (1928–   ). Divorced wife of the poet Yevgeny Yevtushenko and friend of Elena Bonner.

December she came quietly to Gorky to say goodbye to Andrei—they met a few times in the city without me. I was so sick that it had become difficult for me to get out of bed and travel somewhere.

Andrei was sure by then that he would have to announce a hunger strike. He showed Natasha the drafts of his appeal to scientists and his letter to heads of state. Natasha also knew that we planned for me to go to an embassy—at the time we were thinking of the Norwegian Embassy—for the duration of the hunger strike. We showed her those papers when the three of us met on her first day. I carried the papers on my person. Andrei did not keep them in his bag anymore—we knew that bags got stolen.

A few days before the New Year (I think it was Christmas Eve) I was asked to go to the U.S. Consulate. Dr. Jeremy Stone* was waiting for me there. He had brought Andryusha a camera and a calculator as gifts. He said he had spoken with the leadership of the Soviet Academy about Andrei, but unfortunately (for us), the conversation had not been publicized. Tête-à-tête conversations are a game that the Soviet authorities love—they've never done anybody any harm. However, this is the tactic chosen by many of my husband's Western friends.

I told Dr. Stone that Sakharov had appealed once again to the Presidium and the president of the Academy to help obtain permission for me to go abroad for treatment, that he had not received an answer, that he was planning another hunger strike, and that he had written a letter to Andropov. Stone asked me for a copy of that letter and said he would personally give it to Velikhov† to be passed on higher. We think Dr. Stone kept his promise, and that the Academy administration therefore knew about Sakharov's coming hunger strike and what had prompted it. Just like the previous time, they did nothing to avert it.

Vitaly Ginzburg‡ came to Gorky on December 29, and Andrei told him of his plans. Thus the circle of initiates grew wider, which

*Jeremy Stone (1935–   ). Mathematician. Director of Federation of American Scientists.

†Evgeny Velikhov (1935–   ). Theoretical physicist and vice-president (since 1978) of the USSR Academy of Sciences.

‡Vitaly Ginzburg (1916–   ). Theoretical physicist, Academy member.

Andrei felt was to the good: the more people who knew, the more likely the authorities, to avoid a scandal, would simply give me a visa. Perhaps that might have been. But now it seems that all the people who knew decided to keep their knowledge to themselves.

The New Year's holiday came and went. That winter was a very hard one for me. I counted off days on the principle of hoping to make it through each one. In early February I went to Moscow to say goodbye to Natasha. I didn't have the strength to go all the way to Leningrad. While I was in Moscow I had a lot to do and I did it, even if "I didn't have the strength."

I am 63 years old today, and by accident or design I am at Disney World in Florida. I regard this as an unreal existence, though not as a dream. I am here with three of my grandchildren—Anya, Matvei, and Katya—whom I thought of so much while in Gorky. Perhaps because Gorky is so distant—not geographically, but distant in other ways—I had pictured them differently. I feel uncomfortable being with them, and a certain . . . not disappointment, but perhaps disillusionment in not finding what I had expected to find. They are not what I had imagined them to be—not worse and not better, just different. They need a lot of getting used to, but I don't have that kind of time. I guess I will never be able to say what they are like, my grandchildren. In any case, they are enchanted by Disney World now, just as are the adults, and just as I am.

I am here with very good people, calling them friends is saying very little. Their goodness comes not from being our friends, but from the aura they give of liking the world and of mutual love. That love, which they direct at each other, warms those around them.

Being with my grandchildren and with these friends, and in a cloudless place like Disney World—truly a cloudless world, not a single cloud in the sky and at night the stars and moon so bright they seem artificial, like everything else in this microworld—would be happiness, if only . . .

Today is February 15, 1986. What about February 15, 1984? Exactly two years ago on this day . . . and what followed! God, right now the temperature is in the seventies, the children went off with my friend Jill to the beach, music is playing somewhere, everything here seems to be carefree, and the flowering trees confuse me—where's the winter? Two years ago the day was cold, windy, and cloudy. Andrei and I celebrated my birthday as usual with the traditional pie, wine, and candles on the table. And also as usual when we are alone together, we were happy. Then I went to Moscow.

I spent a week in Moscow, then back to Gorky. Soon I had to return to Moscow once again, because I had made a date with the children for them to call me in early March, and because I also wanted to get an appointment with Dr. Syrkin.

As usual, I met with representatives from the U.S. Embassy. The Norwegian ambassador invited me to tea again, and I had a talk with him, in which he said that his government could not get involved in my trip. It would be better and simpler for the Italians to do that, since I was planning to be treated in Italy. The conversation left an unpleasant impression, as if we were supplicants and had not been invited by his government to settle in Norway. They were inviting us and at the same time refusing to do what could actually help.

While in Moscow I had a blood test and an EKG. One day in mid-March I was lying in bed at Galya Yevtushenko's house, where Dr. Syrkin was to come for a consultation. When I began making arrangements for the consultation, Galya's telephone was turned off. She had to conduct all the negotiations with the Academy of Sciences Polyclinic from pay phones, except the first call, which I made myself. And she was followed, like me, by KGB people, who must have been afraid that I would invite foreign correspondents to her house. When I left for Gorky, her phone was turned back on.

Syrkin came, not alone, but with my district doctor, Ludmila Ilyinichna, and with a male physician who had come to see me once when my heart condition was diagnosed. Afterward they discussed something in whispers for a long time. A friend who was then at Galya's house tried to eavesdrop through the door, but could not hear a thing.

After their consultation they told me that I had to be very careful; it looked as if I had had some interruption in my circulation again, myocardial or micromyocardial. Syrkin said that if possible I should not go outside until it was really warm, not just spring on the calendar, but actually warm. With that I went outside and took the train to Gorky. They prescribed medication, which I took with me.

I spoke with the children by telephone and we set a date for the next call on April 8. Based on that I planned to leave Gorky on April 7.

When I returned to Gorky in late March, Andrei's leg hurt a bit, because he had banged it on the garbage pail. There was a small bruise near his knee, but no scrape was visible.

On March 30 Andrei was called into the Gorky OVIR office. Oddly enough, they asked for Andrei, even though he had never applied to OVIR. The head administrator said she had been empowered to tell him that there would be an answer to his application after May 1. Andrei told her he hadn't made any application, that it had been his wife. "I don't know about that, I was asked to pass the word to you and I am telling you that you will have an answer on May 2."

When Andrei came home his leg was hurting more, and as usual, whenever anything hurts (I don't know how they find out), Felix and Maya Krasavin showed up. She looked at the leg, decided it was thrombophlebitis, and prescribed hot compresses, which I began applying. The day after Maya's visit, the physicists arrived, and Evgeny Feinberg said there was a new salve, trioksavazan, that would be good for Andrei.

That time, I think, Andrei Linde* came with Evgeny Feinberg, but I'm not sure. Feinberg knew, perhaps from Ginzburg, that Andrei was planning to announce a hunger strike, and he and my husband had a long discussion. Andrei, who by that time had made a firm decision to go on the hunger strike if we did not receive permission for my trip very soon, showed Feinberg various documents he had written, in particular an appeal to his colleagues and two appeals to Alexandrov. Feinberg was very much against the hunger strike, which was his usual reaction. He insisted that if Andrei had been called in by OVIR and told to wait until May 2, he should wait until May 2.

Andrei felt they were just trying to fool him, that it was an

---

*Andrei Linde. Physicist with the Lebedev Institute.

attempt by the KGB to take the initiative. Besides which—and we didn't understand this then—the call to OVIR was also prompted by the fact that the authorities had decided to wait until May before acting—apparently the conclusions of Syrkin and the other doctors about my condition worried them. The call from OVIR was exactly the kind of step the KGB would take in hopes of making Andrei wait until May. But Andrei decided not to wait.

Following Maya's recommendation we applied compresses for two days, but Andrei's leg grew worse so I stopped them. Despite the pain in his leg, Andrei felt I should not put off my trip, and on April 7 I went to Moscow. I left with a firm understanding between us that I would go to the U.S. Embassy and Andrei would begin his hunger strike. We had decided on the American embassy because Andrei was afraid that if I remained in Moscow alone at the apartment—or, even worse, alone in Gorky—I could be taken away to the hospital or someplace else. There would be no knowing what would happen to me. It was not safe for me to stay home, and therefore I had to go to the embassy. At first he thought it would be best for me to go to the Norwegians, and had asked me to find out if there was a doctor at the compound. They did not have a physician on the premises; when they needed medical treatment, they turned to the clinic for diplomats. Andrei felt that would be unsuitable, so I should go to the American embassy.

I did not like the idea of the American embassy at all. I thought then—and still think now—that if I went there it would make it easier for the government to smear me with all kinds of labels, like CIA agent or Zionist spy. Though I did not go, they call me those names anyway, but at least with less justification even from their point of view. In principle, I was against going to any embassy, because I am not a Pentecostalist,* and know perfectly well that diplomats could not help me resolve my problem. Andrei agreed that we did not need the embassy's help, only a retreat for me.

On April 7 Andrei's leg still hurt, but we thought it would get

---

*Two Pentecostalist families, the Vashchenkos and the Chmykhailovs, took refuge in the U.S. Embassy in Moscow in June 1978, demanding permission to leave the country. They were allowed to emigrate in 1983.

better, and on Evgeny Lvovich's advice, we treated it with some trioksavazan I had found in my medicine chest. Andryusha saw me off, sitting in the compartment with his leg up on the seat because it ached a great deal when it was down. But we did not attach too much significance to it. I blame myself, because I am knowledgeable enough to have been more careful, but I was preoccupied since it had been decided that this time I would not return from Moscow. I would go to the American embassy after informing Andrei of the exact date. On that day he would send telegrams to the chairman of the Presidium of the Supreme Soviet and to the KGB and begin his hunger strike. So I was full of concern about that and did not think too much about his leg.

On April 8 I spoke with the children. I think that they understood preparations were under way for a hunger strike, but did not know the date it would begin.

I met with American embassy officials and arranged for them to pick me up on April 12 to meet with the ambassador. I was to hand him the documents Andrei had prepared—an appeal to the ambassadors and other letters. That was the way he wanted it.

On April 10, Dima Sakharov came to see me unexpectedly and told me he had some days off and was going to see his father. I was glad of the opportunity to send with him some groceries and trioksavazan I had bought. I also gave him money for his ticket.

I spent the night of April 11 at Galya's house. The next day I got home at one in the afternoon, an hour before my appointment with the Americans. I began packing a bag—underwear, a dress, some books—to take to the embassy, and just then I received a telegram from Andrei: "LEG WORSE, HOSPITALIZATION RECOMMENDED, I AGREED." I decided to go to Gorky. I went downstairs at two, but the Americans had not yet arrived. I saw Galya running toward me, waving my bag of medicines. She was there only because I had forgotten the bag. I told her about Andrei's telegram and that I was going to Gorky. She did not know, none of our friends knew, about my plans for the embassy, even though she was aware, I think, that I was doing something out of the ordinary.

When the embassy people came, I told them I was not going to see the ambassador, which I think bewildered them. I asked them to

take me to the train station instead and showed them Andrei's telegram. I said I would return on May 2, and asked them to come for
me on May 3. I would meet with the ambassador upon my return,
if he would agree to receive me.

On the way to the train station I remembered that I had Andryusha's letters and other things in an envelope in my purse. I decided
it would be better not to carry all that back to Gorky, and I asked
the embassy officials to hold the package for me. I said very clearly
that I would meet with them on the third and then they would
return these letters to me; I did not want to travel with them. They
understood. They took me to the train station, and I bought a ticket
for the four o'clock train, which arrives in Gorky at midnight. I went
down to the refreshment stand, and saw the Aeroflot ticket counter.
They had a seat on the six o'clock flight, which would arrive in
Gorky at seven. I gave my train ticket to some man, bought a plane
ticket, and called Galya to say I was returning to her house, since
I had three hours before my flight.

I ate at Galya's. Nelly and Emil Shinberg came over after our
phone call, and they took me to Domodedovo Airport.

The flight was almost on time and I reached the house at eight.
I did not let the taxi go. The house was a mess, and Dima was
smoking and leafing through all the magazines; at least, the table
was piled with magazines and Dima was in this kingdom of smoke,
quite pleased with himself. He told me his father was in the hospital. I went there. They wouldn't let me see him, but they took a
note up.

I wrote: "I'm here, don't worry, I'll see you tomorrow morning.
Kisses. Lusia." In the morning I went back to the hospital. I saw
Andryusha after his boil had been lanced. They importantly called
this period "after the operation." He had had a carbuncle near the
knee, but the joint was not affected.

Andryusha, very bewildered, told me that when he had been
brought to the hospital, during the examination in the X-ray room
and somewhere else, his bag had been taken from him. He felt it had
been in the hands of the KGB. The embassy address, the names of
the embassy people I had talked with, and some other papers were
missing. Copies of the letters to the ambassadors, the appeal, and

other letters remained, but Andrei felt that the bag had been out of his hands long enough for the documents to have been photographed. He was very upset. I told him, "We missed our train because of your leg, or if you like, because of the garbage pail. This time you have to stop."

He replied, "No, I won't stop for anything. I'll do what I decided to do anyway."

He wasn't feeling bad at all. I did not understand why they had hospitalized him in the first place, enforcing a strict bed rest regime. The leg was encased in a plaster cast, cardiac medication was prescribed (well, if that made them happy), and they were giving him antibiotics (that made sense at least).

I spent that whole day with Andrei and left at eight in the evening. The next day when I arrived, I saw that his heart condition was worse. The doctor said he was having many extra heartbeats, so they did an EKG. I had not asked what medication they were giving him. It was only on his fifth day in the hospital, after a detailed conversation, that I learned he was being given Isoptin and digitalis —even though it was known from his last stay in the hospital that both had a bad effect on him. It is generally thought that an extra beat or two per minute do not require treatment.

I had a very nasty conversation with the doctor about the medicine and about why they were keeping Andrei in bed—he could easily have been up and at home. I began insisting that they allow me to stay at the hospital. Andrei insisted, too, that they either let him go home or let me stay with him. Actually the latter was his idea when he realized they did not want to discharge him. "They" were not the doctors, of course; the doctors throughout all this were merely following orders. I received permission to stay at the hospital. But the scene with the doctor over Andrei's medication grew into something larger.

She said she had received a telephone call from Tanya Sakharov, who insisted that her father be treated, that he not be let out of the hospital, that he had many illnesses including dysentery and something else, diseases I had never heard of; I can no longer recall exactly what Tanya had said. A few hours later, the doctor said that Mark Kovner, Sakharov's "friend," had demanded that Sakharov be kept in the hospital, that he be treated, that they not listen to his wife, who is against Sakharov getting the treatment he needs.

At the same time, I learned from Felix that everyone in Gorky was saying that Sakharov had gangrene, he might have to have his leg amputated, and that I was not allowing him to be treated. And yet even as he told this story with indignation, he was repeating the story all over the place. Both he and Maya were horrified that Sakharov was so severely ill and that I was obstructing his treatment. I think they said he had blood poisoning (or maybe it was Kovner). And Felix also said that Kovner worked with the KGB, while Kovner said the same thing about Felix. From all this Andrei and I realized that the KGB had pitted them against each other and against us, or rather against me. None of them dared blame Sakharov for anything.

And then Andrei had an incident with Dima. When his son first arrived, he had said he had to go to work on April 18, that he had finally gotten a job. And that he had come to see his father before he started. On the seventeenth, Dima announced he wasn't going anywhere, that he didn't need to go to work. He could not leave his ailing father, did not trust me, and wanted to stay and take care of his father. Andrei said some harsh words to Dima, after which his son agreed to leave the hospital, apparently to take a train.

As we learned later, he did not leave Gorky immediately, but went to see Mark Kovner to complain about me, how I was destroying his father, and then to Maya and Felix Krasavin with the same story. But all that was of no importance except as it affected our mood and mental state. Andrei could no longer stand the people in the hospital. They were still changing his dressing; he had stopped taking all medication, but his EKG did show many extra heartbeats. At his own insistence, Andrei checked out of the hospital on April 21, arranging with the doctor that he would return to have his dressing changed.

Later, I would be accused of forcing Andrei to leave. We did go to the hospital two or three times for the dressings, and then Andrei asked me, "Can't you do that yourself?" I said I could. And he said, "Well, then I won't go anymore." Andrei did not see the heart specialists and so we didn't know how things were with the extra heartbeats. But he had stopped taking the mix of an anti-arrhythmic and digitalis while in the hospital.

On April 24 I bought a plane ticket and sent Galya a telegram that I would arrive on May 2, that I did not need to be met, and that I would come directly to her place. But apparently my friends decided to meet me anyway. They must have been worried about something, because usually when I wrote that I did not need to be met they believed me.

We lived quietly and normally until May 2, even though I was trembling inside, as I had been in April, dreading the fact that I had to go to the embassy and that Andrei would begin his hunger strike. At the same time I thought that nothing would come of it. For we both were sure the KGB knew all about our plan, but I could not stop it and Andrei would not stop it.

In such a mood we went to the airport on May 2. I still can't understand why I carried in my purse the letters and appeals, which Andrei had rewritten, and copies of my letters to Andrei and the children, which also revealed the hunger strike and that I was going to the embassy. Why did I need them? Why was I carrying them around with me? I don't know to this very day what I was thinking of; after all, they were all (well, perhaps Andryusha's letters were in an earlier draft) in the envelope I had asked the American diplomats to hold for me.

We were both very nervous while I waited to board. I sat, Andrei stood next to me, holding my hand. And once again we thought, "Who can know at the word 'separation' . . ." Those words were the leitmotif of our life in Gorky. When we were being led to the airplane, I was surrounded by about five men. I looked back to the waiting room, but did not see anyone. They separated me from the other passengers, took me by the arms, and led me to a small van like a Black Maria. I realized immediately that I was under arrest, especially since we had anticipated something like this when we said goodbye.

They drove me to the other end of the airport, to a small, low building, second floor, some bigshot's office, where there were two women in MVD uniforms and a man in civilian clothes. He introduced himself as a senior counselor of justice, mentioning some

other titles I don't remember, and his name, Gennadi Kolesnikov.*
He charged me under Article 190-1,† and produced a search warrant.
I was taken into the next room, where the two women did a body
search and looked through the one bag I had. They took copies of
the papers which were in the envelope I gave to the American
diplomats in Moscow. It was clear that Kolesnikov was familiar with
them, because he barely glanced at them. They also took two letters
that should have reached Newton, Massachusetts, before Andrei's
hunger strike. I now have copies of those documents‡ and my two
letters before me.

As I write these words and look up from the paper to see the
quiet, verdant suburban street of Newton, the letters seem overly
tragic and valedictory to me. But they convey my feelings of the
time, how hard it had been for us to make the decision and how
pessimistic I was about our undertaking. I would not write a letter
like that now, but I cannot change them. Andrei copied them over
in his hand (he has a habit of keeping copies). Those copies reached
Newton two years later. Whether I want it to be so or not, the letters
are now documents, and therefore I am including them here.

Dear beloved Mama and children!

Forgive me that in this letter I do not ask for advice but am
informing you of our decision. But Andrei sees no other way.
I have been trying since September to get him to rethink his
decision. But inaction in our present situation has become
impossible for him, and he thirsts for my cure and for my
meeting with you, perhaps even more than I. We know that
many will perceive this as a political act, but it's not politics
that makes me try to become a little healthier and to see my
mother and children. Maybe some will say once again that
Andrei is busying himself with trifles. And they will blame
me of course.

---

*Gennadi Kolesnikov, senior assistant to the Gorky regional procurator, in
charge of overseeing KGB investigations.

†Article 190-1 (of the RSFSR Criminal Code), slander of the Soviet state or social
system, carries a maximum term of three years labor camp.

‡See Appendix V for the letter to the ambassador.

You will have to suffer through that. You know us better than anyone, and I do not have to explain to you how insepa- rable we are. I want my letter to soften and reduce your pain. I have lived quite a long time. There was a lot of grief— Papa's death in prison, the shell that found Seva somewhere near Lyuban, the untimely death of Igor [my brother], the loss of friends, Inna's death. And my never-dying guilt that in a romantic revolutionary impulse I rushed off to save homeland and humanity, leaving Grandmother with two young children to care for in Leningrad, which was under siege; and now in my strange Gorky exile I cannot help lonely and sick Rainka,* and I have left you, Mother, in the care of the children.

And still my life has been happy. I always loved my work: I loved the cries of the newborn, and my girls, and what I taught them. Before that I loved being a nurse, so later at the medical institute I even had doubts about becoming a doctor; I loved my woman's work—washing windows, cooking, laundry, washing floors. I loved my literary work (the hard- est for me) and my fees for it. I loved to dance, I loved our friends and our kitchen—"the inn of merry beggars." All my life I had my first love—I never forgot Seva. I had my sunny years with Ivan, and your births, and how you grew, and how sorry I was that you were growing up. And then—now —that incredible, unimaginable human closeness that fate has bestowed upon Andrei and me. My life has turned out happily.

I am eternally grateful to you, Tanya and Alexei, that you, my children, are my best friends. I am happy that my son-in-law and daughter-in-law, Efrem and Liza, are like family and not strangers to me (that happens rarely). How boundlessly grateful I am to you, Mother, for Tanya and Alexei, that they are good people. You and I were incredibly lucky, Mama—they were always spiritually close to us. That was our great work, and you have a right to be proud of it. I want you to live a long time: for the children you are our

*Raisa (Rainka) Bonner (1905–1985). Doctor, aunt of Elena Bonner.

family, our home. The longer you are with the grandchildren and great-grandchildren the tighter will be their ties with one another throughout their lives. Mama, find the strength to stay on with the children. I love you very much. Forgive me for all the warmth I didn't give you, for my explosive temper —I always tried to be kinder, but it didn't always work. My little, my big Tanya and Alexei, all my eight children.* May our mutual friendships always be with you as well as the roads we went down together, and our campfires, and the wild beaches, and the city you were born in and all the other cities we shared; the music we listened to together, the paintings we looked at together, the books we read together, the poems we loved together. I ask you to remain close, to preserve our family and the spirit of our home—that will help you, and your children need it so much. Take care of Grandmother, remember Andrei. I will always be with you.

I want this letter to be not a farewell, but a promise of our meeting. I kiss you . . . Mama.

Andrei, love!

Our life has become public, independent of us. It is discussed by the press, and by acquaintances and strangers. That is why I am writing this letter for anyone who wants to understand, respond, help. You know how I live and you understand everything. I am tired of slander, of the badgering, of police guards, of constant surveillance—the illegality of everything that is happening to us. I am tired of being homeless, of feeling the hatred of your children, your distrust of them and your expectation that one of them will betray you. I suffer that we cannot help our friends in any way; I worry that the suffering of those who are now in Mordovia, Perm, and Kazakhstan labor camps may be in vain. I am ashamed before the eyes of their mothers, wives, and children. I have the impression that they think you can help. But I know that you

*She is referring to her children, grandchildren, and in-laws.

cannot. I see that the only reality is our immeasurable friendship and respect for them; and our packages to them. My dream—not everyone agrees with it—is one plane for all of them; it doesn't matter for whom they are traded, so long as they are freed.

I am tired of being separated from Mother and the children, of the fact that all disasters, all world boundaries, and the struggle for peace go through me, through my heart: there are nine* of them there, but you and my destiny are here. I love you, and I am grateful to you for that, and no weariness is capable of destroying that feeling. I am very tired of my illness. I can add nothing to your thoughts on why I cannot be treated in the USSR.

In September you decided to start on an indefinite hunger strike to obtain permission for my trip. I was trying to put the strike off as much as I could. Neither pity, nor anxiety for your health, nor fear for your life restrains me now. I know that this is your decision and that any action for you now is easier than inaction. This is something even many of our friends (not to mention our enemies) cannot understand —and they will blame me. It does not seem right to me that you wanted to do the hunger strike alone. I also want (if medicine can do it) to prolong my life, and I do not want to live without the hope of seeing my mother and children once more. You should not be the only one trying to achieve this. For thirteen years we have shared our labors and our troubles and we should not separate them now. Whether we will have the strength is "not for us to know." I am writing this letter with hope. Lusia.

*Including my mother, Ruth. [E.B.]

V

I do not remember a single question from the first interrogation; however, I remember my answer—it was the same throughout the investigation. Sometimes in conversation with the investigator I said other things, but for the record, for the transcript, there was only this one reply: "Since I never at any time anywhere under any circumstances deliberately spread slanderous fabrication defaming the Soviet state or social system, or the state or social system of other countries, or private persons, I will not participate in the investigation and will not answer the question."

The answer, of course, is cumbersome and rather long, but I repeated it during all the interrogations. Several times the investigator said that perhaps we could write down a shorter version, but I would not agree, and he always wrote down the reply in full. I had not noticed at the first interrogation that Kolesnikov's right hand was deformed by a wound and that it was difficult for him to write. Probably my position would not have been damaged if I had agreed to let him write "reply the same" as he had suggested, and not the long one I had made up. The search and first interrogation lasted two or three hours. At the end of the interrogation, I signed a promise not to leave Gorky. After that I was given a summons for questioning on May 3, put into the same van, and driven home.

When I got out of the van near our house, a man said to me, "Elena Georgievna Bonner? Allow me to introduce myself."

I was afraid that some petitioner was trying to meet me in front of all the KGB people who accompanied me, so I quickly said, "Get away; you'll be detained if you don't."

And he replied, "Allow me to introduce myself. I am chief of the KGB of Gorky Oblast."

It was a ludicrous situation. I looked at him, not quite sure what to say, and entered our apartment building. He followed me. I passed the policeman on duty and walked through the door of the apartment.

Andrei rushed over to me and said, "Lusenka!" And I replied, "Andryusha, this is the chief of the KGB of Gorky Oblast." By then I was dying to go to the bathroom. I had left the house four hours before and should have been in Moscow a long time ago. I put my bag down on the floor and made for the toilet. When I came out, they were shouting at a high pitch. The KGB chief was yelling, "I don't even want to talk about her. Bonner is an American spy, an agent of the CIA, and a Zionist spy. We will try her under Article 64. But you . . ." And he threatened Andrei. Andrei was shouting something I cannot recall. The KGB man ran out the door, still threatening me, and Andrei followed him into the hallway, still shouting. A few seconds later, Andrei returned and I learned that he had already begun his hunger strike. He had seen them take me away in the van and he realized that I had been arrested. When he got back from the airport, he sent a telegram to the chairman of the Presidium of the Supreme Soviet and to the KGB letting them know that he was on a hunger strike to get me my trip. He came home, took a laxative and gave himself an enema, and was sitting there drinking water. And all my months of arguing whether he should start a hunger strike or not, is it worth it or not, were just hanging in the air.

I told him that I had been charged, that I had signed a promise not to leave the city, and that I was formally under investigation and had to appear for questioning the next day.

In one sense you could say that Andrei's summons to OVIR on March 30 had been fully justified. They did give their answer after May 1 by opening their case against me on May 2. Andrei was right when he said the whole thing was an attempt by the KGB to grab the initiative.

I did not go for questioning on May 3. We set out, but the taxi couldn't get close to the prosecutor's office. Traffic was blocked, and I didn't feel well enough to walk. I went on the fourth, so they changed my summons from the third to the fourth. I do not remember the questions, even though I wrote them all down at that time.

On May 4 the TV news announced I had entered into criminal relations with American diplomats.*

On May 6 Andrei felt fine, even though it was the fifth day of his hunger strike. I decided to plant some flowers. Andryusha began digging up the bed in front of the balcony while I worked with the boxes on it. Around noon Ira Kristi† came up close to Andrei. She was wearing a beige raincoat and carrying a bag with a bouquet of flowers. Andrei did not recognize her—if he's not prepared, he never recognizes people. I knew who it was immediately. And I began telling her right away that I had been detained at the airport, that the KGB had begun an investigation of me, and that Andrei had been on a hunger strike since May 2. I told her the investigation was under Article 190-1, but they were threatening me with Article 70‡ and even Article 64.** Kolesnikov kept saying that this wasn't 190-1, that I should be charged instead under Article 70. He never mentioned treason, however. It was the KGB chief who brought up Article 64.

I did not have time to explain all this to Ira because KGB men rushed over and dragged her away, literally pulling her into the neighboring building, into the room they called the Support Point for Maintaining Order. We did not see when they removed her from there, even though we took turns watching by the window almost all day. I was so sorry she did not have a chance to give us her flowers.

That was on May 6. The next day I was called in the afternoon, around three, and we took a taxi. While I was in Kolesnikov's office, Andrei waited in the hall. He had his bag and a thermos of hot water, which he sipped. The interrogation was rather pallid and not too

---

*See Appendix II.

†Irina (Ira) Kristi (1938–   ). Mathematician and longtime human rights advocate. Kristi was detained overnight in a Gorky police station after seeing the Sakharovs, but contacted Western correspondents as soon as she got back to Moscow. She was then kept under house arrest for many months. Emigrated in 1985 with her husband and child, and now lives in the Boston area.

‡Article 70, anti-Soviet agitation and propaganda, in ordinary circumstances carries a maximum term of seven years labor camp and five years internal exile.

**Article 64, treason, can result in the death penalty.

long, and at the end Kolesnikov said that he had to speak with Andrei and did I mind if he was brought in. I didn't. He called him into the office and said, "Andrei Dmitrievich, doctors have come for you, you must go to the hospital." Andrei began arguing. Several people in white coats came in, five or six of them, and suggested his taking a ride in a way that made it useless to resist. Then Andrei asked that I be allowed to go with him.

We were taken to the hospital in an ambulance and to the same room where we both had been after our hunger strike on Liza's behalf, and where Andrei had been alone when his leg had hurt. There was a man in one of the beds. We were led into the room and left alone for some time with the bedridden man. My back had been very bad during these days. In fact I felt very poorly altogether, and so I lay down on Andrei's bed, and Andrei lay down next to me. Just then Dr. Oleg Obukhov, the chief physician, came in and said I had to leave. Andrei began insisting that I be allowed to stay with him, as during his last hospital stay. Obukhov categorically refused, but then proposed that I could stay at the hospital in a different section and in a different ward. The way he said it made it perfectly clear that he was going to trick us. Andrei would not agree, but several men came in and we knew they were going to remove me by force. I got up from the bed. Andrei also jumped up and put his arms around my waist and stomach from behind me. They tried to drag me out of his arms. He pulled me toward him; they dragged me away. Then there's a blank moment, during which I ended up in the corridor. They must have taken me away by force and I must have briefly lost consciousness. I could hear Andrei shouting, but they must have been holding him in the room because he did not run out into the corridor. I was forced down the corridor the way children are pulled along by their arms. They set me back on my feet at the end of the hall and gave me my purse. We took the elevator down and I was put in a car and driven home. I arrived about eight o'clock.

I was left alone. I do not know how I got through the night. I was awakened by a ring at the door in the morning. When I opened it, Kolesnikov came in with two women, one in a police uniform, several men, and two women from our building as witnesses. They presented me with a search warrant. This was around nine o'clock, and the search began, a long, boring one. I think they themselves were tired of digging around in Andrei's papers. They took away an enormous amount, listed as 319 items, several of the items were files of up to three hundred pages. They removed many books, all the English and German ones. They also took the typewriter, the tape recorder, the camera and movie camera, and, most important, the radio.

The search was pointedly thorough; they knocked on the walls and the furniture, looking for secret hiding places. Quite unusual and unexpected was the arrival of a man who took samples of our food and medicines, apparently looking for drugs. There was a funny incident. I keep everything in glass jars with labels. But there was one small jar without a label. It contained a dirty yellow crystal powder. He asked me what it was.

"I have no idea," I replied.

He rubbed some between his fingers, smelled it, and put the powder in a test tube. Then he took the whole jar. It was only after they left that I remembered Andrei had once bought iodine salts, and that was what was in the jar.

They left late, around ten P.M. I went to bed, or rather collapsed on the bed, and sank into sleep. I was exhausted.

The next day I decided to go to the hospital in the morning, and on the way asked the taxi driver to stop at a small market so I could buy some flowers. I saw we were being followed by two KGB cars. I went over to a woman selling flowers, picked out tulips, and paid for them; two KGB agents asked what I was doing. I said, "Can't you see? I'm buying flowers. What's the matter? I'm not allowed?"

"No, you're allowed to buy flowers," one of them said. "But you can't go to the hospital. And don't even think of getting near the hospital. You won't be let inside, and you'll experience more unpleasantness." I said that I couldn't imagine any more unpleasantness, that we'd had all that was possible already.

I did not go to the hospital. What was the use? I wouldn't be able to force my way in. So I went home. Thus I spent May 9 without seeing Andrei, and arranged the flowers around the apartment instead of taking them to him.

I had to force myself to do something on this sunny and bright day. The ground in front of the balcony was dug up, and I went to plant seeds I had gathered last autumn. I spent a lot of time outside. I kept in mind that May 9 was a holiday (Victory Day) and that maybe someone from Moscow or Leningrad might show up and it would be good for me to be outside at the time. KGB people were everywhere. I'm sure no one showed up, because I would have seen him being dragged off to the headquarters in the building next door.

After that came more interrogations. On May 10 I was asked about Lesik Galperin and about Irina Borisovna Isat. "I have no idea who she is," I told the investigator, violating my own rule about answering all questions the way I had at the first session. Of course, in the transcript the usual answer was put in. But I told him (this was the first conversation, not for the record) I really did not know who she was and that I was very interested. He never did reveal her identity. I decided that she must have been Lesik's wife, Irina, whose maiden name I did not know.

The interrogations continued all during this period. It was at this time that I received a telegram from Dima, Tanya, and Lyuba. Andrei later sent the text in a letter to my mother and the children in Boston:

On May 15 Lusia received a telegram:
"Elena Georgievna, we, the children of Andrei Dmitrievich, ask and implore you to do everything you can to save our father from this mad undertaking, which could lead to his death. We know that only one person can save him from death—that is you. You are the mother of your children and you must understand us. Otherwise we will be forced to turn to the procurator's office, because you are inciting our father to commit suicide. We see no other way out. Understand us correctly—Tanya, Lyuba, Dima." . . .
This cruel and unfair telegram caused Lusia additional suffering and anxiety in her already horrible and almost unbearable situation. The telegram gave the KGB the "green light" for any action relating to us. . . .

This was a very unpleasant addition to everything that had already happened, and most unpleasant of all was the fact that the telegram became a major topic of the next few interrogations. Kolesnikov kept asking me about it, kept insisting, on the basis of the telegram, that I should be tried also under Article 107 or 103—incitement to suicide or premeditated murder. I sent a reply to Lyuba's address because I did not know the other addresses, all my notebooks having been confiscated.

I wrote Lyuba that I didn't know what had been happening to her father since May 7, that I could not stop the hunger strike or save him, and that their telegram . . . I do not remember what else I said. I do recall writing that I knew Lyuba was not the initiator of the telegram, but that I was responding to it at her address because I had no other.

The investigator, at a later interrogation, kept reproaching me for that reply, for writing that I did not know what was happening to their father and that I had no way of communicating with him. He said I was lying, since I knew that their father was being treated and that he was in the hospital and that I should write that to the children immediately. At the time I did not understand why the telegram had come just then, and why pressure on me was so important just then. Now, I know that on May 11 Andrei had suffered a stroke or cerebral spasm, his condition had deteriorated sharply, and they needed the telegram in case they lost Andrei because of the force-feeding. And perhaps they needed some kind of witness. I figured this out only later, when Andrei told me what he had experienced.

On May 18 there occurred an event I had not expected. Around six in the evening there was a knock on the door. I opened it and there was Uncle Venya putting away his passport, which he had shown to the guards. The policeman let him into my apartment.

I need to digress here to describe Uncle Venya. In 1977 Andryusha, our grandson Matvei, and I were vacationing in Sochi. On the beach we met, or rather Matvei met and brought over, a man whom he introduced this way: "This is my new friend, Uncle Venya." We introduced ourselves: "Veniamin Aronovich." "Elena Georgievna." We chatted as we sat by the water and tossed pebbles into the waves. Uncle Venya walked us back to our hotel. It turned out he was staying there too, and asked if he could join us for lunch. I decided he should be told about my husband. I said that Matvei and I had no objections, but we had to pick up Grandpa, my husband, and my husband was the Academician Andrei Sakharov. I felt it was necessary to let this chance acquaintance know, since he might not want any unpleasantness connected with the Sakharov name, but Uncle Venya was very pleased, not at all frightened, and said how much he admired Sakharov but had never even dreamed of an opportunity to meet him. We went to lunch together and spent our remaining days in Sochi with him.

We also went south in 1978 and 1979, without Matvei, without the children, who had left for America. Each time we were down south, Uncle Venya also came on vacation and stayed nearby, so that we spent a lot of time with him. That was pleasant and fun; he was a very nice man.

Now Uncle Venya told me the following story: He knew and worked closely with the chairman of the Olympic Committee, a big man in the Soviet hierarchy. Uncle Venya had heard about the hunger strike over Western radio and approached the chairman to help arrange a meeting with Sakharov; he would try to talk him out of the hunger strike, which he felt was too dangerous for Sakharov's health. And, he said, he was given permission to come and see me and to see Andrei in the hospital. He tried to convince me to write to Andrei to influence him to stop the strike. I told Uncle Venya that I would write nothing of the sort, that if Andrei had started the hunger strike, even though I was against it, I would not interfere with it now and behave like those who do not approve of it or who are his enemies. What would be, would be.

Uncle Venya ate dinner at my house and went back to his hotel. He promised to drop by and tell me how Andrei was, as he thought he would be allowed to see him the next day. And indeed on the next day, May 19, Uncle Venya did come by. However, I was out. He left a note with the policeman on duty. The note said he was hurrying to catch a plane and could not wait for me, but that he had seen Andrei and Andrei was in good shape and in good spirits.

I believed the note and it was only later, when Andrei was home from the hospital, that I learned these had been Andrei's worst days. He was still shaky and could barely walk, could not write, spoke with hesitation. There could be no talk of his being in good shape or in good spirits. And it was during those days that I received the telegram from Andrei's children. Now I think that Uncle Venya had been prepared as a living witness that I refused to help him end Andrei's hunger strike. But I cannot be sure. Had it been his own impulse to come, and had he received permission because he had influence? Or was he a KGB witness? I do not like to think that everything is KGB-inspired, but it is very hard, almost impossible, to think otherwise.

On May 22 I was not called in for questioning, and a woman came in the middle of the day saying she was a nurse from the hospital. The deputy chief physician had asked her to get Andrei's glasses, teeth, and a book on Pascal. I had been worried all that time that when they took him to the hospital, he had not been wearing his dental bridge, which was uncomfortable and which he kept removing. She told me this—there was nothing written—and she put it this way: "Distance glasses, dental bridge, and the Pascal." An awfully homey term for the book. The book is from the *Lives of Remarkable Men* series; I had just read it before Andrei was taken away, and we had discussed it a lot. But I doubt that Andrei would have referred to it like that to a stranger, without the name of the author or anything. And that's why I decided there had been a note. I told the woman I would give her everything when I got the note from Andrei. She said she didn't know anything about a note, she hadn't been given one, and she left.

There was no questioning for another two or three days. And then one morning Kolesnikov arrived with the handyman and a woman from our building, and the nurse. He had come with a warrant for the glasses and dental bridge, and the handyman and the woman from our building were there as witnesses. He began lecturing me on what a bad wife I was. I clearly wanted Andrei Dmitrievich to continue his hunger strike since I wouldn't give him his teeth.

I repeated that I was sure there was a note from Andrei Dmitrievich and that if they gave it to me I would immediately turn over what he wanted. But my "if" had no meaning, since they had a warrant. I couldn't face their turning the whole house upside down again and having to put everything back. I got the glasses, in fact several pairs, the bridge, and a three-volume Pushkin (I forgot about the Pascal).

The investigator was very surprised—or at least pretended to be
—that I was giving him several pairs of glasses. I told him Andrei
Dmitrievich likes to wear different pairs on different occasions. I said
he even had a special pair he wore when eating. Kolesnikov replied
that only a bad wife doesn't know which glasses her husband needs,
but he took all of them.

About the Pushkin he said, "What does he need Pushkin for?"
It was very difficult somehow to explain that you might need Pushkin at any time, in any of life's circumstances. There's the difference
in mentalities; some people don't know that others need poetry. But
he took the Pushkin too. I also asked him to give Andrei some pencils
and paper. They took everything.

Later I learned from Andrei that he had been given just one pair
of glasses and the others only when he left the hospital. The same
happened with the three-volume Pushkin. It was not given to him
until he left. Apparently they regarded the many pairs of glasses and
the Pushkin as some sort of coded signal.

At the next interrogation Kolesnikov unexpectedly brought up
the documents that had been confiscated from me during the search
on May 2. Later they were added as evidence against me and included
in the second volume of the case file, but they did not figure in the
trial. Kolesnikov said that the American ambassador, Arthur Hart-
man, had given a press conference in which he announced that I was
supposed to hide at the embassy according to an agreement made with
American diplomats. But I knew that the diplomats were not aware of
the plan Andrei and I had made, so I did not believe him.*

Then he read me excerpts from an article in _Izvestia_,† but he
would not let me see the whole article. I learned its contents later,
when Andrei came home. We went down to the reading room on
Beketov Street (which is quite far from our house) and spent almost
two hours there, which infuriated our guards. Andrei managed to
copy out the whole article in that time.

---

*The U.S. Embassy repeatedly denied ever discussing with Bonner her plans
to seek asylum there. On May 18 "a senior official" at the embassy acknowledged that
Bonner, before departing for Gorky, left in an embassy car a letter asking for asylum.
†See Appendix II.

At the next interrogation the investigator said that Dr. Jeremy Stone had written an article in which he blamed me for the fact that Sakharov had been forced to go on a hunger strike three times on my behalf. I did not know anything about the article or whether it in fact existed, until I came to the United States.

> Mr. Sakharov is a patient man, slow to anger, but deter-
> mined once aroused. Yelena Bonner's family raised his con-
> sciousness about the way the Soviet Union is run. He had
> been working in secret laboratories in a cocoon of what, for
> a Russian, is exceptional well-being; the life history of the
> Bonners was quite different.
>
> So, when KGB-inspired articles attack Mr. Sakharov as
> having been "captured" by a Zionist agent, Yelena Bonner,
> there is, amid the anti-Semitic smear, the grain of truth: His
> wife did radicalize Mr. Sakharov's thinking, and he is totally
> devoted to her. It is no accident that two of the three Sa-
> kharov hunger strikes have been in defense of her interests;
> the other was in support of a third party.*

I read it here and I was astonished. Dr. Stone merely repeated everything that is usually said by the administrators of Soviet science about Sakharov and me. He simply did not notice how he had been "trained" during his not infrequent trips to the USSR.

The interrogation lasted for several more days. Around June 5 Kolesnikov read me a note from Andrei. The note contained no news about his health or anything else; there were some very intimate words about how he missed me and how hard it was to be apart. I knew he had written the note—no one else could have expressed those sentiments. However, I was not allowed to see the note. It was only later, when Andrei had been discharged and I learned about his condition, that I understood his handwriting must not have been very good.

I was allowed to send a package to Andrei through the investigator. After they took the bridge, I had assumed that Andrei had stopped his hunger strike and I kept asking for permission to send

*International Herald Tribune, May 29, 1984.

him a food package. Finally I was permitted to send him juices, tomatoes, berries, and greens. During the investigation, Kolesnikov gave me notes from Andrei several times, five or six notes in all, even though it turned out he had written many more. Sometimes I could tell from the text that a previous note had not reached me. They accepted notes from me, usually in response to Andrei's, and twice a week they took food packages.

Later in June at one of the sessions I handed Kolesnikov a statement demanding a meeting with my husband, whom I had not seen since May 7. I did not know how he was. A week later, at my next interrogation, there was a man waiting in the investigators' office. Kolesnikov told me that in response to my request, he had asked Dr. Tolchenov, the deputy chief physician, to see me. The doctor said that Andrei Dmitrievich was in the hospital because of his heart trouble and problems with brain vessels and that he was under treatment. He gave no specific information about the treatment and when I began asking questions, he said he was not involved directly and did not know the answers. It was all under the direction of the treating physician. The doctors felt the meeting I requested would be harmful to Andrei's health and could affect the treatment, and therefore there would be no such meeting. And there was vague talk about how my being with Andrei in general, my nearness to him, was dangerous to his health, which was why the doctors had isolated him from me. Kolesnikov and the doctor did not want to respond in writing, so I received an oral answer. And when I pointed this out to Kolesnikov, he said it was within his rights to do so.

The interrogations went on, and there was nothing interesting in them. At first I had no idea on what they were planning to base the charges. Later I began to think they would be connected with the article in *Izvestia* and the U.S. Embassy. Gradually, by mid-July, it became clear that the indictment would include episodes involving the Nobel ceremony. Other charges would involve two documents of the Helsinki Watch Group, an interview in Moscow, and a story about life in Gorky, printed in *Russkaya mysl' (Russian Thought)*, * that had been confiscated during the search. (That is, before the search of May 8, they had not been planning to use that against me.)

---

*A Russian-language weekly published in Paris.

It seems to me that the charges were selected capriciously and as they came up in the course of the investigation, rather than planned ahead of time. There was only one goal: to show the high authorities how badly I behaved abroad. The only thing determined in advance was getting me to sign a statement that I would not leave Gorky.

On July 25 I was given the charges, but talk of getting a lawyer had already begun on July 20. I told them that I wanted Elena Reznikova from Moscow. The investigator refused and insisted on a Gorky lawyer. These negotiations lasted two days. Then he said I could have anyone I wanted to represent me; I could write a statement saying that I requested Reznikova, and he would accept the statement from me—something he hadn't been willing to do before. When I asked him how to go about it and which of my friends in Moscow I could ask to handle it, he replied that I did not have to do anything now; it could be dealt with later. I wrote my request, and Reznikova came.

We read the case file on July 25, 26, and 27—it took up six volumes. Actually the case itself was in the first two volumes and in part of the third. The fourth contained some papers (though it was unclear to me as to who might need them or why), and the verdicts in the trials of persons I had mentioned publicly in appeals and statements. The fifth volume also consisted of verdicts. The sixth had letters from workers who demanded that I be tried and isolated or punished.

The indictment and the six volumes gave me a better idea of the case against me. My reading revealed to me that on May 10 Andrei had had some things impounded: many documents from his bag, his tape recorder, and a few other items. I also learned about the searches conducted in Leningrad on Lesik Galperin and Irina Isat. They took all of Galperin's private correspondence with people abroad and with me and also his old hunting rifle. They took quite a lot of samizdat and tamizdat* from Isat and some correspondence. But none of that had anything to do with me.

I had thought that they had been searched (the searches took

---

*Samizdat is the generic term for unofficial literature in the Soviet Union, usually circulated in typescript from reader to reader. Tamizdat is literature published in the West and circulated unofficially inside the Soviet Union.

place the same day as mine, May 8) because they had tried to come to Gorky. But I've since learned in America that they had not made any attempts to visit us. I still don't know why they had been searched. All right, I could understand it happening to Lesik Galperin. We were friends; I often stayed at his place. The last few times I was in Leningrad I called my mother and children from his telephone. But why Isat? I only learned from reading my case file who she was. She was Regina Shamina, the wife of Tolya Shamin, and I barely knew her at all. Natasha Gesse was her friend, but I had never been to her place or even known where she lived. I think they made a mistake. The KGB must have heard me say something like "Regina is the closest friend of my life" many a time. Everything Andrei and I say is recorded and analyzed—that search is confirmation. They confused Regina Shamina with my Inna, Regina Ettinger, who died in October 1980, and whose funeral Andrei was not allowed to leave Gorky to attend. So they found a Regina.

It's time to tell about the charges. The first involved the press conference I gave on October 2, 1975, in Florence, for the Italian publication of Sakharov's *My Country and the World*. Andrei called me in Florence and read his introduction for that edition (the Russian had come out a bit earlier in a Khronika Press edition). It was called "Foreword addressed to Foreign Readers of *My Country and the World*." I read the full text and then answered questions.

I was asked to talk about women in political camps, because in his appeal Andrei wrote about the need for political amnesty, first of all for the sick and for the women in the political camp in Mordovia. I didn't speak about the human rights activists who were in the camp, but instead about Maria Semyonova.* This woman, a member of the True Orthodox Church, with the exception of brief periods of freedom, had spent almost her entire adult life in camps. I referred to "the tragic fate of Maria Semyonova." That is my phrase, not Sakharov's. While I was not speaking of just or unjust sentencing or anything else about the verdict, I did use the word "tragic." This phrase was the first count of the indictment: that I had committed slander, because Semyonova had

---

*Maria Semyonova (1923–   ). Member of the True Orthodox Church. Spent many years in forced labor camps.

been correctly sentenced, which was supported by the copy of the verdict in my case file.

At the trial, I attempted to explain that it is truly tragic for a person, even a murderer, to be in a camp virtually his entire adult life, whereas Semyonova was in the camp for her religious beliefs. However, this was somehow overlooked, and my words did not touch the people who heard them. Since she had been convicted (the verdict was in my case file), then any remarks about her "tragic fate" were slanderous.

The second charge was based on another press conference in Florence that October. The topic was religious persecution. At that time the first Sakharov hearings were about to be convened in Copenhagen. Before the hearings, representatives of the official Orthodox Soviet Church (what a strange combination, "Orthodox" and "Soviet," but I don't know any other way of putting it) had come to Copenhagen. They made several appearances, saying that there was no religious persecution at all, and that there was total freedom of religion in the Soviet Union, guaranteed by law and scrupulously observed. In answer to the question of whether they were speaking the truth or not, I said something the investigators deemed criminal. I said: "Well, that, to put it mildly, is untrue." And as an example I referred to Father Romanyuk,* who had been convicted not long before that. So my words about religious persecution were deliberate slander on my part.

The third count in the indictment was the press conference in Rome on November 7, reported in the newspaper *Il Tempo*, where I spoke of Andrei Dmitrievich and his Nobel Prize and discussed the question of whether he would receive permission to leave the USSR. I cannot remember what exactly was found incriminating in that press conference.

Then there was the press conference in Oslo. There, two things were incriminating. First of all, that I said that national discrimination exists in the USSR. I gave as an example the obstacles faced by Jews who apply to institutions of higher learning. And second—and

---

*Vasily Romanyuk (1925–   ). Ukrainian Orthodox priest imprisoned on charges of nationalist religious activity.

this was very actively discussed during the investigation and at the trial—that I said there are two forms of money in the USSR, regular money and certificates.* Andrei Dmitrievich writes about that in *My Country and the World*, and I hadn't been speaking very seriously when I mentioned it.

I've been sitting here, making final corrections on this book, which is sort of finished, but not finished, yet there's no time to do more work—I leave in two weeks. I feel very anxious and upset—for the last few days I cannot stop thinking about the Chernobyl catastrophe. And there was a telephone call from Norway that our friend Tim Greve† has died. He had been director of the Nobel Institute, he had come to Rome to meet me, and I feel that we became friends on first sight (but I feel that way about all Norwegians). We went together in Oslo to lay flowers on the graves of those who died during the war. Now I would like to take flowers to Tim's grave.

The next accusation was a very important one for the investigation. It was based on a document of the Helsinki Watch Group of 1977, "An Appeal to the Belgrade Conference." I was accused of being the author of that document along with Ludmila Alexeyeva‡ and Petr Grigorenko,** of disseminating the document, and taking it abroad to Italy. As evidence that I could have compiled the document with Alexeyeva and Grigorenko, the case file had affidavits from OVIR about when Grigorenko and Alexeyeva left the USSR. One stated

---

*Currency certificates can be used at special stores which are a perquisite of the establishment. See *My Country and the World*, p. 26, fn.

†Tim Greve (1926–1986). Diplomat, director general of the Norwegian Nobel Institute for several years, and editor-in-chief of the Oslo newspaper *Verdens Gang*.

‡Ludmila Alexeyeva (1927–   ). Historian, long active in the Human Rights Movement, a founding member of the Helsinki Watch Group, she emigrated in February 1977 and now lives in New York.

**Petr Grigorenko. (1907–   ). A major general, he was stripped of his rank after becoming a dissident. A founding member of the Moscow Helsinki Watch Group, he traveled to the United States for medical treatment in November 1977. His Soviet citizenship was revoked, and he now lives in New York City.

that Grigorenko left in late 1977, the other that Liza Alexeyeva left in 1981. But they confused my daughter-in-law, who was never a member of the Helsinki Watch Group, with Ludmila Alexeyeva. After reading the file, I demanded that the investigator replace the OVIR affidavit with one about Ludmila Alexeyeva, who left in February 1977. He refused. Later the court refused the same request when made by my lawyer. The information would have shown that I could not have collaborated with Ludmila Alexeyeva, since she emigrated before the document was drafted. But the most important part of this count was the charge that I brought the document to Italy.

Felix Serebrov* was a witness for this episode during the investigation and trial. During the course of the investigation, Serebrov insisted that Grigorenko had told him I had taken the document to Italy "on my person." The case file shows that Serebrov was perjuring himself. There is an OVIR affidavit in the file showing that I left for Italy on September 5, 1977. There is a document showing that Serebrov was arrested on August 18. This discrepancy in dates was overlooked as much as was conveniently possible in the investigation.

I was getting the impression that they were trying to prove I had brought out a document. It seemed very important to the authorities to prove that. It wasn't important that all the evidence be consistent or accurate; what was crucial was that the charge appear in the trial record, thereby making it possible to say: Do not let her go abroad for treatment; she smuggles out documents.

The next count was also connected to Serebrov—a Helsinki Watch document in defense of Serebrov. While in prison, Serebrov began to regard his work in the commission as wrong, and said so at his trial. Thus, the Helsinki group document was considered deliberately slanderous.

The next count was the article in *Russkaya mysl* (March 26, 1981) on Sakharov's life in Gorky, translated from some other language

*Felix Serebrov (1930–   ). Worker, member of the Working Commission on the Misuse of Psychiatry and of the Helsinki Group. He was arrested on August 22, 1977, and sentenced to one year labor camp for an allegedly forged entry in his work book. He was arrested in January 1981 and sentenced to four years labor camp and five years exile for anti-Soviet agitation.

into Russian.* A correspondent in Moscow must have chatted with me and then the newspaper translated his article back into Russian. It is not an authorized text, nor is it my text, nor is it clear what it is. In one paragraph I am allegedly asked what Andrei and I know about world events. And I say that unfortunately we know very little because steady jamming makes it hard to listen to foreign radio. The correspondent says, "Can't you read Russian papers, Soviet ones?" And I say, "Soviet newspapers have nothing but lies." Out of the entire article, which has many important details on Sakharov's life in Gorky, I am incriminated by that one phrase.

The final count relates to 1983, when my heart attack was diagnosed and I tried to obtain hospitalization for myself and for Andrei. I had an unexpected visit from François Léotard, the French politician and public activist, now a cabinet minister, who was in Moscow for a few days. He made a home movie of me answering his questions. I was very ill (that was obvious on the film) and told him about my heart attack and how I wanted to be hospitalized with Andrei or at least to have Andrei come to me in Moscow. That is the right of any exiled person, even officially exiled, to visit a gravely ill relative. Andrei was being denied that. And when Léotard asked, "What will happen to you now?" I replied, "I don't know. I think they are killing us!" And that phrase "they are killing us" was interpreted by the investigator as if a member of the government or someone else were holding a gun and shooting at us.

Reading the case, I had the opportunity to learn who had been interrogated about me. Of those questioned, Sasha Podrabinek,† Slava Bakhmin,‡ and Malva Landa** gave no essential (or unessen-

---

*Apparently this is a translation from the French magazine L'Express, Jan. 31, 1981.

†Alexander (Sasha) Podrabinek (1953–   ). A paramedic and founding member of the Working Commission on the Misuse of Psychiatry, he was arrested in May 1978 for his book *Punitive Medicine*, and sentenced to five years exile.

‡Vyacheslav (Slava) Bakhmin (1947–   ). Computer programmer and member of the Working Commission on the Misuse of Psychiatry. Arrested in February 1980, he was sentenced to three years labor camp for slandering the Soviet system.

**Malva Landa (1918–   ). Retired geologist and founding member of the Moscow Helsinki Group, she was arrested in March 1980 and sentenced to five years exile for slandering the Soviet system.

tial) evidence. While Vsevolod Kuvakin* did not give information important to the investigation, he may have created a negative feeling toward me. He told about meeting me at birthday parties in various homes (I never go anywhere; everyone in Moscow knows that and has stopped inviting me), in particular at Tanya Velikanova's† house. He knows from friends that I play a leading role in the Helsinki Watch Group, and that I collect signatures for various petitions, and he's seen me outside courthouses.

Most important to me—not for my preparation for the trial, but to me personally—was reading Ivan Kovalyov's interrogation. Kovalyov did not present any evidence against me, but he gave a handwritten statement of fifteen pages on the condition of prisoners in the camps. His statement is based on the fact that we both wrote a lot in our group's documents about political prisoners, and much of what we wrote was termed slander. Now that he has become a political prisoner himself, he can give firsthand evidence of the situation in the camps. He writes about the food and the work—about food that is inadequate and leads to malnourishment; about forced labor that is banned by international conventions; about the punishments for uncompleted work, which range from the loss of family meetings, of correspondence, or of privileges to buy at the camp store to being placed in the camp prison (PKT) or the punishment cell. He writes in detail about his 353 days in the PKT, when he received decreased rations and was exposed to torture by cold and hunger. He was deprived of his rights to correspondence and to buy at the camp store.

Appended to Kovalyov's statement is a character reference, signed by the camp administrator. I copied it over several times and tried to send it to Moscow, but apparently and unfortunately it did not get there. The character reference confirmed the length of Kovalyov's confinement in the PKT. It stated that he was not fulfilling

---

*Vsevolod Kuvakin (1942–   ). Lawyer and activist in unofficial trade union movement. Arrested in April 1981 and sentenced to one year labor camp and five years exile.

†Tatiana Velikanova (1932–   ). Mathematician and long-time human rights activist, she was arrested in November 1979 and sentenced to four years labor camp and five years exile.

his work plan, that he was impolite and insolent to the authorities. The reference ends with a phrase which serves as an answer to Gorbachev's statement in a recent interview, that people are not tried in the USSR for their convictions, that the 200 people (his figure) in prison for political offenses are there because of their actions, not their opinions. Kovalyov's character references say: "He has not changed his anti-Soviet opinions and has not started on the path of reform." Thus, this official document contradicts the General Secretary, and shows that Kovalyov was convicted for his opinions and that the aim of his camp sentence is to change them.

I was very pleased that Reznikova came to help me prepare my defense. Her arrival seemed like a release from our isolation. I let her read all the notes I had received from Andrei and told her how he had been hospitalized. She did not approve of my behavior during the investigation—she felt it would have been better for me to answer and explain—and she already disapproved of how I planned to act during the trial. Not that I could or would plead guilty, but she simply did not approve of my position, though at that stage I did not understand why.

On a human level her arrival was a positive, joyful event. She and I had lunch at a café not far from the procurator's office, rather than at the procurator's canteen. Then we would sit and smoke in the small square on Sverdlov Street. I saw it all later in a film shown here in the West. The film did not say, of course, that I was awaiting trial and that I was with my lawyer, but made it seem that I was strolling freely about town with a friend.

I drove her around town a couple of times, showing her some of the scenic places, and took her to our house once. She even got out of the car, went over to the front entry, and saw the police, and the KGB men. It was during those days that the KGB made an obvious blunder.

During the second day of our reading Reznikova and I agreed to meet at a café at ten and then go to read the file. When I got out of the car, she headed toward me. We said hello and a KGB man who obviously did not recognize her grabbed Reznikova and started dragging her away. She was frightened and shouted: "What are you doing, I'm her lawyer!" And she began to pull out her documents. Immediately another agent who did recognize her, rushed over and they let her go. She later said that she regretted shouting that she was my lawyer; she would have been interested to see what they would have done with her and where they would have taken her.

After reading the case, we submitted three petitions. The first was a joint one to call Sakharov as a witness for the trial. We did not know then that Sakharov had already requested to be called as a witness. He received a reply from Kolesnikov to the effect that the investigation did not deem it necessary. Sakharov's petition read:

"If my wife's case has been submitted to a court, I ask to attend her trial as a witness and as next of kin. My confinement in a hospital should not hinder my presence at the trial, since my health is now satisfactory.

"Since 1971–72, Elena Bonner's marriage to me has shaped her public activity, the authorities' attitude toward her, and her position in our society. In particular, I have reason to believe that she committed the acts which are the basis for criminal charges against her in response to direct or indirect requests made by me and while acting as my representative. Therefore, the investigation and indictment of my wife cannot properly proceed without me. I ask to be included in this case so that I can accept my share of responsibility."

Not making Sakharov's petition and Kolesnikov's reply a part of the case file, thus keeping me—the defendant—and my lawyer from learning about them, is a gross violation of procedure. And if the law were to be followed, my case could have been retried.

The second petition by Reznikova was for a request to the military for affidavits of the rehabilitation of my father and my mother. The third was to OVIR for an affidavit on the departure date for Ludmila Alexeyeva to replace the one giving information on Liza Alexeyeva, which was irrelevant to the case. The investigator rejected all three appeals. In response to the request for information on my parents' rehabilitation, he told Reznikova: "Ask for it yourself," so she did.

Reznikova left after reading the case, and I went about preparations for the trial. Of course I did not know when the trial would be scheduled. I could only assume that it would be soon, because the whole course of the case was based on a quick resolution. I kept waiting and hoping: There'll be the trial and then they'll release Andrei.

The time between the reading of the case and the trial passed rather quickly. On August 8 I received a summons to court. The proceedings lasted two days—describing them is tedious, but I must.

The trial took place in the regional courthouse in the middle of town on the main street. The building was the provincial courthouse before the October Revolution—and it is where the hero of Maxim Gorky's novel *Mother* was tried. I do not remember which was his real name, Vlasov or Zalomov, and which the fictional name.* But he was tried in this building, also on the second floor, in a room bigger than mine.

My courtroom wasn't exactly small. I counted eighty-five people in attendance, and one hundred could have fit easily. And there was not one familiar face other than my KGB friends.

The presiding judge was Vorobyov (I don't remember his name and patronymic), deputy chairman of the regional court. Nor do I recall the names of the People's Assessors. The prosecutor was the Perelygin† who had once dealt with Andrei. Judge and prosecutor differed sharply in manner and character of speech from the investigator, Kolesnikov, who seemed legally educated and intelligent. (A rhetorical question: Can a Soviet investigator belong to the intelligentsia?) Throughout the investigation he never allowed himself any violations, any vulgarity; everything was observed formally and strictly. But later, when I saw Andrei, I learned that he had written to Kolesnikov with requests to be named a co-defendant and to be called as a witness. So how can you go by appearances? The judge seemed to be not very literate in general or in matters legal, not very cultured and rather boorish. So did the prosecutor.

My questioning on the stand began. Did I admit that I was

---

*Petr Zalomov (Pavel Vlasov in the book), a young metalworker, sentenced in 1902 to Siberian exile for participation in a political demonstration. *Mother* is required reading in Soviet schools.

†Deputy Procurator of the Gorky Region.

guilty? My answer was: "I categorically do not consider myself guilty because I never, under any circumstances or in any place, spread deliberately slanderous opinions that defamed the Soviet state or social system, the government or social system of any other country, or any individual."

I demanded that my husband be called into the court. The first counts in the indictment were related to the publication of Sakharov's book *My Country and the World*. At a press conference on October 2, 1975, I read Sakharov's "Foreword Addressed to Foreign Readers of *My Country and the World*," and as a result quotations from Sakharov were being used against me. My position was that they could not be deliberate slander on my part; I was merely doing what he had asked—and only he could say whether I did it accurately or not. As for the Nobel press conference in Rome on November 7, 1975, where I tried to present Sakharov's views with precision on the problems mentioned, only he could say whether I had purposely made errors and deliberately slandered, or whether I had made mistakes or confused things because I did not fully understand the material. Sakharov had to be a witness. I also insisted that Sakharov be present in the courtroom as my next of kin. The court denied my demands, even though they were supported by my lawyer.

Then I told about myself in approximately the same tones used in my biography for the suit against Yakovlev. I said that in general it was not I but Yakovlev who should be sued for slander; he had libeled me before millions of readers, but I had been refused the protection of the court.

I said that this trial was in reality a response to my request to travel to see my mother and children. And if I really had committed crimes, then why was I being tried now, when the majority of them went back to 1975? Why were they trying me nine years later? If they truly had been crimes, they should have been stopped immediately. I said that the court was not empowered to try me in the absence of the only and main witness, Academician Andrei Sakharov, at whose behest and in accordance with my own convictions I appeared in Oslo to accept the Nobel Prize since he was not allowed to go there; at whose behest I passed along other documents for publication, in particular the letter to Dr. Sidney Drell,* entitled "The Danger of Thermonuclear War." This letter elicited a stormy response, shall we say, from the workers—after the statement of the four academicians criticizing Sakharov, Andrei Dmitrievich had received almost three thousand letters.

In the courtroom I quoted a few passages from that letter. It is very important for understanding how public opinion is formed on the basis of lies. While I spoke, I was interrupted many times by Judge Vorobyov. He kept saying that this did not have anything to do with the case, but I went on. I had the feeling that he could not force me to be silent; he had to observe all the formalities of the Procedural Code. I used their desire to do everything correctly and said what I wanted to say, even if I was interrupted.

One episode was rather amusing. The charge which appeared to be the most important one in the trial was my remark at a press conference in Oslo about there being two kinds of money in the USSR: money for "blacks" and money for "whites"—meaning ordinary money, which is used to pay salaries and pensions, and in everyday commerce, and certificates. Certificates are received by only a few—diplomats who work abroad and those who are on the same social level: writers, film people, scientists. To disprove my claim, the investigator asked for a statement from the Ministry of Finance. The statement said that there were not two forms of money in the USSR; there was only the Soviet ruble, but there were also checks from Vneshtorgbank (Foreign Trade Bank) of the USSR which are paid to people working abroad, or for publications printed abroad, and so on.

Knowing that this charge would figure in the trial, I brought two rubles, an ordinary one and a certificate one, in my purse. I also had a document confirming that Andrei Dmitrievich receives certificates for the publication of scientific articles abroad. It was a very polite letter from Vneshtorgbank stating: "Dear Andrei Dmitrievich!

*Sidney Drell (1926–   ). American physicist, Deputy Director of the Stanford Linear Accelerator Center and a specialist on arms control. Sakharov's article "The Danger of Thermonuclear War" was written in the form of an open letter to Dr. Drell.

Please let us know in which form you would like your honorarium paid, in Soviet rubles or Vneshtorgbank checks." Usually Andrei responds that he would like Vneshtorgbank checks, and after a while receives them by registered mail.

When we got to that point, I said I was a simple, normal person and saw things the way they were. Here I had a ruble like this and a ruble like that. I know that with one ruble I can buy only certain things, but, sometimes not what I want, and if it is what I want, I have to stand in line or use some special method. I also know that with the other, certificate ruble, I can buy what I want, without a line and of the best quality. I know that one certificate ruble can be exchanged for two ordinary rubles on the black market, sometimes more, and that selling or buying them that way is considered speculation in currency and is punishable by law. Here they both are—I consider that they are two forms of money.

The prosecutor exploded. He began screaming that I was displaying money which I had been paid by the CIA, that I was a paid agent of the CIA, and that they compensated me with those very certificates.

I raised my voice in response and eventually began yelling too —that I certainly was not a CIA agent, that the CIA did not pay me, that Andrei Dmitrievich had received that money for publication of his scientific articles in the West, and here was a document to confirm that. And I offered the court the letter asking which form of payment he preferred.

"The prosecutor has insulted me," I said, "and if he does not apologize I will not participate any further in this trial."

I did not just say that, I shouted it even louder than the prosecutor was shouting. The judge hesitated, and a few seconds later said: "The court will recess for consultation." The court came back a few minutes later and the judge said: "The court has made a decision: the prosecutor must apologize to the defendant." And Perelygin muttered into his chin: "Excuse me."

I was satisfied.

There were two witnesses. The first was Felix Serebrov. Andrei Dmitrievich writes in detail about his testimony in his administrative complaint and I think my lawyer dealt with him in a very business-like and effective manner, proving by dates that Felix was not telling the truth. I must add that Reznikova's remarks on this score were not entered in the trial record, nor did they have any effect on the sentence.

When Serebrov was brought into the courtroom, his physical appearance was that of a very sick, perhaps incurably ill man. I do not remember any prison inmate looking that bad when he was let out. His skin was an earthy yellow, he had lost a lot of weight, his eyes and cheeks were sunken, the skin was tight on his skull, and he wore the blue inmate jacket. He looked like an inmate of Auschwitz in such films as Mikhail Romm's *Ordinary Fascism* or Andrzej Wajda's *Landscape After the Battle*. He made me feel a terrible pity and at the same time, since he told absolute lies, a feeling that I cannot define or name . . . I would never want to be in the same room with him.

Not only did he state facts that had no relation to reality, he also said things that created a general mood. He said something very stupid from my point of view, but which he was obviously told to say: "Elena Bonner has a great influence on her husband, a bad influence. I can tell you a story; once Sakharov wrote a very good article himself ["himself" is Felix's word]. But when everyone started signing it, he refused to sign it because Elena Bonner hadn't liked it."

This quotation, which I give almost verbatim, is false. If Sakharov had written an article, he would not have shown it to Serebrov; he would have signed it and would never have given it to anyone else to sign. He wrote his articles himself and signed them himself, and bore responsibility for them himself. Sometimes he did confer with me about what he wrote, but he never discussed articles with Serebrov—he was not closely acquainted with the man. Serebrov began to visit our house only after Sakharov was exiled to Gorky. He was first brought to us by Masha Podyapolskaya to receive advice from Sakharov before his arrest in 1977, when he was accused of forging documents. Serebrov was still free, but had signed a paper promising not to leave town. Later, in 1981, when he became a member of the Helsinki Watch Group, he came over frequently.

The second witness was Kuvakin. While Kuvakin said in his

written statement that he knew me and knew that I played a leading role in the Helsinki group, giving everyone documents to sign, at my trial he said that he had met me in front of the courthouse during trials of various dissidents and that he barely knew me. He had been at our house once with Vladimir Gershuni.* He said, "I was at Sakharov's house once, but Bonner was not home. And I saw her once as I was leaving Naum Meiman's† house. She and her husband were just arriving." So in fact his testimony had almost no significance. I think he had been called as a witness so that there would be two of them, which is better than one.

The other proofs of my guilt were verdicts, a whole volume of them, pronounced on individuals I had mentioned at any time in statements or appeals. I gave the judge a list of over ninety people whom I had named in Sakharov's Nobel Prize lecture, saying that if you are using these verdicts as evidence of slander, then add some more. You haven't got all the people whose names I have ever mentioned; you might as well have them all. The judge took the list and added it to the case file.

Other proofs of my guilt were the statement from the Ministry of Finance; the article in *Russkaya mysl,* attributed to me, about Sakharov's life in Gorky; and tapes of my press conferences, which I had brought back from abroad quite openly. My lawyer said that since I had carried them without hiding them, I clearly did not consider what was said in them to be deliberate slander. There was also a videotape of François Léotard's film shown on French TV in late May 1983. There was no expert testimony about whether I had spoken slander or the truth.

Actually, I did not understand that term at all. What was deliberate slander? The judge and the prosecutor said that I realized I was committing deliberate slander because of my personality (I do not know what they meant by that).

---

*Vladimir Gershuni. Stonemason, political prisoner in the Stalin era, arrested in 1969 and sentenced to confinement in prison psychiatric hospitals for dissident activity.

†Naum Meiman (1911–   ). Mathematician, refusenik, and member of Moscow Helsinki Watch Group.

In my final statement, which Andrei liked very much but whose words I have forgotten, I repeated that I did not consider myself guilty, and that they would be better off letting me go abroad to be treated and to see my children than putting me on trial. Rather than making themselves the object of worldwide scorn—holding Sakharov in total isolation in Gorky and now also in total isolation from his wife for three months, and putting on a trial with an unprecedented lack of access, without any relatives present in the courtroom, and my husband being kept in the hospital only so he could not appear at the trial—they should re-establish "Soviet legality." I reminded them that it had been done before by Khrushchev, after Stalin's reign of terror. There was no one in Gorky or probably in the entire world who even knew I was being tried.* In conclusion, I reiterated, "I do not consider myself guilty and I have no requests for the court."

The court wrote the verdict rather quickly (or perhaps it had been written ahead of time). The sentence was pronounced an hour or so later. Everything that had been in the prosecutor's charges went into the verdict. I was given five years exile.

I should say a bit more about the documents in my case file. Besides Ivan Kovalev's testimony and the papers on him from the prison camp, there were documents pertaining to my health, with a detailed copy of my record from the Academy of Sciences Hospital. It was then that I learned what kind of heart attack I had had— an anterolateral and posterior myocardial. The record also discussed the situation with my eyes and reported that I had had surgery for thyrotoxicosis in 1974. Overall the excerpts from the medical record were detailed and truthful.

There were documents confirming my army service beginning in 1941 and a certificate stating that I was a group 2 invalid. There were files from OVIR about my travels, my mother's trip, and the emigration of my children and Liza Alexeyeva. There were files on Andrei's health, his diagnoses of cardiosclerosis, ischemic disease,

---

*News of Elena Bonner's trial was first announced by a U.S. State Department spokesman on August 23, 1984. Dates of the trial, erroneously given in the department's report, were to remain unknown for a year.

and atherosclerosis of the brain vessels, but no really new information on the state of his health.

Right after the trial I wrote a very brief appeal. "Please schedule
an appeal hearing, since I do not agree with the verdict." Reznikova
was supposed to draft a detailed appeal from Moscow. I said goodbye
to her hurriedly. I was in a rush to get home, because I thought there
was no more reason to keep Andrei in the hospital and they would
let him out. But my anticipation and hopes were in vain. Andrei was
not released, and my life without him went on.

A few days later I was called in to read the trial transcript and
to write my comments. I had not been prepared for that because I
did not know it was done. I was slightly surprised to find inaccuracies of a tendentious kind as I read the transcript. I spent three days
writing very detailed comments on the transcript and made a copy
for myself. Everything pertaining to the lawyer had vanished almost
completely, which it turns out is allowable. Much of what I said
when the judge kept interrupting me—about Andrei's activities, the
letter to Drell, the meaning of his human rights activities—was
deleted. The transcript looked as if the case had gone smoothly and
calmly, without the prosecutor's screaming or his apology, and this
I noted in my comments.

VI

How did I live that summer of 1984? With great difficulty, and very busily. The trial had been a lot of work. There had been over twenty interrogations; the apartment search, and then cleaning up afterward; tidying the apartment in hopes that Andrei would be coming back; shopping for him—winter shoes, socks, hats, a sweater, winter underwear. I was not sure whether I would be allowed to remain with him and I wanted to prepare him for life without me. For his birthday I bought him a desk. Then Reznikova came; we talked about some problems relating to the investigation and discussed what I should wear to court. I went around town looking for a skirt and blouse, which I bought, and then I had to think about what to wear on my feet. I had shoes in Gorky, but I wanted something more decent.

I continued working on my flower garden. The nicotiana's scent was intoxicating. There were boisterous blooms and the gillyflowers had a strong perfume. On the street level I planted matthiola and malva. So that summer I had a green, gorgeous, and scented balcony and a tiny flowerbed below.

I passed food packages to Andrei, and made jam, lots of jam. I thought that if he continued to be separated from me, he would at least have jam for the whole winter.

On one of my trips to the market, when I was buying berries, I realized I was being followed. I saw that they were using a camera, or rather I thought they were. But it never occurred to me that I was being filmed so I could be shown in the West, and in all these years that was the only time I spotted a camera. Now an incident comes to mind that Andrei once described: he and Dima had gone out—

it might have been Dima's first Gorky visit in 1980—to buy bread, and he saw that they were being filmed. He covered his face with his hands, and then turned and left. He had told me this, but I didn't recall the incident until I was in America. And it was in Boston that I remembered being filmed at the market.

After the trial my contacts with the investigator ended. There was no one to deliver my notes to Andrei, and there was nothing for me to do. As I was receiving no news of him, I sent a telegram to the chief physician with a question about his health and a request for him and the treating physician to tell me his condition. On August 15 I was given a piece of paper which informed me that Obukhov and the treating physician, Natalya Evdokimova, could see me at the City Health Department at two o'clock. (Not at the hospital; they must still have been worried that Andrei might glimpse me or I him.)

I was received by Obukhov and Evdokimova, who were seen in the films shown in the West. Obukhov sits on a bench and turns the pages of a magazine toward the camera, so that Andrei Dmitrievich will not notice but the viewer will see that it is really 1984. Obukhov then walks down a garden path with Andrei Dmitrievich, demonstrating the "healthy" Sakharov to the world. And Evdokimova reports on Sakharov's health (which is fine, according to her), and on how he is being fed and treated.

Those two physicians, however, tried to convince me that Andrei Dmitrievich was gravely ill, with serious arrhythmia and profound disturbances in the brain vessels. They insisted that he could not be discharged from the hospital and that my visits or contacts with him would be dangerous to his health. That was the end of our conversation. Of course, when they told me how they were treating him, they brought up digitalis again. I tried to convince them that digitalis was dangerous for Andrei Dmitrievich, that with extra heartbeats, taking digitalis was like taking poison. But nothing came of my entreaties.

Two days after that conversation I managed to buy a pediatrics textbook in a store that sells books published in socialist countries. The textbook had been translated from Bulgarian. I sent it to Obukhov, underlining the parts that said that digitalis should not be taken in cases of congenital or youthful extrasystoles that remain for life.

This is how I lived until September 6, knowing nothing about Andrei except for what Evdokimova and Obukhov told me, longing and lonely, trying to keep a grip on myself. On that day the secretary of the court came with a summons to appear the next day for an appeals hearing. It was unprecedented to have a judge of the Supreme Court of the RSFSR come to an appeals hearing in Gorky.

This was done so that everything would be properly observed, even the opportunity to appeal for the convicted defendant, and also so that no one in Moscow would know that I had been tried and found guilty. Two years later, I learned that people in Moscow had waited for an appeal and tried to find out when and where it would take place—or if it had indeed happened. They never did learn, just as they had not learned about the trial until much after the fact—my lawyer had not told anyone.

On September 7, Reznikova came from Moscow and repeated her arguments before the judge. I was allowed to speak my piece. I reiterated everything I had stated at my trial and added I did not consider myself guilty. The judge handed down a decision that did not differ at all from the verdict, and I formally became an exile. Directly from the hearing courtroom, where I was videotaped throughout the session, I was directed to a certain room on the first floor to see the chief of the Fifth Division of the MVD of Gorky Oblast. He took away my passport and gave me a certificate saying that I was an exile. He told me I did not have the right to go to Moscow for my things, that my place of exile was Gorky, that I could not travel beyond the city limits of Gorky, and that I retained all the rights of a citizen of the USSR except the right to leave that city.

I told him I was a war veteran and that as an invalid of the war I wanted the special food allotment I was entitled to and all the other privileges. He was slightly taken aback, but did not argue. My entire conversation with him lasted five or ten minutes. He also informed me that I had to appear on September 12 to receive my official exile documents from the MVD of the Prioksky District of the city of Gorky, and named the man I was to see.

I once again said goodbye hastily to Reznikova and hurried home in the hope that Andrei would be there. But he was not.

I have skipped many things in my narrative. I had to ask for emergency medical aid several times that summer. Once I was so sick, moaning, that the KGB agents called an ambulance. I knew that it was important for them to get me to the courtroom in good health and I did not fear doctors as I do now. Interestingly, throughout the trial a doctor and nurse were on duty. I was offered a shot before each session if I wanted it. I had analgin with papaverine and noshpa twice. So there are instances when even Gorky medicine can be trusted.

Throughout the investigation Kolesnikov himself offered and obtained medicines for me, indicating they knew perfectly well that I needed it. Once, when he gave me Timoptik, he complained about how it had to be imported from Finland. At first, he took money for the drugs from me but then stopped, saying that since I was a war veteran I didn't have to pay.

It even reached the point where he would ask me if I needed anything. I told him I needed instant coffee. "Needed" is a flexible concept here—I could have bought the lousy coffee sold in Gorky, but I told him I needed it. A day or two later he handed me two jars of coffee at six rubles each, the price when it is available. (But it never is available.) They tried very hard to make sure I got to the trial alive and well and satisfied.

On the day after the appeal, around two o'clock, I went to the MVD to bring them papers asking for the return of the items confiscated during the search—in particular, my radio, typewriter, and tape recorder—and asking for permission to go to Moscow to get my things; otherwise, I claimed, I was not only being sentenced to exile but was also having my property confiscated, as I did not have access to it.

On the way I was stopped by a highway patrol car. When I pulled over, a woman in a white coat got out of the KGB car that was following me. This time just one black Volga was escorting me —I am always under surveillance when I drive. I recognized Valya, the nurse who always took care of us, the only nurse allowed near us when we were in the hospital after our hunger strike to get Liza out, and when I was with Andrei during the period of his leg problem. She said, "Elena Georgievna, you are asked to come to the hospital at five o'clock to see chief physician Oleg Obukhov."

I asked how Andrei Dmitrievich was. She said, "I don't know anything." And she went back to her car.

I drove to the MVD and handed in my application. Then I bought bread and a few other things at the market—it was late, around four, and the market has a poor selection then.

At the hospital, with Obukhov in his office was Professor Vagralik, a cardiologist who "treated" us during our hunger strike for Liza. He went to see Andrei in one hospital and then me in another and kept saying in answer to our questions about the other that he did not know a thing. Also present were Professor Troshin, a neurologist; Dr. Evdokimova, the treating physician; Obukhov; and someone I don't remember.

They all chorused that Andrei Dmitrievich was in a bad way, that he was on the brink of death, that his extrasystolia was very bad, that he was suffering from grave atherosclerosis in the brain vessels, and that he had either Parkinson's disease or symptoms of it. (When I asked a direct question, "Is it Parkinsonism or symptoms of it?" I did not get an answer.) And that I should not worry him. They practically said I should not tell him about the trial or anything like that.

I yelled at them, telling them that as doctors they should understand that a man in that state of health cannot be kept isolated for four months from the only available person dear to him; that they should be thinking about how to change his situation; and that what they were telling me was nonsense. They had given him digitalis and had brought on his worsened condition themselves. I told them that I thought this was the only thing they did that was not premeditated, that they had simply lost their heads out of fear of the KGB. Everything else they were doing to Sakharov was a crime. (I said all this before I knew that they had tortured and humiliated him with forcefeeding and its consequences.)

In general, we had a very unfriendly talk, after which I started to leave, accompanied by Obukhov. I don't remember what I said to him, but he responded with a line from Pushkin that seemed to express sympathy for me and implied that it wasn't his fault, it was just the circumstances. As we were going down the stairs I was still cursing and blaming everyone, including my judges. Obukhov said suddenly: "Be indifferent to praise and slander and do not dispute with fools." I replied, "Ah, look how educated you are: you not only know how to perform vile deeds, but you also know poetry." He did not respond. After our frequent arguments (and my family and friends know well how sharp my tongue can be), he always pretended at our next meeting that nothing had happened.

I left the hospital, and in about fifteen minutes, Valya came along, leading Andryusha by the arm. He was wearing the same light coat in which he had been taken away in early May from the procurator's office, and his beret. It didn't seem as if he had lost weight; on the contrary, he looked almost bloated. We embraced, both of us in tears. We got in the car. I couldn't move. We just sat and wept with our arms around each other. About twenty minutes passed.

Then Andrei began asking questions about the trial. I told him everything "briefly and in detail." Basically, what was there to tell? The sentence, that was it. The rest would come later.

We left the hospital, taking the bypass road—there's a hill from which you can see the Volga River. We stopped on that hill and sat in silence. Then Andrei began telling me what had happened to him, which is all in his letter to Alexandrov.*

Andrei did not mention some matters in his letter, thinking them unimportant. I did not attach any importance to them myself until I came to the West and learned what information people have here about us and what was being disseminated about us from Moscow.

On May 9 I had not been let into the hospital. On the tenth, Andrei's documents had been impounded. We later discovered that, along with the documents and objects listed in the record of the search, Vsevolod Bagritsky's book *Diaries, Letters, Poems* was also taken from his bag. I had brought the book to Gorky because I always kept it with me. Ever since Yakovlev had launched his slan-

*See Appendix VIII.

derous typewriter into action, we were very worried that it would disappear, and so Andrei carried it in his bag. Well, it did disappear; it was not impounded officially, it did not appear on the list, but the book was gone. They simply stole it.

The night of the tenth, Obukhov woke Andrei and said that doctors from Moscow had come to see him. He brought in two men in white coats. These people asked a few meaningless questions and left. Back then in 1984, Andrei did not assign much significance to the visit. But in 1985, when he was back in the hospital and the big KGB boss, Sokolov,* appeared, he recognized him as one of those two men. We did not know anything about the other man until I heard talk in Moscow and the West that in 1984 Andrei had been visited in the hospital by a psychologist or psychiatrist who tried to hypnotize him in his sleep or something like that. If it was "in his sleep," then Andrei couldn't have known about it. Later Andrei and I decided that those two men had been called in to give permission to force-feed him.

Andrei described what happened during the force-feeding. I was wrong when I thought that he had halted his hunger strike when they came to the apartment for his false teeth—it happened a week later. He could not explain to me why he stopped, but in the letter to Alexandrov he said he could not stand the torture. I think that is the correct explanation. So I had been right in not turning over the teeth and glasses because I thought there had to be a note from Andrei. There *had* been a note and it was not given to me, because his handwriting was affected by the stroke (or spasm) and he repeated the same letter over and over in a word. Apparently they did not want me to see the note, assuming *quite rightly* that I would realize things were bad with him.

This makes it harder to understand the note left by Uncle Venya, saying that Andrei was perfectly fine and feeling good. Uncle Venya saw him on May 19, and Andrei could not have felt fine that day. He still had trouble walking, and there were hesitations in his speech.

Andryusha did not receive all of my notes, either. He understood

*KGB official. Elena Bonner first met him in November 1973, when she was interrogated about the sending of Eduard Kuznetsov's *Prison Diaries* abroad.

that. He made copies of all his notes and in addition kept a diary, which, strangely enough, was not taken away from him. When he came home, he let me read it. It records everything that happened to him. How they tormented him with talk that he had Parkinson's disease, and how Obukhov brought him a book on Parkinsonism and said that he had gotten the disease from his hunger strikes, adding things like "You will become a total invalid, unable to unfasten your own trousers," and, "We won't let you die, but we will make you an invalid."

Judging from what Andrei told me, and from the remaining symptoms he still had in September and which partly remain (involuntary jaw movements), I think he suffered a stroke, or a severe cerebral vascular spasm.

At home, Andryusha's condition was rather strange. On the one hand, he was very happy we were together again; we literally were not apart for a minute's time—we followed each other even into the bathroom. On the other hand, he began berating himself, almost from the first day, for not continuing his hunger strike and for giving in to them: he had threatened another strike for September 7, but they discharged him on September 8, and he did not persist, unable to be apart from me any longer.

His mood was rather grim. When I told him he had to learn to lose gracefully, he said, "I don't want to learn that, I want to learn to die with dignity." He kept repeating, "Don't you understand, I was not just on a hunger strike for your trip, not so much for that as for my window on the world. They want to turn me into a living corpse. You kept me alive, giving me a connection to the world. They want to cut that off."

After my hearing, I had started reporting in as an exile. I was told I needed a photograph made for my exile document. I decided we should also have a picture of the two of us together. Andryusha got dressed up for our picture. In the photo, Andrei does not appear emaciated in the least, because over three months had passed since he ended the hunger strike. But I can't say that he looks good; rather, he looks oddly bloated.

I went to the district MVD on September 12, where I was fingerprinted (like all criminals) and photographed, mug shots, full face and profile, for my file—not as a defendant, but as a convicted person. And our joint and happy life went on.

We visited the hospital once more in September—they had made Andrei promise to go. That trip to the hospital, shown in one of the films, where I say that he has no heart pains at all and that he is sleeping well at home, was, I believe, our first visit. I think that I went with him twice—once in the fall and once in the spring.

By late September Andrei said he would start another hunger strike, and arguing with him was impossible. He became more irritable on the subject than before. He said, "They tried to scare me with Parkinsonism, which I don't have; they scared me with this and that; they think that they've broken me. No, I will go on a hunger strike."

But in the meantime we lived happily. We each bought a winter coat. And we purchased a radio. When our radio had been confiscated during the search, I tried to get another one, but a KGB agent in the store said, "What, are you planning to buy a radio?"

"Yes."

"I don't recommend it," he said. "We'll come with a confiscation order."

I believed him and thought, why waste the money?

But in September we went to a radio store, and Andryusha bought a radio—an Okean, very bulky and heavy. In 1985 outside the house, especially in the summer, I used it constantly.

Andrei began his letter to Alexandrov and his administrative complaint. At the same time he decided to quit the Academy; he needed Reznikova as his lawyer to sell his dacha, so we would have funds to live on once he left the Academy.* He sent a letter to the Lebedev Institute of the Academy of Sciences, telling them he was prepared to receive colleagues. I wrote Reznikova, asking her to come help us write the administrative complaint about my trial.

The physicists and Reznikova arrived in November, one right after the other. By then Andrei had a draft version of the complaint

---

*Sakharov continues to receive a monthly stipend of 400 rubles as a member of the Academy, plus a salary from the Lebedev Institute. He still owns the dacha in Zhukovka, near Moscow, which he was awarded for his part in the development of the H-bomb.

and a draft of his letter to Alexandrov. Reznikova had some sugges-
tions about the administrative complaint which he did not like. He
made some changes and sent it in late November.*

With the physicists Andrei discussed our situation and said he
would be writing to Alexandrov. He was both appalled and depressed by the fact that Reznikova and the physicists did not react
at all to his detailed description of his hospital stay. They were like
statues, or corpses. He was astonished by their deliberate indifference, their desire to alienate themselves. He was more upset by
their attitude than by anything else. He had sought and hoped for
compassion.

Both the physicists and Reznikova mentioned the movie *Scare-
crow*. Soon after their visits it played in Gorky, and Andrei and I
went to see it. It was a short, humid day with wet snow. What can
you expect from the weather in late November? My back hurt very
much. Our tickets were for the seven-o'clock show. We drove to a
café around five o'clock to have something to eat, and when we came
out, our car was dead. What had they managed to do to it? We had
no doubt that this was the first response to Andrei's conversation
with his colleagues, to the fact that he was going to take action again
to resolve the issue of my treatment.

We left the car where it was—Andrei would pick it up in the
morning—and went to the theater by taxi. We saw the film: we
wept, we were horrified, we suffered. The film was one of the
greatest events of recent years in Soviet life. We came out of the
theater dumbfounded.

But I couldn't walk—my back gave out. I leaned against a wall
while Andrei tried to hail a cab. The KGB agents were angry that
they had to be out in the snow because of us. Finally he got a taxi.
When Andrei told the driver the address, she asked: "Where Sakharov lives?"

"This is he," I said.

We started to talk, and amazingly, after the pogroms and threats
provoked by Yakovlev, this woman's attitude toward us differed
from so many others', and I was moved to tears when she said, "But

---

*See Appendix VII for the administrative complaint.

one can see how much you love each other. I'm going to be sixty myself soon—I'm retired already, I'm just working my two legal months—and I could see right off that things are good between you." I often recall her words: "good between you."

That excursion to the movies was the start of the cardiac deterioration I suffered during the winter of 1984–85. And after that trip, I was placed under an eight P.M. curfew.

So we didn't go out in the evenings. We weren't allowed to visit anyone, but who was there to visit? That makes it the perfect time to talk about our everyday life.

VII

I would like to tell the story of our car. It's an old one, born in 1976. And the KGB has subjected it to its persecutions, too. As soon as it was widely known that Andrei and I were planning a hunger strike to get Liza an exit visa, the car was stolen—this was in the fall of 1981. Rumors were spread around Gorky that I had driven the car to Moscow and hidden it, so that we could accuse the state of stealing it. When we were on the hunger strike and not leaving the house, afraid of being grabbed on the street and forcibly hospitalized, it was suddenly found, and the traffic police kept calling us to come for it. Andryusha said that we didn't care about the car now, but they argued that it was so valuable a possession that our hunger strike could be interrupted. But at last, unable to lure us out of the house with the prospect of getting our car back, they simply broke down our apartment door and took us by force to separate hospitals.

After Liza's departure, the car was returned to us, but only its remains—everything that could be unscrewed had been taken, and the tires were replaced by bald ones. Half the parts had been removed from under the hood and everything taken out of the interior—even the ashtrays. Liza left on December 19, but we did not get the car back into shape until May. In the years that followed a strange situation developed with this inanimate object. Whenever the authorities did not like something, it was our car that suffered. Either two tires would be punctured, or a window smashed or smeared with glue. This was how we knew that we had done something bad by their standards: perhaps we managed to talk to someone on the street or at the market, or had gone to the wrong place, or refused to see Dr. Obukhov or another doctor.

There are many sins and only one car, so it suffers, poor thing. And as the limitations on us increased, they reflected on the car. That first summer we decided to go for a swim in the Oka River—exactly twelve kilometers from our house. We swam and sat on the shore. As we were driving onto the highway from the river road, I was stopped by a traffic policeman, which surprised me as I had not committed any violations. Then I saw that there was also another police car next to the traffic vehicle. Snezhnitsky (then a captain, now a major) got out and headed toward us.

Here I have to mention another episode involving him. This was at the very beginning of our life in Gorky. On February 15, 1980, Yura Shikhanovich came to see us on my birthday. He was immediately dragged off to the "point for the protection of public order," where Snezhnitsky began questioning him and working him over. Andrei and I burst in. The agents started pushing us out, and I slapped Snezhnitsky. We were dragged out, of course, and dropped in the corridor—we were like beaten dogs.

Then there was a trial which I did not attend. (Perhaps it wasn't a trial, but something administrative.) I was fined thirty rubles. I had the occasion to tell Captain Snezhnitsky that it wasn't expensive—thirty rubles for the pleasure of slapping him. Incidentally, history shows that in the years of Nicholas I the police chief in the central part of Nizhni Novgorod* was a certain Snezhnitsky—perhaps it's a family profession.

On this summer day, Snezhnitsky came over to us and declared that Andrei had violated the rules of his regime by going beyond the city limits. He wrote out a report which Andrei refused to sign. However, we no longer went there together. I went by myself quite often, because the local Sovkhoz has a stand there, and three times a week they sell very good cottage cheese and sour cream. Andryusha would wait for me on the side of the road inside the city limits. Once it was pouring, and the traffic police (they're not all KGB) invited Andrei to wait out the shower in their little booth.

That also happened when I gave an old man with a Leo Tolstoy beard a ride to the bus station in the rain, while Andryusha sat in

---

*Gorky was called Nizhni Novgorod until 1932.

a traffic police inspector's car. He waited for me once when I decided to take a look at what was on the other side of the big Volga bridge. But I did not enjoy driving alone; it was lonely and I felt sorry for Andrei. That is why I never went to Pushkin's estate Boldino nor to the village of Vyezdnoye, where the Sakharov family originally came from. I naively expected better times when we could go together. But from the moment that I signed an agreement not to leave the city, I stopped going too.

In those early years we often gave lifts to strangers. Then, without any explanation, we were forbidden to do that. At first the ban was not total—that is, when I was driving alone I could pick up people, but if Andrei and I were both in the car, I couldn't.

The authorities underscored the ban by puncturing our tires and that sort of thing. Then, seeing that we still did not understand fully, they began hauling passengers forcibly out of the car. I remember one horrible scene when Andrei was driving. He took in two women —one was very elderly and could barely shuffle. As soon as he started the engine, our escort ran over, stopped the car, and with shouts and curses pulled the two passengers out. The old woman was so frightened she could have died on the spot. We were forced to drive away.

Another incident occurred in the summer of 1985, when I was without Andryusha. A man stood by the side of the road holding a screaming child of four or five. I stopped. The boy had a broken leg, which the man was supporting. I started to help them in. My guards ran over and began pulling the man from the car. I think he would have fought with them if he weren't holding the child. Everyone was screaming—the child, the man, the KGB agents. And I started to yell louder than everyone, scaring them. I rushed at one of the guards, and I think I was prepared to kill him or die. I shouted for him to get in the car and drive. I think my behavior frightened the KGB man. He got in the front seat with me. I put the man and boy in the back and we drove to the first-aid station near our house. When the man and boy were gone, the KGB man said to me: "You are not allowed to stop. You know that, and if you try it again, you can say goodbye to your car." I did not reply, simply slamming the door. I shook for a long time.

Another incident was funny. Tires do go flat occasionally, a car's a car. It's hard for me to change them, so when I get a flat I tell the KGB escorts that I will flag down a truck. Any driver is happy to do it for three rubles. Sometimes the KGB man will give me permission on his own, sometimes he radios for advice. When I have permission, I flag a truck. Once the van driver was surprised by my request, since he saw a strapping young man near my car. When he was done and I offered him a three-ruble note, he said: "Don't bother, Mother, but you should teach your kid a lesson. What's the matter with him, is he sick or something that he can't change a tire?" "He's not mine, he belongs to the Committee,"* I replied. "Ah . . ." said the driver, and hurried back to his van. I still don't know what he thought. But at the last moment he gave me a look that made me think he knew who I was.

Our guards talk to us in the language of breaking or taking our car. They also speak in another way—the language of the loss and subsequent return of other things. A pair of glasses disappears and then resurfaces in a place where we both have looked. At first, I used to hiss at Andrei that he was being forgetful and that the KGB had nothing to do with it. But then it started happening with my things too. I began keeping notes. For instance, this silly notation: "My toothbrush is gone, and both Andrei and I have looked in the bathroom in the glass," with the date. Then more than a week later: "Hurrah, the toothbrush is in the glass," with the date. Obviously we are not crazy. Books have vanished like this, and so has Andrei's dental bridge, which turned up when Andrei was released from the hospital. When I was alone for ten months I often felt an inner anxiety from the knowledge that they were constantly entering the apartment when I was out. They were doing things, looking for things. What would they take away? What would they leave? The sentence from my trial vanished, and various papers disappeared during Andrei's absence. This whirlwind of moving objects creates a feeling of a Kafka-esque nightmare on the one hand and on the other that you are on a glass slide of a microscope, that you are an experimental subject.

A few days after Andrei had discussed the latest hunger strike

---

*Euphemism for the KGB—the Committee of State Security.

with Evgeny Feinberg, he was unwrapping the packages with scientific reprints when suddenly a dozen huge cockroaches scrambled out. It was nauseating and frightening. Later Andrei wrote about it in his diary:

> This happened yesterday: when I opened a package sent from the Lebedev Institute of the Academy of Sciences, cockroaches began running from it in all directions. I managed to kill five. I doubt that they climbed into the package at the Lebedev Institute. More likely, this is a demonstration of the KGB's scorn. As if to say, you are starving roaches. Of course, this is an interpretation, maybe the fruit of my imagination. The Greeks had difficulty guessing the meaning of what the Scythians sent them (an arrow, a frog, and something else like that: check old history books).

Another such language—albeit less revolting—is that of gestures, such as sealed envelopes arriving empty instead of with letters from friends.

Our isolation grew in terms of telephone communications. Even though we could not make long-distance calls between 1980 and 1983, at least we could make calls within Gorky. There was no one we wanted to phone, but still there were several times when I was sick that Andrei got in touch with Felix and Maya Krasavin and sometimes Mark Kovner. Once, when I was very sick and did not want to remain alone, Andrei dictated the text of a telegram to Newton, Massachusetts, to Kovner and asked him to send it; sometimes we requested him to buy some things for us at the market (Andrei did, I never called Kovner), since he lived nearby. Sometimes we called our friends the Khainovskys, and we phoned various movie houses to get the schedules. Starting in 1984, however, we were forbidden to approach telephone booths. Soon after that I became an exile, but some Soviet government officials claim that Andrei is a free man who has chosen to live in Gorky of his own free will. If that is so, he should be able to use the telephone.

Once he had decided to start a new hunger strike, Andrei began thinking seriously how we would be able to get information out of

Gorky. The attitude toward the hunger strike on the part of the physicists and my lawyer did not inspire great hopes. Who else was there? We had not seen Kovner or Felix since early April. They had obviously been forbidden to visit us, and anyway how could we try to transmit information through them—it would be horrible to get them into trouble. Andrei remembered that an acquaintance of ours was often in Gorky. He began asking me what I thought of him—in writing, of course; we did not utter a single word about it aloud. In the past, in Moscow, we often had to resort to writing instead of speaking. Andrei called people with whom you communicated that way—usually on magic slates—"slate buddies." I had great doubts that we would be able to seek out this man, meet with him in a way that would appear "accidental," and be able to pass something to him. And whether he would be willing to take the risk. I reminded Andrei of a story that had taken place more than two years before. . . .

Another train. How sick I am of trains. "What will I do in the Arrow, in the train that's left town. I walked the earth like a hero of a successful novel." This time I hadn't guessed right—there was something interesting to do. All night, until the first roosters, I worked out my relationship with a chance traveling companion, an old acquaintance. I hadn't communicated my feelings, stayed up all night clearing the air, in a long time; these heart-to-hearts had receded into the distant past, along with my youth and healthy heart. Along with the days when in our kitchen on Chkalov Street a bib hung on a nail on the wall with a little ditty above it:

> Working out relationships and meanings
> Never happened without a dribble.
> Put on the bib, then go ahead and quibble.

The poem wasn't gorgeous, but just like everything else we had around the place. And its message didn't affect the use of "work" time. Our discussions, and those of our friends, on "loves me, loves me not," "good or bad," "pro and contra," dragged on for hours and started up again and again. Wonderful days. I just want to cry out from today—"Give us our bibs back! My dear children, let's clear things up!"

But back to my story. In the late winter of 1982, Shikh and Emil saw me off to Gorky. I had more things than I could fit into one car. Leonid Shcharansky brought some of them to the station and Emil the rest. We unloaded Leonid's car and let him go. Then we got a porter and headed for the train. I had a berth in the sleeping car. In Moscow I could often get a good ticket, using my privileges as a war veteran. That's almost impossible in Gorky—in all those years I had a place in the sleeping car only twice, once with Zhzhenov, which I've described. The second time would come when I took my trip abroad, my American vacation.

Why is it so hard to get a good ticket in Gorky? Simply because they are not on sale in the normal way; they do not ever get to the city ticket office, but are sold instead at the Gorky Kremlin where the regional soviet meets.

I had too much luggage for my seat. That fall our car had been taken apart. We were putting it back together and I was bringing two wheels, a battery, and a suitcase full of smaller parts. That did not include my usual luggage—two larger chiller bags with food.

The conductor would not let me into the car. She was polite, but said that only if the passenger who was sharing my compartment did not object could I get on. We were waiting on the platform for my neighbor, who finally showed up. I did not see him until after I heard the conductor read his ticket (berth 15; mine was 16) and ask him if he minded my luggage, pointing at me.

He looked at me and started to blush. It was a slow process. I think everyone saw it. He blushed and blushed, and I began worrying about him. But maybe it all happened in a flash.

He said, "Of course," and went into the car. My friends (we had let the porter go, and anyway, what porter would have waited?) began dragging the wheels and things into the car. Then I went into the compartment. He was not there. I said goodbye to Shikh and Emil. I changed into my robe and lay down, covering my legs. My feet were always cold that winter (during the hunger strike and afterward). The train started. I took out a book and found myself half-reading, half-dozing, to the clickety-clack of the wheels.

I thought that perhaps my neighbor had slipped unnoticed into another compartment or even another car. But then he arrived, embarrassed and smiling. He shut the door and began talking.

I had the impression that he had been waiting for the train to start. He probably thought our conversation could not be overheard once the train was moving. We knew each other in a strange way. We had met in early youth, but came into direct contact only in our fully mature years. In the past it had always been through mutual friends; he knew people I had once been friendly with—my class-mates and, as we used to say (perhaps people still do?), people from our crowd.

He was happy to see me. I also felt a greeting from the past, from my youth. He was still good-looking, tall, and to my taste handsome. But they tell me my taste in men is off the mark. Ages ago I said about a certain Leningrad poet, with whom I was head over heels in love (and he with me), that he was the handsomest man in Lenin-grad. My girlfriends still don't let me forget it, and say that I must have been blind—this was before any of my eye operations. But I was serious then. And I was serious now.

This man was still handsome. I find that important; I always feel that beauty, charm, and sex appeal are gifts, blessings that make a person better, gentler, happier (if not in any concrete way, then certainly in outlook).

At first we shyly spoke of mutual friends, their children and lives. One had committed suicide; that was strange. Not as a teenager, but at our age, having lived through life's tragedies and uncertainties, a successful man in the humanities. Forgive me for using such a gen-eral, vague word—I do not want to be precise. I do not want you to recognize the man I am talking about. My subject is Andrei and myself; anything else I write about has to have bearing on that.

My traveling companion suddenly started asking about Andrei. They had been at school together once. When we first started living together, Andryusha and I were astonished by the number of mutual acquaintances we had, especially from our youth. We kept saying our paths should have crossed before, here and there. Then my companion began speaking about himself. How hard it was to live (not in the material sense, but spiritually), how it angered him to have to keep himself in check: how you never can allow yourself to say and do what you want. Worse—how often you don't even allow yourself to think.

Then he started talking about Liza, rather, about our hunger strike, how people in Moscow's intelligentsia, scientific, and literary circles kept discussing our hunger strike. Everyone disapproved. But our victory and Liza's departure changed their minds, and gradually everyone said that they had been in favor of it from the start.

He spoke a lot about the fact that Andrei and I could not even suspect how often our lives, our destiny, and our actions became not only the topic of conversation, but the background of the existence of many people, even though that did not mean that they approved of our way of life. Most often they did not. But we always kept them from living in peace.

He also said there was animosity toward us, and particularly toward me. He had tried to understand why, what people knew to be concretely bad about me, or what they thought I had done in the past or now. He could never find out. And he laughed sadly and said that the reason was banal—they were simply used to the simplest explanation: "*Cherchez la femme.*" But why or for what, they didn't care.

He was sad and so was I. He kept asking why I didn't talk much —and really he did do most of the talking, I listened, thought, and watched. He was so big and so handsome. He was older than I and was still so good to look at. So successful, smart, a Russian intellectual; his family was known for generations in our culture and history. I felt sorry for him. I could not forget that in 1980 one of our friends had asked him if he would go to see Andrei in Gorky, and he had said he couldn't because he would get fired. I told Andryusha and then asked him, "What would you do if he were in Gorky and you had that job?"

"I would lose the job."

Around four in the morning he asked, "What sleeping pill do you take?"

"I? Nothing."

"What about Andrei?"

"Nothing."

"You're lucky," he semidrawled, flirtatiously. I felt the air of friendship, which had come from the distant past and had been floating around us, start to thin.

"You're lucky," an Academician once said to Andrei and me. We were strolling along Lenin Avenue on a sunny spring day. He had been walking toward us and stopped to talk to Andrei. They spoke about a *festschrift* for a deceased scientist. The Academician complained that he was afraid the censors would not pass something and he thought it would be better to remove it himself. Andrei said there was certainly no point in rushing to do it himself. The Academician replied, "You wouldn't rush to do that, of course [and this was said to both of us]—you're lucky."

There was a time when it all was just beginning. 1973, the article in *Literary Gazette*, when the editor Alexander Chakovsky said that Andrei "coquettishly waves an olive branch." The article criticized him harshly, and it was a full column. I remember standing on the staircase at the Academy hospital. The wife of a corresponding member was going up the stairs, saw me, and rushed over. (She had known me a hundred years, and when I married Andrei, she told half of Moscow what a sweet girl I was.)

"Lusia, how are you and Andrei feeling? That's so horrible in the *Litgazeta*; my husband practically had a heart attack!"

I was embarrassed by her outburst, because I realized she did not know Andrei at all; they hadn't really met. I felt guilty that just because she'd known me since childhood she thought it gave her a right to talk so familiarly about him. And I was angry with myself because I didn't have the nerve to say, "He's no Andrei to you, and I haven't been Lusia to you for a hundred years, either. You used to call me Lusia before my father was arrested. And then?"

But all I said was, "We feel fine."

Incidentally, that was the truth.

And she said to me, "You're lucky."

Yes, we are lucky—but what can you do about it?

How do we live? Tragically. Buried alive. And at the same time, strange as it may seem, happily. On the seventh we celebrated our thirteenth official wedding anniversary; we did everything right, a party for two—Lusia went all out (cake and cheese pie, a "goose" [i.e., chicken] with apples, fruit liqueur), thirteen candles in a pretty design. Every postcard from Ruth Grigorievna, every photo is a great joy for us. We kiss you. Wish you good health. Kiss the younger children for us. Every night at bedtime, Lusia knocks on wood eleven times, with thoughts of you and of us, naming everyone and wishing them well. Kisses. Andrei."

January 15, 1985. From a letter to the family in Newton
from Andrei

Everyone agrees on one thing—Andrei, too. And so do I. We are lucky! I'm knocking on wood.

As for passing on information through our friend, nothing came of it. Andrei could not even get close to a telephone booth to make some calls and find out about him from mutual friends.

VIII

I'm lying on the beach in Miami, looking at the sea. A yacht with a crimson sail is passing, and behind it, one with a white sail. Crimson sails.* I just can't believe it. The miracle of Andrei's resistance, and the miracle that after my incredible operation I am spending my second day by the sea—it is all very hard to describe and even harder to accept as real. Just as it is difficult to imagine the lack of freedom in Gorky to which I will soon return. On the one hand, soon, and on the other, not so soon, for Andryusha has been alone for almost three months. And I know what it's like to be alone there, for I spent four months in 1984 alone in that special prison designed for Andrei, and six months in 1985.

The day before yesterday, February 18, I was given an extension. I simply cannot understand why the KGB needed to go through all that nonsense. Why they needed Novosti Press Agency to claim I could have had the operation at home, why they needed Victor Louis† to announce that I had been given the extension. Now even the waiter in the luxurious Fontainebleau Hilton Hotel and the salesclerk in a store yesterday congratulated me on getting a three-month extension. But it is impossible to explain anything to anyone. Even Aase Lionaes,‡ a wonderful and brave person who knows everything about us, said to me on the telephone two days ago that

---

*Crimson sails—an allusion to a book by Alexander Grin (Grinevsky) (1880–1932).

†A Soviet citizen who works as a stringer for English newspapers and has ties to the KGB. He has been the source of several videotapes of the Sakharovs bought by the German newspaper *Bild.*

‡Aase Lionaes. President of the Nobel Peace Prize Committee in 1975.

she wants me to go home via Norway and to stay in her house for a bit. It is impossible to explain over and over that I cannot return the way I want or the way my friends want. I have to ask for permission for everything. And that permission is not granted easily for anything.

The children flew back with my friends Jill and Ed Kline. I am alone in Miami, which I know from novels—the name was always alluring, and God only knew what went on in this city (again, in the novels). No sooner had the car with the children melted into the rush hour crush than a feeling of incredible lightness, of not being burdened by anything at all except myself, engulfed me with a power I had not experienced in a long time. Which should I seek out first —the city or the sea? I don't have a bathing suit, but I wasn't going to buy one at the Hilton. That morning, on our way to the museum, some side streets had caught my eye, and I decided to go back into town. I decided so quickly that my taxi could have caught up with the one taking the children to the airport. (A fine grandma who needed to be alone to work I would have been!)

I managed to explain to the cabbie everything that I wanted to see, the most interesting things, where I wanted to go, and where I was from. It's interesting, and it's something I checked several times afterward: in the north—more precisely, in Boston and New York—Russia elicits at least a superficial interest, while in the south, it gets none at all. For them we Russians are not exotic or anything else—just from some distant provincial place that they've heard of. But my statistical base is small and perhaps I am wrong.

We drove down the long and beautiful shoreline of a lagoon, and I looked at the villas and then handsome, ultracontemporary multi-storied apartment buildings—clearly housing and not banks of offices. Then came the lovely old streets, filled with shops, restaurants, and people. And I wandered around them, had some coffee, and bought a bathing suit. Then it didn't seem like enough, so in another store I bought a beach jacket, and some espadrilles. I stared at everything and was happy for no reason. Then felt sad because I was alone, and because Andryusha was alone in Gorky under steady surveillance—alone with the cameras.

I got back to the hotel and went to the beach after sunset. I was afraid to go into the water, so I sat down on a chaise longue at the edge of this beach. The sea was calm. I had not sat on the shore for a long time.

A bearded man walked by, came back a few minutes later, stood around by the water, and began asking me questions. I could not understand him at all. He sat down on the chaise longue next to mine and talked a lot. When he stopped, I said, "I do not speak English."

He slapped his thighs, laughed, and said, "That's wonderful," and something else which sounded like a curse, but I didn't understand his words.

Then we began a conversation. He understood my "Please, slowly," and I heard a whole novella about the American beach bum. He was twenty-seven; he had been a bum for four years; he had studied in several colleges, but just wasn't interested in anything. At first he didn't seem sick or anything, but then I got a vague, unpleasant feeling—was he on drugs perhaps?

We spoke about his country and mine. What was good and what was bad. I said, "We don't have freedom."

"We do—to jump in the ocean."

"Where do you sleep?"

"On the beach."

"Where are you headed?"

"California."

"Why?"

A shrug.

"What do you eat?"

"Whatever they give me."

"Can I give you some money?"

Another shrug. No offense, no interest. I opened my purse, which was on my lap. And suddenly I grew afraid—my money, and ticket, and precious Soviet passport, and all my phone numbers, everything was in there. But he was still indifferent, he took some money and stuffed it in his pocket. After a silence, he said, "You are an amazing woman, you understood everything I said. Who are you? Who?"

The question became persistent and somehow unpleasant. I remembered that as a student, and later, I had been afraid of the mentally disturbed. He suddenly took my hand and kissed it. I didn't have time to be frightened.

A wave overwhelmed me, the sense of an unwashed body, not a toiling or healthy one, of alcohol, and of something sickly sweet (narcotics, maybe). I forced myself not to gag. I got up. "Goodbye." "Goodbye, ma'am. Good luck." It was he who wished me luck.

What was the point of the conversation? Perhaps so I would leave my purse at the hotel and wander around after that with just a wallet?

I went to eat dinner. I decided against the hotel where I had dined with Jill and Ed, not because the luxury scared me off, but because I was really hungry and was afraid that I wouldn't be able to work out the complexities of the menu. And I don't like being served by three people at once. When I was in Iraq I felt like my own person and didn't mind, even if there were five of them, but here, at any moment someone might say that I wasn't me but the wife of Academician Sakharov.

In the back streets behind the Hilton I found a restaurant. Practically a canteen. There were no free tables, but a woman was sitting alone, a young woman compared to me, but actually middle-aged. I asked if I could join her and received a completely surprised nod in response. I sat down and only then realized that it isn't done here.

A waiter came over. I ordered with difficulty—or rather, I pointed, for luckily someone nearby had just gotten a plate with a piece of meat and a mound of French fries. And salad and coffee sound the same in Russian and English.

Even before I ordered, my companion told the waiter that we were not together. She saw that I had understood and looked embarrassed. I thought, "Why, you're a foreigner, too." Just then a young and handsome man came over. "Are you Elena Bonner?" he said, and then went on with all the usual about respect and so on. But not for long. This is a different country, and people here do not go on expressing their respect for long.

The waiter brought our food. At first we were busy eating in silence. Then she spoke. She was surprised at herself for not recognizing me, and then told me she was from Warsaw—that is, she was born there. She had been in Europe after World War II—first in

France, then Italy—and now in the United States. She was divorced, living on her ex-husband's pension, and her daughter had brought her here since she gets depressed sometimes. She was happy to have met me and was prepared to spend time with me in Florida.

"Just what I need," I thought. "First that beach bum and now you—other people's business, other people's faces, when I can barely handle my own." But I only thought that; out loud I said, "I'm leaving in the morning."

We left together. I decided to go for a walk along the beach. She said that Miami was dangerous at night. But it wasn't night yet, only nine in the evening. We said goodbye and I went out on the beach. The water was still, and along the marina as far as the eye could see there were yachts, yachts, yachts. For sale and for rent and just docked.

In the morning, having sat my fill at the water's edge, I swam for the first time in five years and found out that I am afraid of swimming and of water—I guess because of the surgery. Then I went to a yacht auction: I could come aboard and look at the luxury of the cabins—an old lady in thick glasses and three-ruble (excuse me, three-dollar) shoes. You'd think it was obvious I wasn't going to buy one. Maybe the salesmen enjoyed me in the absence of real customers as much as I enjoyed the yachts.

Wouldn't it be great to own a yacht like that, for mother, Andrei, and all the children? No—no children. We're all like that: "Apart I miss you, together . . ." Better without them; let them be happy on their own. Happy and peaceful. Everyone lacks something. Happiness? Peace? Andrei and I don't need to live anywhere, we could just sail, fly, drive—live. So long, Miami—no, farewell!

From the air Los Angeles seemed endless—the stripes of lights, in two colors, gold and silver, like foil chocolate wrappers. All I had seen of this city were a few streets and the trade center. I proved to myself once more that the only way to absorb a place is to be alone. It's like sitting at the typewriter for me—it's work.

At the airport I was met by a boy with whom I had studied at our alma mater—the First Leningrad Medical Institute. I write "boy" intentionally. Almost all of my fellow students, except for a few who had been demobilized like me, were five or seven years younger, and they've remained junior to me forever.

I was a first-year student. Mother and my aunt Raisa, a doctor, who had helped my grandmother as best she could all the years that mother was in the camps and who loved me and my brother very much, opposed my studying at the medical institute. They were worried about my eyes, and my eye doctor was against it. Together with the doctors, they would later object to my having children, which I decided to do despite all the doctors' warnings. I often think now what kind of person I would have been and what a life I would have experienced if I had followed doctors' orders and not gone to school, not gone to work, not had children.

So, it was February 1948. The money reform had gone through and no one was too hungry anymore. We were celebrating my birthday—I had invited my fellow students. Mama spoke irritably of one of them, a sturdy, rosy-cheeked teenager. "He is one of your colleagues too? Right out of kindergarten." I could hear her scorn because I spent time with "children," because I stubbornly left the house every morning at seven for my classes. She had hoped that I would skip classes and somehow drop out. She was angry that every evening I made her read physiology or biology to me, or even write outlines in Marxism for me. That way I cut down the load on my eyes.

The boy at the airport, Dr. Levran,* was one of those rosy-cheeked youths. Now he had three boys of his own, plus a girl. Los Angeles is a big city but we got to his house quickly. Or did it only seem that way because we picked up so easily and simply at the very point where we left off decades ago, years that had flashed by so swiftly?

And suddenly, a funny encounter from 1949. A young woman in a big round hat. I don't know what the hat situation was in the world then—our borders were locked tight—but in Leningrad hats like that were very fashionable and wildly expensive for those days.

---

*Arye Levran. Physician, classmate of Elena Bonner at Leningrad Medical Institute, now living in California.

She is either smiling or about to smile. I like her. Why? Maybe because she is unfamiliar. I had never seen that picture before. Levran forgot to give it to me (that happens to amateur photographers often), but now he's sent it to Gorky and I had confirmation that it got there.

From Sakharov's letter of March 18, 1986: ". . . a good letter with a big picture of you in 1949; I didn't recognize who it was right away, someone who resembled you. . . . I put the photo on my desk. The hat is like Marlene Dietrich's."

I decided to publish the picture in this book, even though I know it smacks of middle-aged coquettishness! "I was never beautiful, but I was always damned cute."

More about old photographs: a photograph of me from 1942 and my service record. This is not coquettishness, but documents for fighting back against Yakovlev. He writes somewhere that I hid out in a medical train at the end of the war. In the picture I still don't have shoulderboards—specialists know that means the picture was taken before 1943. It was far from the end of the war. And the service record gives the exact dates, and incidentally corrects me.

In my autobiography for the court I wrote that I had been sent to the Belomorsk region in May 1945, but the record which I found with the photograph makes it June—when the train, VSP 122, was being demobilized. I came to it just before New Year's 1942 from Sverdlovsk Hospital, still shaky from my wound and concussion, and for three and a half years it was my home and my front. All the officers of the train are in the picture—the chief, the doctor, the chief of the administrative section, the two senior nurses, the pharmacists, the other nurses, the sergeant, and, I almost forgot, the deputy political officer.

Lunches, dinners, good people—there were quite a lot of good people. Of course, you can't invite too many for lunch; it would have been better without eating, but with friends. Pasadena, San Diego —trained killer whales, and I'll never get over the fact that I saw them and Andrei didn't.

In San Diego I visited more good people and those they invited me to meet were also good. The hosts understood my aversion to lunches and dinners, and they arranged my meetings without them.

But the cakes and pastries, coffee and tea, fully compensated for lunch and dinner. It reminded me somewhat of our Leningrad-Moscow tables, when you get everything all at once—from breakfast to dinner. But the most important part was the lively eyes of the hosts and their friends, lively when I spoke about Andrei, lively when they asked me questions.

And how wonderful and alive were the people in Berkeley and San Francisco, what remarkable Americans in the theater department of UCLA, in Palo Alto and Menlo Park, at the New York Academy of Sciences, at Columbia University, at the Russian Research Center at Harvard, in Congress; all the receptions, lunches, and dinners in people's homes, in formal ballrooms and restaurants, and at my children's house in Newton, at the National Academy of Sciences, the Federation of American Scientists, the Boston Academy, the American Physics Society. I need these lists; for the moment, I do not want to talk about people as individuals.

The Americans I met were varied—primarily Andrei's colleagues, scientists, but not necessarily physicists; there were also politicians; people involved in the press, writers, actors—on the whole I would say they were the intellectual elite. I kept thinking that each of them seemed smarter than Andrei and me: they've all seen things, heard things, met people, read, and traveled—while we've been limited in those ways all our lives.

Many of these Americans speak out on questions of disarmament, war, peace. They talk about nuclear winter, star wars, pollution. About all the horrors that await mankind. They are all competent in their fields—or seem competent to those of us who feel incompetent. But when you meet them you understand that they are interested in living and that these problems interest them, too. They have no fear for the future—their own or humanity's—not the doctors who are against nuclear war, not the scientists who carry on nongovernmental talks about disarmament, not all the many specialists. They constantly speak and write about all these horrors in an almost professional way, sometimes totally abandoning their original work. But in their daily lives they are not troubled by what they talk about. They have their work and vacations planned far into the future, their purchases or remodeling of houses, new tax write-offs;

breakfast at home, a business lunch, dinner with wife and friends. I like the way they live.

And they sleep peacefully. They do not notice that they have depressed and ruined the sleep of millions of other people. Physicians are especially interesting in this regard. I don't know what they've said, but there is an epidemic of insomnia, neuroses, and borderline mental states, which if they have not created they certainly support with their activities. In Gorky a woman who works at the post office said to me (when we were still allowed to talk to people) that she was planning to redecorate her one-bedroom apartment and to buy a new rug. A while later, she said, "I don't know if it's worth starting all that, they say there'll be a war soon . . ."

Maybe here in the United States the so-called simple people (what is simple about them, I wonder?) think the same way as that woman, that it's not worth buying a rug, but the intellectuals certainly don't. It's an interesting phenomenon, but it's not for me to try to understand it.

I am going to try to limit myself to their attitude toward Andrei —and to me, since now that attitude can be expressed only in tandem and through me. Most of them don't need us at all, but almost all of them show formal interest (at dinners and receptions it is so formal that sometimes I just wanted to ask a person expressing his respects, "Do you at least know who Sakharov is?"), almost all are ready to sign something (there should be more petitions offered around), and yet many know very little. And not only about Sakharov's problems. Typically, they don't feel that this knowledge is necessary. I had the feeling that politicians sometimes possessed just as little information on other issues. It is not knowledge, but something else that leads them to act on problems (be it Nicaragua, energy, medicine, education, human rights), some other stimulus. Maybe it's a question of prestige, the important thing being to understand what's prestigious and what isn't. A few had read a book of Andrei's statements. At Scientists for Sakharov, Orlov, and Shcharansky,* everyone at the

---

*Scientists for Sakharov, Orlov, and Shcharansky (SOS) is an international organization of scientists with headquarters in Berkeley, California. It has been effective in mobilizing the world scientific community on behalf of Sakharov.

meeting was handed a copy; they must know their own people. It was there that I found a group who were seriously involved in human rights and did not just talk about it. But there are people in other places too who want to know and who accomplish things, and they were the ones I hoped to talk to, because I sensed compassion, saw animation in their eyes, and not the alienation and emptiness that Andrei described in his Soviet colleagues who came to see him in November 1984 and February 1985.

There are those who talk a lot about their work and about us . . . but. Now I have to explain one of my difficult discoveries. I'm thinking about people who know Sakharov's name, even know his work and views, who always sign everything, who sometimes take the initiative and call upon others to join them, who speak about Sakharov to Soviet scientific or government administrators.

I divide these people into two categories. For one group Andrei is alive, and everything relating to him hurts them like their own pain; for the others, he is a symbol, a game, politics, even personal success—a dead concept, I am afraid to say it, a dead man. I understood this when I was invited to meet a high official in Washington.

IX

You probably do not know that the White House has a back door
—in Russian, we sometimes say a back alley. I know it. Accidentally.
A passageway the width of an average street leading from the administrative building. On the other side of the security checkpoint
we were met by my old acquaintances, American diplomats who had
served their term in Moscow. (That's the truth. To "Everyone has
his term," I would add, "and his place.")

Maybe now they are "policy makers." No! They're not making
anything. The expression on their faces reminds me of an old story.
When my son, Alexei, decided to marry Liza by proxy, we had to
have Liza's signature notarized on a document that stated she was
giving her proxy to our friend Edward Kline to represent her in the
wedding ceremony. We turned to the American embassy in Moscow for help, because we knew that no Soviet notary public would
notarize such a document.

Two sweet consular employees—we later became friends—told
us, "Yes, sure, we'll talk to our lawyer." The lawyer (older than they,
but also young; Americans aren't afraid of giving responsibility to
the young) said, "Sure," and all three said, "We'll ask the State
Department. We think the answer will come quickly."

For the next four months I went to see them every week, making
a special trip from Gorky, once even leaving a sickbed. Their faces
grew more and more tense each time they saw me. I think even the
timbre of their voices changed, as they said week after week, "You
know, the administration is changing, there hasn't been an answer
yet." And finally, "They gave permission."

The next day I went back with Liza. You should have seen their faces glow! They stopped being embarrassed by us and perhaps by their bosses, who spoke so much about the humanitarian problems of the Helsinki Accords (why wasn't letting two people get married one of the problems?). Once Ed Kline got the proxy he became "our bride" (Andrei dubbed him that, and it became a family joke).

Today Efrem, Alexei and Ed (our groom and bride), came with me to the White House. They don't know that expression, half-sympathetic and half-guilty, with which my old acquaintances met us. I wonder why they invited us—me? "I didn't ask to be invited," I thought. "I'm just sitting here quietly, fixing the primus stove," as Mikhail Bulgakov put it.

The passageway is not wide, there are cars parked all over the place, and at the end loom two guards, and there is no pomp or majesty. It's not like the Kremlin, where I've also been. I didn't invite myself there either; I was invited by Anastas Ivanovich Mikoyan.* He also had a rather guilty look in his eyes. He was alive, while my father . . . They had been friends, and fought together through their youth, once even on the same horse. In the Kremlin there are many guards, some on each level, on each floor, all in parade uniforms, at attention, while here I'd say they were "at ease."

Beyond the passage was a small door, very ordinary. At the Kremlin the doors are really doors—twice the height of a person, and made of oak. At least, they ought to be oak. I don't know anything about woods used in furniture or building, but the doors said oak to me. And wide and heavy. And they open silently. Compared to the Kremlin doors this one was provincial. But the door was in a white wall, the house truly was white.

But why make comparisons with the Kremlin? The Kremlin is so far away. You can find something closer, like the Capitol. Everything is broad and expansive, and there is an abundance of everything—halls, windows, doors, rooms, corridors, stairs. In the Capitol the stairs are symbolic of something that leads both across and up—stairs as in Eisenstein's *Potemkin*.

In the White House, the staircase beyond the little door is as

---

*Anastas Mikoyan (1895–1978). Old Bolshevik, in 1964–65 President of the Supreme Soviet Presidium, and a colleague of Elena Bonner's father.

narrow as one leading to a tower chamber, and beyond it the rooms are small and the ceilings low. From this entrance, the White House is like a chamber work.

We were led into a small room. Besides the four of us and my two acquaintances from the Moscow embassy, there were three people waiting for us, and it seemed very crowded. The old Russian saying "Crowded but happy" flashed through my mind and melted away instantly; it didn't suit the mood. We were received by Admiral John Poindexter, Reagan's national security adviser. He spoke of the profound respect he felt for my famous husband. He also said that the American administration was profoundly worried about the fate of my husband and many others, but at the present time it felt that the best way to help them was through quiet, nonpublicized actions. That was why I had been invited to Washington, and why he instead of the President was receiving me.

I had the impression that the national security adviser was not well informed on the concrete work of Sakharov, on his role in the ratification of the Moscow partial test-ban treaty, on his scientific activity, and in particular on his pioneering work in the use of thermonuclear energy for peaceful means. Of the entire complex of problems on which Andrei Sakharov has been working for many years and which were reflected in the title of his Nobel Peace Prize lecture, "Peace, Progress, and Human Rights," only one aspect is often noted. And then the extraordinary personality of Sakharov and the significance of his free voice in the modern world are not understood. I must say that this erroneous view of Sakharov as simply the most important Soviet dissident—because he is an academician—is still frequently encountered in both scientific and political circles and speaks only of the narrowness of historical concepts.

I did not ask to be received by the President, and certainly not by Admiral Poindexter. But when I learned of his invitation I asked Dr. Moncure to put off the angioplasty and let me out of Massachusetts General for three days. I thought that the admiral was planning to tell me something important, or at least something new. But quiet diplomacy in the defense of human rights is such an old song. Was it so necessary just then for an official "instead of the President" to see me and thereby involve me in some political game that was harmful to the defense of my husband and other human rights activists?

Academician Sakharov considers publicity the main weapon in the struggle for human rights. In that sense I am a faithful and consistent student of my husband. I think that neither the admiral nor I came to accept the other's argument.

When we said goodbye, the President's national security adviser asked me to convey his respects to my husband. Of course I will. Our meeting did not take long. Once again we were led along narrow staircases. Downstairs in the tiny vestibule, a small group of people rushed past us, almost at a run. Alexei told me later it had been Vice-President Bush and his bodyguards. Without returning to the administrative building, we went along the passageway past the guards and into the city. I'm sorry I didn't see the famous Oval Office, or the garden where the President signed a proclamation declaring Andrei Sakharov Day. I won't be able to tell Andrei what they look like, but I will certainly describe the backstairs to him.

X

Human rights. Vastly different people and organizations talk about them and work on them. And the attitude toward them may be quite varied: sometimes only theoretical (that is, abstract), sometimes alive and human. I always recall President Carter with sorrow. Once he said: we will deal with the problem of human rights, but we will not deal with individual cases. And in saying that, he destroyed the deepest respect people had felt for him after his inaugural address. There can be no defense of human rights without the defense of every person who needs protection. Today, there are politicians and public figures who say they are concerned with the problem but not with each individual case. In fact, they are not really concerned with the problem either; they merely talk about it. And then there are those who are concerned with the person, with his fate.

Often the work of both types on behalf of Sakharov coincides—usually for some date or event: a celebration of Sakharov's birthday, the proclamation of Sakharov Day, at a prestigious reception, before an election, and so on. On the other hand, the work may diverge completely. One group may say: do not irritate or annoy; we will do it, but quietly. The other might say: do everything in public; we're not thieves. The former go to Moscow to meet with the scientific establishment and talk about disarmament, contacts, exchanges, and Sakharov. Why not, if it's in someone's office and done quietly, so that no one learns of it? That won't even annoy the Soviets and you can report back to the West that you did have the talk. The Soviets figured out that game a long time ago and they accept it. Europeans and Americans pretend not to know that it's a game.

But they do know it's a game, a special kind of doublethink. People claim that doublethink is characteristic of totalitarian societies, but unfortunately it's not limited to them. (I discovered "Western" doublethink.) A scientist recently told me that the White House does not like him any more than the Kremlin likes Sakharov. When I asked him why he was there (we were at a fancy reception in Washington) and why he had permission to go to Moscow so often (not to mention all his important positions), he did not reply. He probably had no answer.

People are very odd about their attitude toward Andrei. Apparently many do not want to understand, or cannot (a different mentality), that Sakharov must not be left in Gorky anymore; that it means death, if not today, then tomorrow. But they will ask if articles reach him. Sometimes they do, and sometimes they don't, and sometimes they are accompanied by cockroaches. And at the very instant when the KGB decides that articles need not reach him anymore, they will stop arriving. Western scientists are concerned about how often his Soviet colleagues go to visit Sakharov. Don't worry, the colleagues come as often as it is necessary to cloud your minds, dear friends; to make you think that the situation is ideal for Sakharov to pursue his scientific work.

Even after the publication of Sakharov's letter to Alexandrov, there is still talk about organizing medical help for him in Gorky. Who would give it? The doctors whom Sakharov called "the Mengeles of today"? He cannot remain in Gorky, and that must be understood by those who are concerned with human rights—anything can be done in Gorky and no one would know.

The world will go on watching the movies which Victor Louis sells, passing on the fees to the KGB filmmakers. Everyone will discuss how Sakharov looks in each new film and what he actually said. But films like that can be pasted together and released long after one or both of us is no longer living.

Another question. Are my husband's colleagues going to continue nongovernmental negotiations on disarmament and other issues without his participation, thereby overlooking the only voice that is both independent and competent?

On April 27, as a guest at a garden party at the National Academy in Washington, I was introduced to a physicist who is working on the problem of peaceful use of thermonuclear power. He hopes for cooperation with the Soviet Union.

I asked him, "Without Sakharov? After all, he did the pioneering work in that field and he is still alive. It seems unethical and amoral to behave that way."

"But it is rational. However, we do remember your husband."

"Remembering him that way is like remembering the dead, isn't it?"

"Perhaps."

That scientist does not suffer from doublethink. He is a realist. But those whose reason is replaced by doublethink are not much better. As far as I'm concerned, it's easier with realists—at least they do not try to delude you. Perhaps the reason Hitler's Germany lasted only twelve years is that it did not cloak its goals with pretty words. Its ideologists spoke frankly—they did not suffer from doublethink or doublespeak.

I will not start cursing. I will hope. After all, I know there are people who understand everything and whose hearts are not overgrown by indifference. It is better to curse someone not enough than to curse someone unfairly.

For the second group of people, Sakharov's name usually does not bring gain, success, or popularity, and often their honesty and lack of compromise actually involve them in loss—they lose an election, or do not receive an invitation, or are turned down for a visa, or are not given an honored post—but through them we live, and to them I say: "Dear, sweet, good people, save Andrei Dmitrievich!" And Andrei says to them, "Help us, we are counting on your help."

XI

And now we come to the final stage of Andryusha's struggle for my trip. It was long and as tortured as the previous one, but in a different way. It began in the fall of 1984, when Andrei was writing his administrative complaint and letter to Alexandrov. He had shown the first draft of the administrative complaint to Reznikova early in November, and he finished it later that month. He also wrote an amended version of his letter and made an attempt to get it out to the West in late 1984. He made a second attempt in early spring 1985.*

I wrote a petition for a pardon. At first I did not want to write it at all. I have a strong dissident reflex or clichéd response, according to which a petition for pardon is tantamount to repentance. Andrei had never felt that way and he managed to convince me otherwise. By the time Reznikova came in March, I had written my petition. I wanted her to turn it in to the Letters Office of the Supreme Soviet in Moscow.† We felt that was the best way. But she refused. She said that you do not write for clemency that way, that I had to condemn my activities. I replied that I knew how petitions for a pardon were written, but that I would not rewrite mine. I sent my petition by mail in late March or early April.

---

*See Appendix VIII for the text of the letter to Alexandrov.

†The Letters Office receives letters and petitions from Soviet citizens addressed to members of the Supreme Soviet, the legislature.

To the Presidium of the
Supreme Soviet of the USSR
From Bonner, Elena Georgievna,
residing at 603137 Gorky,
Gagarin Avenue, 214, apt. 3

PETITION FOR PARDON

On August 10, 1984, the Gorky Regional Court sentenced me to five years of exile under article 190-1 of the Criminal Code of the USSR.

Eight charges were mentioned in the verdict: four relate to 1975, when my husband, Academician Andrei Sakharov, was awarded the Nobel Peace Prize and at his request and as his representative, in accordance with my beliefs I accepted the prize on his behalf and participated in the Nobel ceremony. The next two episodes mentioned in the verdict are drafting, signing, and circulating two documents from the Moscow Helsinki Group (1977 and 1981); the seventh is an oral account of Sakharov's life in Gorky; and the eighth is an interview I gave to a French correspondent who had visited me three days after I had been diagnosed as having a myocardial infarct. All of the above were deemed by the court to be criminal actions, for which I was pronounced guilty. . . .

In 1977 my children—son and daughter with their families—were forced to emigrate from the USSR and reside in the United States. I want to see my children, four grandchildren, the youngest of whom I have never met, and to see my mother, who is with them at the present. She is a Soviet citizen and may return to the USSR but she will have to live alone in Moscow at the age of eighty-four (my brother, a navigation officer in the Soviet fleet, died on a voyage to Bombay in 1976) or to live with me in exile, in total isolation. In effect that will mean I would be asking her to serve another exile-camp term; her first, seventeen-year term ended after the Twentieth Congress of the CPSU with a posthumous—for lack of formal charges—rehabilitation of her husband, her own rehabilitation, and reinstatement in the Party, of which she has been a member for over sixty years.

In September 1982 I applied for a trip to treat my eyes (in the past I have had treatment and surgery in Italy three times) and to see my children, grandchildren, and mother. I have yet to receive a reply.

I ask for a pardon and permission to travel to see my children and mother. Six months ago I suffered a myocardial infarct, and this request is that of a person who cannot count on a long life. If you do not deem it possible to grant me a pardon, then allow me to travel to see my mother, children, and grandchildren for the last time during a suspension of my sentence; and, if I am allowed, to receive the treatment necessary to save my life.

I am writing my petition for a pardon or for a suspension of my sentence in the year when the USSR and the whole world by decree of the United Nations will mark the fortieth anniversary of the victory over fascism—a victory to which I contributed portions of my health and strength. I assure you that the only purpose of my trip is a meeting with my family; our separation has continued much longer than World War II itself lasted. I assure you that I will return to the USSR to serve out my sentence for as long as my strength endures.

Honorable Chairman of the Supreme Soviet! Honorable members of the Presidium of the Supreme Soviet! I appeal to you as the highest government powers and as people, trusting in your kindness and humanity! Deem it possible to show mercy to a gravely ill woman—a daughter, mother, and grandmother; a veteran of World War II and a group 2 invalid of the Great Patriotic War. Your refusal will condemn me to death without seeing my mother, children, and grandchildren.

February 12, 1985   Elena Bonner

We had no evidence that the documents Andrei was sending out had reached the West. Andrei hoped that even if the documents did not get out, the physicists who had visited him twice would tell their Western colleagues everything he had told them, and that Reznikova (who had seen us on March 25) would inform Sofia Kalistratova* about his plans. Thus, the West would understand

*Sofia Kalistratova (1907–   ). Retired lawyer who defended many dissidents and joined the Moscow Helsinki Watch Group. Advised Andrei Sakharov on human rights cases.

what was happening to us in Gorky and what Andrei was planning.

He asked Reznikova to tell Sofia Kalistratova that Ira Kristi should hold a press conference in Moscow on April 16 to announce that Andrei had started another hunger strike to obtain permission for my trip.

Why Ira Kristi? Andrei felt she was in least danger of the camps or Siberia because she had a small child and because she had applied to emigrate, and probably they would resolve the problem by letting her out. Therefore he felt that it was even to her benefit to be asked to do something like that for him.

We did not know that Ira Kristi had been under house arrest for several months after her visit in 1984 and that her husband was very upset by it. After Andrei began his hunger strike, we received a telegram saying that Ira Kristi had been called into OVIR and was gathering her papers to be able to leave quickly, that she was receiving permission. By then, Andrei felt that his documents had fallen into the hands of the KGB, and to hell with them, but at least Ira Kristi had received oral instructions and she would follow them. The fact that she had been called in by OVIR seemed confirmation. But it wasn't like that at all. The KGB had outwitted us, Ira Kristi, and all our friends.

On April 16 Andrei began his hunger strike. The date was not chosen in any serious way. Andrei thought that the authorities would pardon me on the anniversary of V-E Day, May 9, and he would not have to strike for long; also that it is easier to bear hunger in the spring than in the cold; also I kept asking him to wait. He had wanted to start it in March, but I said, "Can you imagine what that will be like for them in Boston? Tanya's birthday, and you're on a hunger strike." Then I asked him to wait until Easter —I wanted to bake *kulichi*, the traditional cakes. Not so much eat them as bake them. So we agreed that on Easter he would eat *kulich* and *paskha*, the Easter cheesecake, and then begin his strike.

Andrei never went to church in Gorky. I will not write about his feelings toward religion, because they are too serious and too intimate. (He writes about them in his book.) In Moscow we sometimes attended services on Easter eve (sometimes on Maundy Thursday or Good Friday), most often alone, sometimes with the children, and often we did not even go inside but stood nearby.

I went to church in Gorky late on Good Friday in 1981. We have a sweet little church not far from the apartment, just over the bridge. After the service, I sat down on a bench in the churchyard. Several women my age were nearby and two men stood next to them. They were having a quiet, peaceful conversation.

One of the men said to the woman sitting next to me, "Let's go. It's getting dark, and the streets are full of hooligans."

The woman got up, and one of the others said: "They ought to be shot."

The man supported her. "That's right. All of them."

"Well, shooting them all may be a bit much," I said.

"No, all of them," the second man insisted. "They've gotten out of hand. There's no order."

The third woman said, "Things need to be tightened, tightened."

"It used to be tighter, as tight as it could be," I interrupted again. Feeling that this could lead to an unnecessary argument, I got up and left the bench, but I could hear their disapproving comments behind me, to the effect that I personally had let things get lax.

I stopped going to church. I told this story once to Vera Lashkova and she said, "Why does that surprise you; it's like that everywhere." Now Vera is no longer in Moscow, either. I missed her terribly once she left.

So the date after Easter was chosen because of *kulich* and *paskha*. The night of April 16 I gave Andrei an enema, and he took a laxative. He was going to fast alone. I felt horrible—it all seemed hopeless to me, but I did not have the physical strength to do what Andrei was doing. So, once I had stopped objecting to his fast, I meekly agreed that I should not fast with him, that I would simply complicate things. I was just being cowardly, I suppose. Not because of the hunger strike itself, but everything connected with it. In those days I realized as never before how illness changes a person.

Around one o'clock on April 21 our doorbell rang. It was Obukhov with six men and two women. He said he had come to take

Andrei Dmitrievich to the hospital, but Andrei refused to go. The women stayed in the corridor. One of them gestured, and I took her to be beckoning to me. I did not understand why, and I went out. I don't know how they did it, but they pushed me into the little room off the corridor. The women sat on either side of me and even though they did not hold me I knew I would not be able to move or escape. They shut the door to the corridor.

From the big room I heard a shout: "Lusia! They're giving me an injection!" Then Andrei shouted: "Bastards. Murderers! Protect yourself!" And then: "Lusia! They're giving me an injection!"

I called out to him, but I didn't know if he could hear me. (When he got back home afterward, he told me he had.) There was a scuffling noise, and then silence. I heard the door slam and then footsteps. The door to my room opened and the women vanished instantly. A man who obviously was in charge of the whole thing stood alone in the corridor. I rushed up to him and said, "Where and what can I learn about my husband?" He said, "You'll be informed." Then he added, "All the best," and shut the door behind him.

I went into the big room. The table was pushed against the window. One of the chairs lay on the floor, and there were signs of a struggle on the couch, with its cushions and everything else scattered and crumpled.

The next day, when I went to the car, an elderly woman living in our building walked past me and whispered: "They took the old man out on a stretcher yesterday." She must have heard the screams. It was from her that I learned how Andrei had been hospitalized.

So a period began when I knew nothing about him. As opposed to the previous year, when Investigator Kolesnikov told me things, whether they were true or not, and passed along packages and notes, this year there was nothing. But I began receiving letters from Moscow. Many letters about Ira getting ready to leave, about her husband being sick and then being discharged from the hospital. There seemed to be great agitation about Ira's departure. Her friends clearly did not understand why she was leaving; but I did.

I began sending telegrams. I know for certain that from April 21 until October 23, I never used the words "we," "Lusia and Andrei," "Kisses from us," or anything in the plural. Never. Not once. Anything from the period that is in the plural is a forgery. But the postcard dated April 17, which temporarily confused my children, was not a forgery. It was written on the seventeenth—that is, before Andrei was taken away.

I sent telegrams to friends, asking them to get in touch with our lawyer. I began to realize that Reznikova had not said anything to Sofia. Perhaps the latter was ill or something; I didn't know. I kept writing to them, "Meet with my lawyer," "Meet with my lawyer." I sent Reznikova a telegram saying she should not continue with the dacha sale until she had seen her client. When I got an answer from her, I figured she must have understood something.

But instead of *my* telegrams, Masha Podyapolskaya, Galya Yevtushenko, and Ira and everyone else were receiving completely different texts. It got to the point where I sent Masha a telegraphic poem: "I can't understand it, I can't stand it, you're wining and dining, of envy I'm dying." Because all Masha wrote about was the Moscow high life, whose birthday it was, who was being seen off. No reaction to my telegrams.

On Andrei's birthday I received an amazing number of congratulatory telegrams. At the same time I received presents for Andrei: candy from Flora,* tea from Lydia Chukovskaya, a cake, chocolates, other things. Books and letters or telegrams from Ira, saying she was leaving, sending kisses and congratulations to Andrei.

I gathered up all the presents and sent them to a friend in Moscow with a request that she give them all back, with a list of what belonged to whom. While I was at the post office, a telegram from Masha arrived, and they gave it to me right there. Ira had left; the telegram was sent from the airport.

That evening at home I could tune in Radio Liberty without any jamming. There was Ira Kristi at the plane saying she could assert with confidence that even if Sakharov had been on a hunger strike, he was not on one at the present time. The sound was so clear and pure that it was as if the KGB were saying to me: "Here, listen, and do what you want. Beat your head against the wall—no one will ever know, go ahead and hang yourself."

*Flora Litvinov (1918–   ). Retired biologist.

I was furious with Ira. The anger lasted two or three days. Then I learned on the radio on my way to the cemetery, that my children had received a forged postcard and they realized that the telegrams were also fake. And I saw that things were beginning to come unglued. I stopped being angry with Ira and even worried that she might be taken for a KGB spokesman. People in the West like doing that. I knew she would rather die than knowingly do something the KGB wanted.

That was on May 24. Later, in Newton, I read the forged postcards and telegrams to my children. Not one contained my own unadulterated text. There was no mention of my wanting to see the lawyer. They were all signed as if Andrei and I were together.

I saw a receipt for mail—Ira sent us something and got back a receipt. It has my signature and my words: "I alone wish you a good trip." I thought that the words "I alone" would alert everyone, especially, of course, the "I." The receipt was delivered with "We" instead of "I." The correction is obvious, but it was noticed only in Massachusetts. The people who do this sort of work did not consider it enough and added Sakharov's signature. Two forgeries aren't that much if they convince many people throughout the world that everything is all right with Sakharov.

I came to think more and more frequently of an old acquaintance of mine as I looked at the forged signatures. This man had a hobby, the signatures of the famous and the great. He could easily run down a blank sheet of paper, signing *Pushkin, Dostoevsky, Tolstoy, Gorky, Lenin,* finishing up with *Stalin.* Many people requested one of those pages to keep. Somewhere in my debris on Chkalov Street I have one.

I learned of another incident that took place in Moscow. In August a letter came from Marina, Andrei's granddaughter. She wrote that she was entering the university. I wanted to congratulate her and sent her a tape recorder as a present. On the postage form I wrote, "Dear Marina, I am happy for you. I am certain that when your grandfather can learn of this, he will be very pleased, too." You would think that I had made it clear Andrei was not at home. But in Newton I learned that all of Moscow was saying that Grandpa had sent a gift and a telegram. That meant he was home.

I am writing this down in detail as a warning for the future—not to believe anything except direct contact. I don't think that modern technology has reached the point of forging telephone conversations, though perhaps I'm not up on the latest developments.

As soon as I realized that Ira was leaving because of her involvement with us, I started working on getting Lesik Galperin out. I began writing letters, knowing full well that all my postcards and letters went straight to the KGB as soon as I mailed them. The agents saw me posting letters, no matter which box I used. But still I drove to other parts of town and pretended to mail things secretly. I wrote to N. and to I. I wrote to other addresses in Leningrad that I could remember. I made appointments for a secret rendezvous at the cemetery with Lesik, promising to pass something to him, to leave a note in secret by a grave.

And I started going to the cemetery every day. I also went, because during these vigils for Lesik, I discovered that the radio reception was pretty good there. I listened to the radio for long stretches, from four in the afternoon until sundown. Since it stayed light until late, I disregarded my curfew. I felt that reporting for check-ins was enough, and that the curfew was something they had added and which I did not have to obey. I hoped that if Ira Kristi got out because Andrei had asked her to do something for him, then perhaps I could help Lesik leave by asking him to come and get instructions from me.

On May 30 I received a summons to appear the next day at eleven o'clock at the executive committee of Prioksky District to see its deputy chairman. I thought I was being called in connection with violations of my exile and for breaking curfew. I had been getting home around nine and even ten, leaving the cemetery when it got dark or when the mosquitoes started biting. Those were my deadlines. It was unbearable being home. I would leave in the morning, buy a bun somewhere, and sometimes I'd bring a thermos of coffee with me or a can of juice.

But it turned out that they wanted to discuss my petition for a pardon, which I had forgotten about after May 9. Before Victory Day, I kept hoping, "What if they do it? After all, it's the fortieth anniversary."

The deputy chairman informed me that my petition had been

reviewed by the Supreme Soviet of the RSFSR—I had sent it to the Supreme Soviet of the USSR—and denied. When I asked him the date of the decision, who had signed it, and the number of the document, he said he had not been given that information.

I inquired, "What if I decide to reapply? I have to refer to something, to a document that has a number, etc."

"I was not told any of that. I was empowered only to tell you that your petition was denied."

I said, "Listen, you work in an office, in a state office, a Soviet one. And you are educated enough to know that every reply and every form has a number, in and out; there is someone's signature, and naturally a date. If you don't know it and you don't tell it to me, then you can consider that you have not informed me of anything. I have never seen you and do not know you. And you haven't seen me."

I turned and walked out. And indeed, I placed so little store by this reply that later, when I saw Andrei, I forgot to mention it.

Then the next day I happened to pick up a block of wood on the roadside, to use instead of a stool, and put it in the car. No sooner had I done that than the KGB agents who followed me demanded to see it. At first I didn't even understand what it was they wanted to see. I took it out and showed it to them. They examined it from all sides, knocked on it, and I realized they were looking for a secret hiding place. Now I knew that something was up, since they had become awfully attentive to everything, even a block of wood. I used to pick up planks of wood all the time and they had never examined them.

That evening I was called on by the KGB. A young, handsome, elegantly dressed agent told me to be ready at nine-thirty the next morning as they would be coming to take me to the KGB. Very politely he asked, "You don't mind?" To which I replied, "What's the point of minding? If I mind, you won't take me? You'll take me anyway, if you have to."

And for no reason, not long after he left, I began to think they were calling me in because Andrei had died. My fears were groundless, but I couldn't help thinking it. And I kept thinking about it right up until my appointment with the KGB. I did not cry; I was in a stupor.

The next morning we had to go up to the third floor, which was rather difficult for me. I was panting and using nitroglycerine. I went into a large office, obviously belonging to a VIP, where I was met with a smile and practically open arms by a familiar-looking man about my age—sleek and solid, wearing a well-cut gray suit. He said, "Elena Georgievna, we've met before, remember during the investigation of Eduard Kuznetsov's diaries? My name is Sokolov."

I had forgotten what he looked like and would never have recognized him, but I did recall his name, and I remembered the conversation that took place before I began dealing with the investigator. During my first interrogation at Lefortovo Prison in Moscow, Sergei Sokolov had chatted with me a rather long time. This time he also spoke at length, for two hours or so. But before he could begin talking, I started crying. I could tell from the look on his face that Andrei Dmitrievich was alive, that nothing like what I had been worried about all night had happened to Andrei. I cried and cried, and he kept asking, "What's the matter?" He didn't understand. I explained that I thought Andrei had died.

Smiling joyously, he announced, "Oh no! Everything is fine with Andrei Dmitrievich, fine. Everything is very good."

"How can it be good when he's on a hunger strike," I said through my tears.

"What hunger strike? There's no hunger strike."

I went on crying, but I understood that . . .

"There was no hunger strike, really. Last year you worried in vain, there was no hunger strike. Just three days or so."

I began to see they felt that if there was force-feeding, then there was no hunger strike. That was such a convenient way to present it to the world, and to their bosses, to Gorbachev or whomever. No hunger strike; it's just a fantasy of Western propaganda—there is force-feeding, but you don't have to talk about that.

I gradually got hold of myself—I can't call it "calming down." First Sokolov tried to scare me. He told me that things would get worse for me, that he knew I was trying to get information out and that I would be punished for that and that I couldn't even imagine how severely they would punish me. On the other hand, he said I would never go anywhere and never see the children. My mother, well, what about her? She can come back at any time, today if she wants—there is no problem with your mother. No one will restrain your mother. But your children, they are very bad. He berated the children. And repeated several times that I would be punished for trying to pass information and, second, that my children were very bad, and, third, that my mother could come at any time, and, fourth, that there was no hunger strike and that there hadn't been any last year, either. We parted on that.

At some point in the conversation he had said that I would never see the children, but on the other hand, if I were better behaved then maybe I would. And then he reverted to scare tactics. I started talking back, and he said, with a sweet smile, "Elena Georgievna, how many heart attacks will it take?"

"For what—for me to change? No number will do that."

When we were saying goodbye, he said he would be seeing Andrei that day. I asked if I could meet with him after he had visited Andrei Dmitrievich, just for a few minutes. He said, "No, I can't promise you that. But if you need anything, anything at all, please ask me."

That was the meeting with Sokolov on June 2. I now think that when Sokolov met with me and tried to frighten me and then saw Andrei, Gorbachev had already given orders to the KGB to settle our case. But the KGB said, "There's no hunger strike; there's nothing," and went on as usual. So there may have been a struggle between them, and it wasn't clear who was stronger—Gorbachev or the KGB.

After all these events I realized I had basically won my game by summoning Lesik to meet me at the cemetery. It looked as if the main part of Sokolov's talk, that I was trying to pass along information, was related to that. On June 2, I sent a telegram to Lesik. I wrote: "CONGRATULATIONS ON THE ACHIEVEMENT! KISS MOTHER AND THE CHILDREN."

Lesik got the telegram on the fifth, as I had wanted, on his birthday, but before he had informed me that he had been summoned to OVIR. And naturally, understanding my message, he was truly amazed at how I had known about it on the second. Right after being called into OVIR he wrote me a letter in which he said that he wanted to meet me to say goodbye before his departure, but he did not know where to apply for permission and asked me to take the appropriate steps. I received this letter on June 13 or 14.

On June 15 I brought an appeal to Sokolov to the KGB of the Gorky Oblast, asking for permission for Galperin to come to Gorky to say goodbye. I did not receive a reply, but very soon after I got a letter from Lesik. He wrote it the night before he left:

> You will receive my letter when I am already beyond the borders of the USSR. I understand that our departure is somehow tied to you and to Andrei Dmitrievich, but I do not know how. I would not like to be a figure in the KGB's game against you and Andrei Dmitrievich. I am grateful to fate that I met you and later Andrei Dmitrievich. I hope to see you again.

It was a good letter of parting, and at the end Lesik wrote, "Leaving is so hard. It is at the limit of human strength." The letter is sad, of course, but it was a great joy for me that Lesik left, that we managed to trick the KGB about something.

I went on living. I listened to the radio and was aware that the whole world was worried about Sakharov. Along with the actual facts of our life that were known abroad—the forged postcard among other things—there was a lot that was vague, or incorrect. However, on the whole it added up to a very active concern for us —it was clear that we were not forgotten. That even put me in a good mood. But it was horrible that there was no news about Andrei. I had no idea what they were doing to him.

How did I live then? It is difficult to describe, because time seemed to stand still, and yet it moved rather swiftly. I will try to re-create my daily schedule. I got up late. I forced myself to eat breakfast, usually two cups of coffee and cottage cheese. I bought cottage cheese regularly; although I had no appetite, I found I could eat it anytime without forcing myself. I was normally done with breakfast by eleven. Then I did my daily chores, which were not too time-consuming, and if the weather was good, I'd drive off, most frequently to the cemetery. I would take a thermos of coffee, berries (when they were available), or apples, and a sandwich. And I would

Elena Bonner in uniform, 1943.

As a medical student in Leningrad, 1949.

Bonner and Yuri Shikhanovich visit friends in exile in Uvat, Siberia, 1971. *Left to right:* Boris Vail, Ludmila Vail, Bonner with Dmitri Vail, Shikhanovich.

Sakharov in Gorky, 1982.

Photographs of Sakharov (OPPOSITE) and Elena Bonner (ABOVE)
provided by Victor Louis and distributed by the West German
newspaper *Bild Zeitung.* The alleged dates are May 15, 1984, the
fourteenth day of a hunger strike, and May 12, 1984.

Sakharov in his and Bonner's apartment in Gorky, December 1983.

OPPOSITE: Sakharov in the Gorky apartment, November 24, 1985.

Sakharov and Bonner on the balcony of their apartment, March 1985.

OPPOSITE, ABOVE: A policeman on duty outside the Sakharovs' Gorky apartment, viewed from their front door. BELOW: The yard behind the Sakharovs' apartment building.

This picture was taken in a state photo studio on October 25, 1985, a few days after Sakharov's last hunger strike.

ABOVE AND RIGHT: A forged postcard from Bonner to the family in Massachusetts. In the first line the number 1 was altered to 21 (April) in order to deny rumors that on April 16, 1985, he had begun another hunger strike. On the second line and three lines from the bottom the

№21 21 апреля. Здравствуйте мои родные, родненькие. Вот и прошел апрель! Мы сегодня делали грандиозную уборку в парадной горнице и занимались наведением красоты в кухне — там действует Вася, что несмотря на все у всякий мысли быт берет свое и не всегда быт неприятен, особенно когда он как у нас главное приложение жизни. Читаю я какую-то ерунду — все эти номера журналов не интересные и все время что ворчу в тональности которая мне не всегда понятна не скоро при приятна. Но в N Мире две проблемных "вещи — Бонд-арев и какой-то Ебаки — Император" как я поняла из писем друзей — в мосиве интеллигенция их обсуждает, хотя что так обсуждать непонятно. Мы получили вашу телеграмму а вот получили ли вы две мамины день рожденческих подарков не знаем когда получите напишите. У нас хоть и не очень тепло но ручьи текут и снег тает. И все светит. А как у вас. Будьте здоровы все. Целуем крепко всех. Мама.

tense of verbs has been changed to make the text correspond to the new date. However, the forgery was exposed because the card contains a question to which Bonner had already received an answer, as was indicated from her own April 3 postcard.

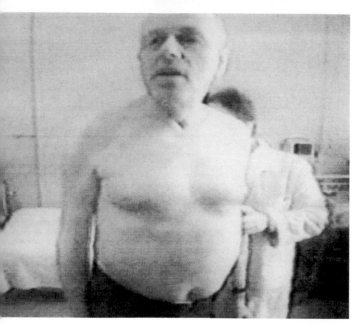

Sakharov undergoing
a physical examina-
tion—this is from a
film released to *Bild
Zeitung* by Victor
Louis in July 1985.

Bonner with her
grandson Matvei on
arrival in Boston,
December 7, 1985.

Bonner talking to her mother, Ruth, on her first night in Newton, Massachusetts.

Christmas in Newton. The grandchildren are Matvei and Anya Yankelevich.

A family portrait: *Back row, left to right:* Efrem Yankelevich, Tanya Yankelevich, (inset) Katya Semyonov, Alexei Semyonov holding his daughter Sasha, Liza Semyonova; *Front row:* Matvei Yankelevich, Elena Bonner, Ruth Bonner, Anya Yankelevich.

Elena Bonner and her son, Alexei Semyonov, visiting Washington in April 1986.

At Disney World in Florida: Matvei Yankelevich, Anya Yankelevich, Elena Bonner, and Katya Semyonov.

The view from Bonner's
Moscow apartment,
June 1986.

Bonner writing *Alone Together* in
Newton.

After her meeting with French Prime Minister Jacques Chirac in
Paris, May 26, 1986.

A visit to 10 Downing Street with British Prime Minister
Margaret Thatcher, May 30, 1986.

A meal with her friends Emil Shinberg and Galya Yevtushenko,
June 2, 1986, on her return to Moscow.

In the train station and on the train to Gorky, June 3, 1986.

spend the whole day out of the house, getting back after nine or ten at night. All that summer I was never reprimanded officially for missing my eight-o'clock curfew.

Listening to various short-wave stations, I had a sense of belonging to the world. I knew that our situation was causing great concern, and I knew that our children traveled and made many appearances. I heard a broadcast from Ottawa, where there was a conference on human rights in the framework of the Helsinki Accords. I knew that a plane bearing the message "The path to peace is through Gorky" was flying over Ottawa. I heard Alexei and Tanya, badly distorted by jamming devices. I heard Efrem's speech in London.* It was clear to me that when there were broadcasts about Sakharov, the jamming increased in Gorky and Gorky Oblast —I don't know about other places.

The fact that I could listen to the radio in the summer of 1985 made my situation somewhat bearable. A year before I had thought that the memory of us was still alive, but probably nothing else. I realized that the children were worried and were doing something, but I had nothing concrete to go on, as I did in 1984.

On rainy days—the summer was not a good one that year—I tried to find work in the house. I made shelves for the pantry; I organized our household products—soaps, detergents, and so on; I spent almost two weeks on those shelves. Then I made a shelf for journals along the top of one wall in our spare room, with supports resting on the wardrobe, measuring almost two-and-a-half meters long. On it I put the *Advances in Physical Sciences, Scientific American,* and *Physics Letter,* thereby unloading Andrei's study a bit. Before, he would stack them on the floor and on the wardrobe.

I found, as I sawed and planed the boards on the balcony, that the attitude of Gorky residents to my work was quite negative. Once two women walked by and one of them said loudly, so I would hear, "There's Sakharov's wife making a coffin for herself."

I gathered boards for the shelves along the road. All kinds of

*Efrem Yankelevich spoke at the Fifth International Sakharov Hearing, London, April 10–11, 1985. The hearing reviewed the human rights situation in the USSR in the ten years since the signing of the Helsinki Final Act.

scrap wood is discarded in vast amounts; I think you could pick up enough to build a house. My collecting wood really upset the KGB agents who accompanied me. I would wash the wood in the tub at home, dry it on the balcony, and then set to work on it.

I spent a lot of time on flowers. My bed under the balcony was not doing well—in part because it got trampled, and in part because I couldn't work the soil properly. The soil wasn't soil at all, but a nightmare. You would have to bring in top soil to plant there successfully. The flowers on the balcony did very well, however. There were lots of nicotianas, stock, petunias in all colors and shades, marigolds, and forget-me-nots. The nicotianas and stock were so aromatic that you could smell them as you approached the house. Through the open window the flowers filled the room with their perfume, and in the evening it was like being in a garden.

One report that no one was living in our apartment and that the windows were dark must have been based on someone walking by and seeing the closed blinds, the unlighted windows on the side that fronts on Gagarin Avenue. I did not spend time on that side. When I got home, around ten, I would make myself a quick meal in the kitchen and go out on the balcony. I sat there sometimes until one in the morning, and then went to bed, to read. I read many popular science books on physics. This was my basic project in the summer of 1984. I had no English books. I read a lot of interesting things in Soviet "fat journals," the literary magazines. I read Eidelman's *Herzen Against Autocracy,* which astounded me with its parallels to our own situation; then *Emperor's Madman,* which elicited so many associations that I had the feeling it had been written about us. (I've forgotten the author's name.)

I cannot say that my time was empty. I obtained special pleasure in tending my flowers, because it was communing with something alive. Besides which, I bought a bookcase, a round table, and rearranged the furniture slowly. And I tried (total success is never possible) to bring some order to the books, which were taking over once again. I washed the walls and ceiling in the kitchen, the walls in the hallway, in the bathroom. Slowly, because I could not work with sustained speed for long. But I did not go back to the doctors when my cardiac symptoms reappeared.

In the summer of 1984, doctors had not seemed dangerous to me
—I sensed that they wanted to get me to court at any cost, if not in
a healthy state, then at least an ambulatory one. But in 1985, I thought
that they might have different intentions and it would be better not
to approach them. I had rather severe attacks of myocardia, three so
bad that I prescribed bed rest of several days for myself. It didn't take
much forcing; I was so weak that I couldn't go out. I didn't even feel
up to reading.

I was not on a hunger strike, but apparently I was under severe
stress or nervous tension. I developed an aversion to food from the
moment Andrei was forcibly hospitalized, and I had to make myself
eat regularly three times a day. For lunch at home I usually cooked
something, fried eggs and potatoes, vegetables or a salad, and ate a
sandwich in the evening. I liked berries with sour cream. Nonethe-
less, I kept losing weight, and in the period from April 27 to the end
of June my weight dropped from 147 pounds to 109. All my bones
stuck out, literally, and I developed an irritation on my backbone
which looked like the beginning of bed sores. It hurt to lie down or
to sit, and I had to buy a cushion and camphor spirits to put on the
skin in that area. I was afraid I would develop real bed sores.

On July 11 I was home—the weather had not been good in the
morning, and I wasn't feeling well. It cleared up around three, but
I still didn't want to go anywhere, so I was sewing. The doorbell
rang. Dr. Tolchenov and a woman, who introduced herself as a
doctor from the local clinic, were at the door. Dr. Tolchenov was
Obukhov's deputy, the man who had taken Andrei from this house,
in whose presence Andrei had been given an injection and dragged
away on a stretcher on April 21.

They told me that Andrei was being discharged and would be
home in two hours. Tolchenov said the woman doctor would be
available to help him if he needed medical attention. Andrei was not
well—he had extra heartbeats—but the doctors had decided to send
him home, where he would be better off. They had come to let me
know in advance. There wasn't a word about the hunger strike—as
if it had never happened.

I felt very strange about this announcement. They had taken a
new position: before, the doctors had maintained that it was worse

for him at home. I spoke very harshly, as I always do with those doctors. "Why are you here then? Andrei will come home and he'll explain everything to me himself."

"No, we wanted you to know, so you could meet him."

I didn't understand that I should do just the opposite. They left, saying Andrei would be home in an hour. Their "meet him" stuck in my mind so much that I went down to the street and waited an hour for Andrei.

A black Volga drove up. (I think it was a black Volga, but it could have been a hospital car.) Then Andrei got out (no, not from a Volga) and behind him came the nurse Valya, who was carrying some of his things—or maybe Valya hadn't come this time; that was another time. We kissed and went into the house.

It was only later, here in the West, that I realized why they wanted me to go downstairs to meet Andrei. I understood that I had done a stupid thing by meeting him on the street. They filmed the scene and showed how Andrei was brought home from the hospital like an ordinary sick man, and his wife calmly greeted him. Any Soviet would have seen a lie in this. No relative is ever told that a family member is being discharged from the hospital and brought home. The patient usually calls from the hospital himself and his relatives go to the hospital to pick him up. They don't wait at home. But they wanted the scene for their fraudulent movies.

Once he was home, Andrei told me many of the things that had happened to him. He said he had made regular attempts to get some information out about himself through the various people he ran into, despite the constant KGB surveillance. The first thing he told me was why he had been discharged: he had stopped his hunger strike that morning. He had done so because after Sokolov's visit on June 30, he had written a letter to Gorbachev. It occurred to him that the letter would be viewed more positively if he ceased his hunger strike.

But the speed and alacrity with which they discharged him made him think he was making a mistake. A few hours after he announced his decision he sent a note to Obukhov, saying he was stopping now, but if he did not receive an answer from Gorbachev in a reasonable time, which he considered to be two weeks, he would resume the hunger strike.

He was very thin. But he was calm and had greater inner strength than he had in September 1984 when he was released from the hospital. He suspected they had been giving him psychotropic drugs in the force-feeding and that it was under their influence that he had written the statement about ending the hunger strike. But the main factor had been, of course, his concern for me and not knowing what was happening to me.

Sokolov had a long conversation with him on June 30, in which he said, on the one hand, that Andrei Dmitrievich's request would never be granted and, on the other, that he had to disavow his former public statements and especially his letter to Dr. Sidney Drell, "The Danger of Thermonuclear War." He spoke about how I was a bad influence on Andrei and gave no promises at all about a positive resolution of Andrei's situation.

Andrei also said that the force-feeding went much more easily than in 1984, because he had learned not to resist as hard, and that in general he had become a real, experienced *zek*, or inmate. He said that as before there was another person in the room with him, allegedly a patient, but presumably from the KGB. In the next room there were two KGB men, plus two KGB agents on duty in the hall, one on the stairs and one by the exit. He walked twelve to fifteen miles a day in the corridor. He told me that, unlike 1984, he was not taken out into the garden for a walk, or even out onto the balcony. The balcony door was blocked and he was told that the balcony itself was in a dangerous condition. So he had had no fresh air for three months. Soviet penal regulations state that even in prison an inmate must be taken out for a half-hour walk daily.

At first, Andrei was allowed to go into the corridor to watch TV. But then the TV was removed from the corridor and all the patients in the section were deprived of it—they were told the set had broken down.

The first evening home, Andryusha was agitated. We went to bed around midnight, but we were excited and went on talking. Andryusha was trying to convince me that he definitely had to start a hunger strike again in two weeks. Then he said that he had hopes, that maybe we could manage without a strike. I think he was afraid and really wanted to avoid a repetition. When we stopped talking he soon fell asleep. I lay without moving, my hand on his chest, feeling his heart beat. I couldn't count the extra beats—I didn't have a watch and it was dark anyway—but his beat was unimaginably strange. First there would be several normal beats, then uneven beats, then two or three, followed by such a long pause that I thought . . . God knows, I thought everything. And I remembered everything. The first time I felt his extrasystoles with the palm of my hand —big deal, one or two a minute, just like an adolescent's heart, and I laughed, and Andrei asked what was so funny. And then I listened with my ear. Those extra beats had never worried me until they had done all those things to him in Gorky. There were different breaks in the rhythm now, and I did not understand them. This was no longer an adolescent heart.

XII

Andrei slept badly the first night home. He cried in his sleep, and I woke him twice. In his sleep he thought he was still (or once again) in the hospital.

July 12 was dreary—gray, rainy, and windy—and we stayed home. On the thirteenth we went out to the cemetery to listen to the radio. There was a lot about Andrei, and that cheered him up somehow. Hearing his name on radio broadcasts, he saw that there was concern for him in the world.

July 14 was a good day, and we decided to go to the market for food. In the two days at home with me, he had gotten better, the expression on his face was different—softer, I suppose—and he was gentle and kind. After his first night at home, we did not think about his going on a hunger strike again in two weeks. We just lived. Andrei called that period "time for living."

We went to the market and bought various kinds of fruits. I remember we bought the first peaches, which he did not like. We got some very good apricots. On the way back to the parking lot, which is rather far, we purchased *pirozhki* or buns and ate them on the street, and then as we passed the movie house we saw a poster for a French film called *Men's Games,* something about bicycle racing and a murder, a typical and not very good mystery, which I've practically forgotten.

We decided to go to the movie, but first we drove down to the bank of the Volga to have a light lunch of fruit and buns.

That day was filmed by the KGB and shown as a typical day in the life of Sakharov. The films depicting Sakharov's "normal" life in 1984 and 1985 which I saw in America have scenes that were shot in 1980, 1981, and other times. They were edited to create the impression of a normal life, a normal state of health. Actually, it is one big hoax. One big lie, a horrible lie. That kind of documentary lie can create the impression of truth, and it is harder to refute than an absolute lie.

It was sheer chance that, beginning with the forged postcard, my children managed to unravel the complex knot of disinformation that bound us. Another time they may not be so lucky. The world could watch films about our well-being when we are no longer alive.

These two weeks were a radiant time. Every day we drove out to listen to the radio. We bought a small Rossiya radio and decided that Andrei would try to take it with him the next time he was hospitalized.

Our breakfasts literally took hours, because that was the time when we talked to each other the most—about how we had lived without each other. We were outside a good deal during the day. We drove to small groves with shade and a hint of the real outdoors, and gathered mushrooms in a narrow strip of forest.

The weather was basically good, even if not too warm, and the days were clear. The KGB followed us constantly—two cars of them—and they walked in the woods between the trees. In fact we were never alone for a minute, and the films are proof of that.

On July 25, two weeks after Andrei was released from the hospital, he began another hunger strike. Once again he took a laxative, gave himself an enema, and sent a telegram to Gorbachev. The twenty-seventh was my son Alexei's birthday. When he got out of the hospital, Andrei had asked if I had sent a telegram to wish Efrem a happy birthday on June 25. I said I had not, that ever since I realized our telegrams were being altered,* I had stopped sending them to Moscow and to the children. But Andrei felt we had to send one to Alexei. I said something like, "He'll survive," but he tried to convince me that it would be excessive cruelty not to congratulate him on his birthday.

*The date and two words on a postcard sent by Elena Bonner on April 1 were altered by the KGB to make it appear the postcard had been sent on April 21 (after Sakharov's hunger strike began). Bonner's family in Newton detected the alteration, which alerted them to a number of other cases of KGB forgeries in communications received from Gorky.

The morning of July 27 began as usual. Andrei went out on the balcony, and I shut the door firmly, so he could not smell the aroma, and had my coffee. Then we started getting ready to take a drive. We did not hurry and I still had laundry and other chores to do. By the time I got it all done, it was half-past twelve. Incidentally, I had a cellophane bag packed in the corridor, with Andrei's shaving and washing kit, the Rossiya radio, paper, eyeglasses, and other necessities. So we understood that they might come for him at any hour of any day. But even so, when they do come, it's a surprise. Andrei felt good; it was the third day. He was full of energy and did exercises in the morning.

We were just about to leave, at around one o'clock, when the doorbell rang, and Dr. Obukhov appeared again with his crowd of men and women; he had about eight people with him. And there was something playful in his voice when he said, "Well, Andrei Dmitrievich, we're back for you." When I pictured them throwing Andrei down on the couch and giving him an injection and all the rest, I couldn't stand it. I went over to him and said, "Andryushenka, just go; don't."

They took him by the arms and half-dragged him but he didn't resist too much. I handed the cellophane bag to one of them, and they left.

And I was alone again, and again I did not know for how long. Again with the feeling that he was completely in their hands, that they could do whatever they wanted, beat him, inject him, kill him, have mercy on him. Anything.

I got myself organized and drove off to listen to the radio, though even as he was leaving, Andrei said, "It's Alexei's birthday, remember?" "I remember." But I did not want to send a telegram. I thought that it would confuse everyone. I don't remember if it was that same day or the next that I heard about the film, which showed us going to the movies and how happy and healthy we felt. My God! That broadcast horrified me. Horror because there was no way to counter those lies. It was absolutely impossible to know where or how they would falsify our lives again.

And another string of empty days, fast and slow. Reading, mending things no one needed, washing walls, sometimes necessary and sometimes not, and fussing with the flowers. All despite my weakness, holding myself as tight as a fist and forcing myself to go on. I did not lose weight—that aversion to food and the daily weight loss which I had experienced in the previous three months of Andrei's absence were not repeated. I did not gain weight but remained stable. In the evenings, like a pendulum, pacing about the balcony, I read poetry aloud, to keep from forgetting how to speak. And to answer my question, "Who needs poetry and why?"

I kept trying to send out information about us. There was one episode which I still cannot recount in detail. I don't know yet what happened. Even though everything was done so that information about the summer of 1985 would get beyond the city limits of Gorky, something went wrong. Sometimes I think that it didn't go wrong, that it was ruined by people I had trusted; that's why all that mail reached Newton ten months later, when I was already in the United States.

Andrei made similar attempts. I know that in one case his information reached Moscow back in April. Unfortunately, those who got it were afraid to pass on his handwritten text. They edited his letter and even translated it into English. It must have been a lot of work. But the effect was that our children in the States did not accept the information as authentic. I probably would have had doubts, too.*

The days in August passed. Mother's birthday. A telegram from Lenya Litinsky with a request to tell him the date of her birthday. I did not reply. I did not send Mother a telegram. I heard more and more about us on the radio, and I saw that my tactic of not sending telegrams even on birthdays was the right one. If everything is being altered, then we must be silent.

On September 5 I was home during the day. I had heard on the radio that my son Alexei was on a hunger strike. There was talk about it (and us) every day. I was planning to go out to listen to the radio, when Andrei walked in.

I rushed to him, and he said warily, "Don't be overjoyed; I've

---

*Sakharov's letter, allegedly received by an unnamed friend, had been reported by the Associated Press on May 16, 1985. A retyped excerpt from the letter reached the West three months later.

only got three hours." I must have looked puzzled, because he immediately added, "Sokolov came to see me again; he wants me to write certain papers." Without listening to anything else, I got upset and shouted, "The KGB can go f--- itself!" Andrei said calmly and quietly, "Just listen to me." I shut up.

He said, "They want you to write that if you are given permission to travel to see your mother and children and to get treatment, you will not hold press conferences, see reporters, or this, or that." When I realized that all they wanted was for me to keep my mouth shut in the presence of the press, I said, "With pleasure!"

Then I asked, "What do they want from you?"

"The same." I somehow got sidetracked from finding out what they were demanding from him. We began telling each other what had been happening in our lives. And I forgot to mention that my petition for a pardon had been turned down.

Andrei said that Sokolov had come to see him that morning. He demanded that we sign such papers and said that Gorbachev had given him orders to handle the Sakharov case. When I sat down at the typewriter, I asked him to whom my paper should be addressed. Then I said, "No, I won't address it to anyone." And I did not write anything in the corner for the sender's and the recipient's names. I left the first few lines blank, and then I began: "In case I am allowed to travel abroad to see my mother, children, and grandchildren, and also for treatment, I will not hold press conferences or give interviews. Elena Bonner. September 5, 1985." I gave the paper to Andrei.

He showed me a draft of his own statement, which said, "I accept the Soviet authorities' right to refuse me permission to travel beyond the country's borders, since I did in the past have access to especially important secret material of a military nature, some of which might still be of significance even now. However, this does not mean that I accept my exile and isolation in Gorky as being legal. In the future, if my wife is allowed to travel abroad for treatment and to see her relatives, I plan to concentrate on scientific work and on my private life; however, I retain the right to make statements on public issues in extreme situations."

I don't actually recall the exact wording, but this was the gist of what Andrei wrote. He was in a big hurry to get back to the hospital. After we composed the statements, we went out onto the balcony. I showed off what remained of my flower garden. We stood there with our arms around each other's waists. Andryusha said that I felt a bit heavier to his touch, and he was probably right. And then he started hurrying, worried that he would be late; they were going to pick him up outside at six. He was afraid they would trick him, not come for him, and then they would be able to say he had ended his hunger strike or something like that.

He probably believed that the statements we had written would help me get an exit visa, that the problem was almost solved. Still, whatever the reason, I think he wrote under duress. The separation from me of four and a half months, with a break of two weeks, the isolation, and the force-feeding—all put pressure on him. When I tried to talk to him about that, he replied that he didn't see anything bad in his statement; he really did believe he knew secrets; he really didn't want to deal with social issues anymore because he didn't have the strength for them. He felt sick, tired, and all he wanted was to do scientific work and be with me.

In his diary, he wrote: "I want to be with Lusia so much. I never wanted anything so badly in my life."

September is autumn in Gorky. I think I saw it arrive and felt it physically when I was standing with Andrei on the balcony, feeling his ribs even through the jacket he was wearing. My dear, sweet, skinny love! He hurried to get back to the torture of his hunger strike and our separation. And it was autumn for me, the nasturtium leaves were thick and light yellow, the asters were fading, and it was time to collect seeds. I gathered them at the cemetery and listened to the radio. Alexei was on his hunger strike in Washington right next to the Soviet embassy; the announcer said it was hot there. It was getting cold in Gorky and the days were growing shorter.

Andryusha, when he had been home for those three hours, had spoken about Alexei's hunger strike in a heightened and even joyful mood. He knew about it, as he did about many other things going on in the world. The transistor radio worked well and he was up-to-date on everything. He thought Alexei's act was the right one at the right time and in the right place. Later, when I was in Moscow, I was told that a physicist who did not approve of Andrei's hunger strike or our way of life said, "Look how cruel she is [meaning me]; she's even making her son starve, too." When someone responded, "How can she force her son—they're not in communication," he replied, "She'll find a way for that."

Andryusha said: "Looks like your children will pull us out of a black hole." And as confirmation of his words I heard the resolution of the U.S. Senate and House of Representatives, after which Alexei ended his hunger strike.*

I suddenly felt such weariness that I thought I could not take any more. But every day I said to myself, "Well, just one more day or two, and everything will be decided." And I lived with that. I marked every day of our separation in 1984 and in 1985 on the calendar and made notes of what happened each day on the pages. For even though it seemed as if time were standing still, it was passing, and events were taking place in the world and in my solitude. When I was leaving for the United States I bought Andrei a flip-page calendar. He had read my entries when he got back from the hospital. Now, when I return from my American holiday, I will read his.

For the first few days after our three-hour meeting, I was sure Andrei would be home soon, that everything would be cleared up and made right. But the days passed.

Just before the October holidays, Gorbachev gave an interview to *Time*, made a trip to France, and held a joint press conference in Paris with Mitterrand. All of it was shown on Soviet TV. It was interesting, if for no other reason than the fact we had not been spoiled with that much proximity to our leaders in many years. It was scary for me, too, because there was talk of Sakharov everywhere, and it was all so hopeless—it gave me the chills. The broadcasts of Western radio stations were also interesting—for there was a lot about Sakharov, concern and worry for him, and confusion as

---

*Concurrent Resolution 186, September 10, 1985, "expressing solidarity with the Sakharov family in their efforts to exercise their rights. . . ." The resolution urged the President "to protest in the strongest possible terms and at the highest levels, the blatant and repeated violations of the Sakharovs' rights by the Soviet authorities. . . ."

a result of the disinformation and the absence of real information. Then came the Nobel Peace Prize for the Soviet and American doctors.* Ten years after Sakharov's prize.

I listened to the news broadcast twice. The first time, at night, it was almost impossible to hear any of it. The second time, in twilight, Tanya's voice came over very clearly.† The first snowflakes of the year fell on my windshield, then the snow began falling in earnest. You have to make a wish during the first snowfall. Lord, how many superstitions there are in the world! You want to make things easier in any way possible. I got out of the car, gathered up a handful from the hood, and put the snow in my mouth. It was cold. Why did snow taste sweet when I was a child? I don't think I ever counted the days like this in any of our previous separations.

It snowed again. It was very cold in the apartment. The heat wasn't on yet, and the wind blew out what warmth there was. It was down to fifty-five degrees in the big room, and was even colder where I slept. I stopped sewing and mending; I did not wash the walls and doors. I sat, bundled up in everything I could find, including blankets, and waited. For what?

My heart ached either from the spasms, or the loneliness, or the cold. The morning of October 21 was so dark that I couldn't tell if dawn had come or not. More wet snow was falling. I really didn't want to get up on such a cold day. Suddenly the doorbell rang. I pulled on a robe and went to the door. One of the most obnoxious of our guards—they are distinguished only by degree of obnoxiousness.

"You are ordered to appear at the MVD Directorate at eleven A.M."

"I won't be able to get there by eleven; it's already ten."

"I don't know about that. Second floor, room two hundred

---

*The 1985 prize was presented to the International Physicians for the Prevention of Nuclear War (IPPNW). The organization includes doctors from many countries; the co-heads were Evgeny Chazov from the USSR and Bernard Lown of the United States.

†Tanya Yankelevich traveled to Oslo in October 1985 and attended a meeting to commemorate the tenth anniversary of the announcement of Sakharov's Nobel Prize. The speech she delivered there was broadcast to the USSR.

twelve, to see Evgeniya Guseva, and you must be there at eleven."

"I said I won't be able to make it." And I shut the door. It's the way I am. I can't get ready quickly and even though I didn't drag things out, I didn't leave the house until eleven.

There was snow on the car and I had to clean it off. The defroster wasn't working on the rear window. I just wasn't ready for winter. Finally I got started and reached the building around noon. There is parking only for official cars, but I parked anyway. I was angry at my legs and my heart for hurting; and at the wet snow and the piercing cold; and at the city, at which I wanted to scream, "I've seen you in your grave, wearing white slippers!" And at the summons. I thought they were calling me either for a meaningless talk or to punish me for violating curfew, for being out after eight P.M. the past summer.

And the fact that I had to see a woman merely confirmed my theory. I had noticed that in Gorky it is the women in the MVD who supervise convicted people, those who serve their sentences doing heavy labor but are not confined in prison or camps. There are a lot of them in Gorky, along with minor offenders, such as people who don't pay their alimony. And, based on my example, exiles too are handled by the women, though I think I am the only exile in Gorky —one in 1.5 million residents.

I thought I was being called in to see a woman inspector of a higher rank than usual. At last, I found the right entry and noted on the lobby directory that she worked for OVIR. I was surprised, but it did not occur to me that they would let me go on my trip.

I went to get a pass and saw a sign that said: "Today, because of a meeting, OVIR is not open."

"That means they're waiting for me." I was used to the fact that the authorities tried to keep me from any contacts, even random ones in a line. They would often close down a department or section for this reason. This had happened to me at the regional executive committee office and the procurator's office.

I spoke to the young woman at the reception desk and said that I had been called in to OVIR. "Are you blind or illiterate?" she barked at me with a practiced air. "There's the sign. We're closed today."

"But I was called in," I said, raising my voice and speaking loudly, so that everyone in the bureau would hear my usual opening: "I am the wife of Academician Sakharov . . ."

But a fellow ran over and simpered: "Elena Georgievna, come this way; they'll be right down . . ." He got me out of the crowded reception area to the staircase, where there was only one guard and no people.

To those readers who think I am like a child who has forgotten to include the guard in the category of "people," I haven't forgotten; I simply don't include him in it.

A few minutes later a woman in an officer's MVD uniform (with a wide band on her shoulder boards—she was a major) came down the stairs and also simpered: "Elena Georgievna, come with me." We went up to the second floor. She saw me in a large office, in the middle of which stood a desk with chairs on either side. Along all the walls there were chairs. The room looked like a hall or waiting room. And the desk looked like a recent arrival.

Later, when I saw myself at that desk in a film, I realized that my impression was correct. Doors on the right and the left led to other rooms. I am describing it carefully, because now that I have seen the film of my chat with Guseva, I keep wondering where they could have placed the camera and why didn't I hear it. Maybe they have silent machines now.

Guseva said: "You have applied for an emigration visa. You are being asked to fill out the forms again."

"I never applied for an emigration visa. Only for a trip," I answered immediately.

"No, no, I didn't mean that; it just slipped out. Sit down comfortably and fill out the application."

"You mean right here and now by hand? But you require that it be typewritten and in two copies."

"It's all right, it can be handwritten and in one copy."

I filled out the forms—name, surname, residence. The next question was, where to. She dictated: "To Italy." I began telling her that I had asked to go to Italy, but now I wanted to go to the United States as well as to Italy, that I wished to bring back my mother. She was with the children now, but she hoped to return. She wasn't an emigrant; she was on a trip. (That part was on film.) I wrote "to the U.S.A. and to Italy." The rest I filled in without thinking. Sometimes she dictated the answers to me and I wrote down her words. So, in answer to "When do you plan to leave?" she prompted: "As soon as I get the visa," and that's what I wrote. And for "Via which border point?" she said, "Via Sheremetyevo Airport," and I wrote that too.

I finished the application, gave it to her, and made ready to go home. I realized that the authorities must have come to some decision concerning us, and it just might be positive, but I had no certainty about it. And in truth by halfway through the application (all that writing took over an hour) I was in a hurry to get home. I thought Andrei must be there. His return was the reality I was striving for. The trip—that was still something unreal.

But Guseva delayed me. "Go now and have pictures taken and bring them to me tomorrow at ten." "Who will do pictures so quickly for me?" "Our people will go with you and it will be done. It's nearby on Zvezdinka [a street in the middle of Gorky]."

I was photographed without having to wait in line and told, "You can have them tomorrow at nine-thirty." I rushed home. I was lucky not to run into any highway police, or I would have had a violation marked on my driver's license for sure.

Andrei was not home. I waited so expectantly that I didn't go out on the balcony, even though I didn't need to hear the doorbell. For two years or so we have not taken the key out of the front door, it's just there. At first the policemen demanded that I take it out, but I refused, and apparently they weren't allowed to do it themselves. The reason we left the key in the door is that people go into our apartment all the time when we're out, and they don't seem to have very good keys. They kept breaking the lock, and I got sick and tired of it.

All night, instead of sleeping, I kept rehashing my appointment at OVIR. And I realized that, one, they wanted me to leave soon and, two, without seeing Andrei. I was sure that the decision had been made and that I would receive permission to go. What was going on now had nothing to do with the decision; it was all KGB stuff.

In the morning I still hoped that Andrei would come. But there was no news of him by nine, and I went for the photographs and then to OVIR. Once I got the pictures, I decided not to rush over to OVIR and stopped by a beauty parlor. My escorts in two cars seemed more upset by this than by my usual excursions. Apparently they expected me to rush headlong to OVIR, and the beauty parlor could have been a place for a secret assignation.

The behavior of our outdoor guards during the time remaining before my departure from Gorky was peculiar. After all, I had received permission to take the trip, and thereby the right to communicate and to have contacts. But they increased their vigilance and scurried around me, and later, when Andrei was released, around both of us, more than ever.

When I arrived at OVIR with the photographs on October 22, Major Guseva met me downstairs. (The KGB men waited outside, and she brought me out to them later.) I told Guseva I wanted the application back because I had to make some changes. For one thing, I would not leave as soon as I got the visa, but only after being reunited with my husband, whom I had not seen in six months, except for a brief interlude.

At first Guseva resisted, saying I did not even have permission, and already I was making a scene. And that it was not up to her to decide whether or not I could have the application back. Then she went off to telephone. I was alone, there wasn't a soul at OVIR—perhaps that's the way it always is there. No, it can't be. I know that the city has refuseniks and applicants for visas. Now it is clear to me that they had let the employees off, because they were filming from the other rooms and did not want people to know about it.

The KGB trusted Guseva, but not the other workers. When I go to check in at the regional MVD office, my KGB agent goes into the room with me. Apparently the KGB does not trust Lieutenant Ryzhova, to whom I report.

Guseva was gone for over an hour. Upon her return, she gave me the application. In the place "What else do you want to say about yourself," I wrote that I was going to Italy and the United States to see my relatives and to get treatment, that I would leave in the usual time frame—that is, within three months after receiving permission; and where it said that I would depart from Sheremetyevo, I think

I substituted "any border point," but I don't remember exactly. She took the application and told me, "You'll be called."

I rushed home, but Andrei still wasn't there, and I spent another sleepless night. In the morning, without changing out of my dressing gown, I lay down most of the time; I did not plan to get dressed or go anywhere. Around three in the afternoon there was a knock —it was the nurse Valya. She needed clothing for Andrei Dmitrievich. He had left in his jogging suit and was still wearing it, even though it was winter now. I collected a jacket, a warm hat, shoes, slacks, a sweater, and gave it all to her, asking: "When are they planning to discharge him?"

"I'll bring him right away, as soon as I give him his clothes and he gets dressed."

After she left I thought: maybe they'll give me back my husband and maybe I'll get to see my children and my mother. I didn't figure that maybe my heart would work again, too. I seemed to do a hundred things at once: gulped some nitroglycerine, set the table, baked an apple pie and stewed a chicken, washed, and put on my pink dress. I did it all and even placed candles on the table and lit them.

Just before five Andrei appeared in the doorway. In his fur hat and jacket, which seemed too big for him. A very thin small face, all gray. He did not even kiss me, but said, "What's happening?"

"You don't know? I've been called into OVIR."

And suddenly his face was transformed, in fact his face disappeared; all that was left was his eyes, alive and glowing. (Writing this five months later, I cannot refrain from smiling as I recall that face and the whole scene.) And he wiggled his rear end, as if he were dancing; I'd never seen Andryusha make a movement like that.

"Well, then, did we win again?"

"We won!"

And in violation of all the rules, he went straight to the dinner table from the hospital. And our conversations began.

Andrei didn't know anything; he had simply been told an hour ago that he could go home. He had not stopped his hunger strike and no one had talked to him about it. He had not seen anyone except the nurse who had brought him his clothing—not the treating physician, nor Obukhov. And he did not know what was awaiting him as he rode home. He told me little about his latest stay at the hospital. He said that among his roommates, who changed every week, there had been one who spoke English. He had introduced himself as a translator of specialized technical texts. The man offered Andrei some English-language journals to read and Andrei took them. Thus the film clips of Sakharov reading Western magazines in the hospital, including magazines that are not on sale in the USSR. All our foreign journals and magazines had been taken away during the search.

Andrei was also surprised that one day they brought several packages, mailed from the United States, of scientific reprints, which they made him sign for. That had never happened before, and whenever he did get packages, they came to the house, without our having to sign every time. Without suspicion, he had signed. So the films show that the mail from the West comes normally and that his signatures are not forged.

Andryusha also told me that one of his rotating neighbors in the room kept talking about me. No matter how hard Andrei tried to stop him, he kept on. They were long monologues in the style of Yakovlev. Andrei thinks that the man had been specially prepared, because things slipped out in his tirades which had not appeared in the Soviet press—only in *Russkii golos* (which is published in the States) and in *Sette Giorno*.

At last, Andrei decided to stop him once and for all. He demanded that the man be taken away. They would not do that. Then he blew up. He told me that he can bring himself to a state of hysteria, that it sometimes helps. He began screaming, dragged his pillow and blanket, pushed his way out into the corridor, and made himself a bed there out of three armchairs. It was evening, almost nighttime—and either they were intimidated by the screaming, or higher-ups weren't there, but in any case, they left Andrei in the corridor. After Andrei's three days and nights in the corridor, the Yakovlevologist was taken away.

Before Sokolov's last visit to Andrei, on September 5—he had forgotten to tell me about it during our brief three-hour meeting— he had not been force-fed for three days. He had been told that the doctor who headed the women's brigade was sick (or someone in her family was sick). Thus he had to go through the hardest first three days of total fasting all over again. That's how they prepared him for his meeting with a VIP from the KGB. The same thing had happened before Sokolov's visit in June.

I must relate everything that Andrei told me about the women's brigade. These were large, sturdy women, very healthy and strong. They had come to force-feed him last year too. Their commander is a large woman doctor. They would push him down and tie him to the bed. All the unpleasant and disgusting moments that occur in force-feeding are psychologically harder for a man to bear when it's done by women. Andrei felt they used women on purpose, to make it more difficult for him. Obukhov talked about it openly in the summer of 1984 when he threatened Andrei, who had stopped his hunger strike but was demanding to be called as a witness at my trial and to be let out of the hospital which had been turned into a prison for him. Obukhov would say, "Watch out, Andrei Dmitrievich, or I'll send the women's brigade again."

I cannot rid myself of a thought that pursues me constantly: Aren't some of the people who tortured my husband members of the International Physicians for the Prevention of Nuclear War? Dr. Chazov* is a cardiologist, and I know that people tried to talk to him about the possibilities of real, serious treatment of my husband's heart trouble and about my heart—to no avail. Was he or any of his associates involved in the decision to force-feed Sakharov in the summer of 1984, with such horrible consequences? One of the films states that consulting cardiologists came to see Sakharov from Chazov's All-Union Cardiological Center in Moscow. In Moscow and in the West, there is often talk that Sakharov was "treated" by psychiatrists too. Dr. Rozhnov† is named in this connection. I don't

---

*Evgeny Chazov (1929–   ) is a cardiologist, a member of the Communist Party, and an Academician. In 1973 he signed one of the letters denouncing Sakharov published in the Soviet press at that time.

†Prof. Vladimir Rozhnov, a Moscow psychotherapist, specializing in hypnosis, head of the department of psychotherapy of the Institute for Advanced Medical Training of the Academy of Medical Sciences. Persistent rumors of Rozhnov being regularly flown to Gorky to administer drugs to Sakharov, or to treat him by

know about him, but I am aware that among the doctors struggling for peace an important role is played by Dr. Marat Vartanian,* implicated as one of the chief figures in the misuse of psychiatry for political purposes.

---

hypnosis, circulated in Moscow in July and August 1984, and were discussed in the Western press.

*Psychiatrist and director of the Scientific Center for Mental Health, and an officer of IPPNW.

XIII

In February 1986 I visited friends of my husband in Palo Alto. At a reception in my honor, Donald Kennedy, president of Stanford, gave me an invitation for Andrei to come to his university. When I was introduced I realized that this sweet man who was offering an invitation for Andryusha had recently received Marat Vartanian. I lost my presence of mind and did not say what I should have said: that I couldn't remain there following the footsteps of Vartanian. Yes, I was a coward. Everything was so proper, so polite, so beautiful and intelligent. Everyone was speaking such warm words about Andrei—and even about me while they were at it. Perhaps people sincerely believe that their words can help. That's why they go to Moscow, talk there to grownup people, academicians, and try to educate them along the lines of "this is good and this is bad," although never publicly, only tête-à-tête.

Perhaps they sincerely believe that in handing me an invitation, they have saved Andrei from being turned into a living corpse in his isolation. Perhaps they do not know that their colleagues in Physicians for the Prevention of Nuclear War are a weapon of the authorities in this crime.

I did not say any of this out loud. I emulated my hosts and became polite and silent. There were so many nice people, delicious hors d'oeuvres, flowers, grandiloquent words, Joan Baez singing about freedom. And I became unfree and swallowed my tongue. Suffering in silence, I lost my chance to speak.

There was also a slight misunderstanding. I kept waiting for the host to say that the guests wanted to hear me speak. But apparently the guests didn't. I went over to the president again, and I told him everything that I thought about their reception of Dr. Vartanian. I told him and realized that my behavior was imitating theirs. I was also teaching a grown man, an academician, tête-à-tête, "what was good and what was bad." Lord, I'm still ashamed of myself!

Perhaps if I had said all that aloud to the group, it would have made possible an honest and serious discussion.

Something similar happened later with Dr. Wolfgang Panofsky,* with the difference that I found the strength to say what I thought. Probably that is why neither he nor I felt any bitter aftertaste from our meeting. In fact, it gave me the hope that perhaps Andrei's friends would realize in time how they can help my husband and others. And that this "in time" will come before it is too late.

I also had an unpleasant discussion with Dr. Marvin Goldberger, president of Cal Tech. I did not want to hurt his feelings, but I had to say that the mistakes of Sakharov's Western colleagues in their dealings with Soviet science and government authorities had a direct and tragic effect on our fates. His colleagues should at least know that. I am sorry that at Cal Tech so few people came to meet me. Were they the only ones concerned with Sakharov's fate?

Now about some good things. If we put aside (which in real life I would never do!) the most important thing in our lives (i.e., the closeness between Andrei and me, "You are me") then there aren't many good things in this book. On October 23, toward the end of the day in Gorky, I went outside with the garbage. It was clear and frosty. The snow, which had been falling since morning, had stopped. The first whiteness covered everything, even the puddle outside our apartment—it's just like Gogol's Mirgorod puddle, and it reigns over the entire landscape at our end of Gagarin Avenue. The snow covered the cars parked by the house. On our windshield someone had written: "Bravo! Congratulations!" Nothing had been said on the radio yet, no one but us, the policemen, and the KGB knew I had been to see OVIR. One of them must have written that on the car. I will always look into their faces and think, "This one? No, this one."

*Wolfgang Panofsky (1919–   ). Physicist, director of the Stanford Linear Accelerator Center.

On October 25 I went with Andrei to OVIR at one o'clock. Major Guseva was not downstairs. I asked the guard if I could use the house phone to call her. One of my escorts—he had been off duty the last few days and was not fully informed—jumped at the phone like a wildcat and pushed down the button. He did it so fast and so abruptly that he must have pushed me accidentally. My heart went into spasm, and I grabbed my nitroglycerine.

The other KGB agent politely said, "Go ahead and call, Elena Georgievna; he didn't know." He began quietly to rebuke the phone grabber. I called, the lady came down for us, and we went up with her.

In her office, in a chair next to hers, sat a man in the uniform of an MVD colonel or lieutenant colonel. He did not introduce himself.

His speech boiled down to this: Permission has been granted, you've seen your husband, now you must pay two hundred rubles and bring the receipt here. Tomorrow you're going to Moscow. You will be given a ticket; a seat has been reserved for you. In Moscow you'll need money for exchange and for the ticket. So, tomorrow evening you're leaving!

I blew up. "I'm not going anywhere until I have lived with my husband for as long as I see fit. He's been fasting; he's emaciated; I have to bring him to a condition where I'm not afraid to leave him alone. If you're pushing me out or throwing me out, then tell me so. I'm not going anywhere."

I went on shouting about many other things, about the hospital, about Andrei's isolation. Andrei did not speak, merely looked at me and sometimes smiled, as if my shouting had nothing to do with him. So we sat—on the one side, Andrei and myself on two chairs, on the other side, on two armchairs one boss man and one boss lady.

The colonel began yelling at me that he could not make that decision, that my behavior was outrageous, that they tried to meet me halfway and that I was risking loss of the trip completely. And I said, "So I'm risking it, that's all I ever do is take risks, so I won't go . . ."

And suddenly we both got tired of screaming. I said in parting that I wanted to go after Gorbachev's meeting with Reagan and after the "courageous doctors" received the Nobel Prize—I did not want to be asked about that by the press. And he said, "All right, wait." And he left.

We waited a long time, maybe over an hour. He came back angry. He had obviously gotten it (as they say) from his higher-ups for not being able to make me leave right away. Without looking at us or Guseva, who was guarding us all that time, he said, "Write an application. How much time do you need?" I said, "Two months." Here Andryusha smiled and said so calmly, "A month will do." Well, I wasn't going to argue with him, so I wrote, "One month."

We left the MVD bosses and went to have pictures taken. That night, or the next, we heard on the radio that Victor Louis said I was arriving in Vienna the next day and could go from there wherever I wanted. Then there was an announcement that the possibility of my going to Vienna had been confirmed by the ambassadors from the USSR in Vienna and in Bonn. We were called back to OVIR. The boss wasn't there, but there was a woman who said that my request had been granted, that we had to bring her a receipt for the payment of two hundred rubles for a passport. Later, she told Andrei on the phone that I could buy my own ticket.

We demanded a telephone conversation with the children. We insisted that they would never believe anything Victor Louis said and their skepticism would create even more of a furor. She said she could not decide the issue and we would have to phone her. I never dealt with her again. Andrei went to see her, and he brought her the receipt. He phoned her several times regarding the permission for the telephone conversation and about the ticket to Moscow. Then another question arose: what documents would I use for travel? Andrei called her again, to remind her that exiles had to have a travel order; otherwise I might be detained. "No one will detain her," she said in a tone more appropriate for "Go to hell."

The OVIR conflicts were repeated when I got to Moscow, but from a slightly different angle. At the city OVIR office, I was told they didn't know where my passport was and would let me know when they found it. A day later they informed me that I had to see Colonel Kuznetsov (a bigwig) at the All-Union OVIR. Emil and Nelly Shinberg drove me there as I could barely walk then.

Kuznetsov said, "Give me your passport and you'll get your foreign travel one."

"Passport? I don't have one; I'm an exile."

He was confused.

"Would you like my exile ID?" I offered.

He said, "Wait," and went out. He returned quickly. Disdainfully, with two fingers, he took my ID—a small piece of cardboard, but with a photo. Then he handed me my passport, saying, "We've put in the Italian visa here, and you can get the U.S. visa in Rome."

And then I saw that in the section indicating where I was going, it said only Italy.

"I will not accept a passport like this."

"Why not? They'll add America in Rome; we'll send orders to our comrades there."

"No, everything should be completed here. I don't even want to see your comrades in Rome; I'll see your comrades in Rome in their graves."

I was shouting by then, I threw the passport at him, and went out into the waiting room. Emil and Nelly looked pale—they had heard my screams. Kuznetsov caught up with us on the stairs and said, "Come at three o'clock."

"Well, that's different."

We went out. Nelly said, "You're going too far. I'm afraid you're not going to go anywhere now."

At three I got my passport. It said: "To Italy–United States," and the preceding page was stamped void. One of the films shows my exit passport. Naturally, without that page.

But I've run a month ahead. "Your children have pulled us out of a black hole," Andrei said once again after the first telephone conversation with Mother and the children. So the struggle was over. Packing began. And feeding. We ate five times a day. We both needed that sanitorium diet. I didn't have time left for much else, because five feedings take most of the day. We also had very long conversations, lying in bed every morning, sitting up at night. Together, together all the time. We were very happy.

But in two weeks I felt that time was passing, there were fewer days left ahead than had already gone by. Soon we would have to part. I feel the same way now, the calendar is contracting! I can see the shagreen pattern of my freedom tightening, my opportunities to see the children, the grandchildren. My mother, oh, Mother . . .

No, that will come later. Most urgently, I had to do something about my teeth. A crown had broken while Andrei was away, and I had filed the sharp edge with a nail file. That had been a painful operation. Besides which, several teeth were loose. Apparently, they needed immediate care. I couldn't eat or speak normally—it was too painful—and on top of everything I had a papilloma in my mouth. Who knew just what it was, but I was very unhappy with it. What should I do? We went to Obukhov. We weren't allowed to see anyone else.

Obukhov organized immediate first-class treatment for me, including a temporary denture. I am shown telling Andrei and Obukhov about it—simply because Andrei is in his office. All this is on film, with me sitting in the dentist's chair. I didn't hear the camera clicking or humming that time either.

We were filmed at the market and in a store. Andrei, talking on the telephone about a ticket for me from Obukhov's office, Andrei drinking tea with Obukhov and discussing disarmament. We kept wondering why Obukhov wasn't working, talking to Andrei two and three hours at a time. And in his conversation he raised such issues as disarmament. How did he find time for hospital work when he had become such a movie star?

When we were in the last session of that joint project of Soviet filmmakers and dentists, we saw an announcement in the hospital lobby that Obukhov had been awarded the title of People's Physician of the USSR. I wondered: was all of Sakharov's suffering within the walls of the Semashko Regional Hospital included in the man's achievements when he was given the nation's highest award for a physician?

The roads were very slippery my last evening with Andrei. I did not want Andrei driving home alone from the train station, so we took a taxi. When we reached the station, where we hadn't been in two years, we found the whole square dug up: the city was completing a subway system. The taxi stopped very far away. My bags were rather heavy and Andrei lugged them, stopping frequently. He would not let me carry them, but I was barely moving even without luggage. I was not feeling well.

There were five or six KGB men following us. When we stopped to catch our breath, I said to one of them, "You could at least help."

"Don't be silly; we're not allowed. You'll manage, you're healthy people!" he said mockingly. We reached the train, and Andrei brought in my bags. There was a small woman with a repulsively familiar face in my compartment, and the equally repugnant face of a KGB agent was visible at the end of the car. Later I saw them in a film.

I think we were both afraid again. "Who can tell at the word 'separation,'/ Just what kind of separation is in store . . ." We had to bear it again—separation for both of us; loneliness for him, my problems and their treatment for me. But all this was happening in an aura of triumph. Two days ago in a telephone conversation between Gorky and Newton, Andrei answered my question, "How are you?" with "I'm living in a mood of victory." And I recalled the fall of 1984, when I had said, "Andrei, you have to learn how to lose graciously." And he had said, "I don't want to learn that, I would rather learn how to die with dignity."

In the morning I arrived in Moscow. I had not been there in twenty months. Is that a lot? A little? I was met by Boris Altshuler* and Emil Shinberg. At home Masha Podyapolskaya was waiting for me with hot cabbage pies. So were the policemen. Three men at the apartment door on the seventh floor and a whole carful down at the street entrance. Well, all right, they were waiting for me and I can understand that, but why so many men just for me?

It turned out that they had been on our landing all twenty months. Night and day—they even had a cot so they could rest in shifts. What had happened in the apartment? That first autumn the wind had blown open a window. And the apartment stood open to the winds (and the dust, and dirt, and rain, and snow) all that time.

---

*Boris Altshuler (1939–   ). Physicist who lost his job and, in December 1985, his telephone because of his assistance to the Sakharov family.

Our friends weren't allowed in to clean up (to flick off the surface dirt at least) until two days before my arrival. I cannot describe how many decayed and ruined things they took out of there. There had been food left in the refrigerator, which had broken down, and the food had spoiled. It's disgusting even to think about.

It reminded me of our room in post-blockade Leningrad, when I arrived in August 1945.

Interestingly, my friends had wanted to hire people from the Zarya cleaning service, but they weren't allowed to do that, and not all of our friends were allowed to work in that "sewer" either—just Masha, Galya, and Lena.* They pleaded to have at least one man join them—there was furniture to be moved and, most important, many things to be thrown out, but . . . "no men allowed."

And here I was in the house. Mama had been allotted this apartment at the very beginning of apartment assignments for the rehabilitated in late 1954. She moved in with nothing but an umbrella. Tsilya† brought a beautifully embroidered tablecloth as a housewarming present, even though there wasn't a table. Someone else brought a cot. And Mother had a home—something she hadn't enjoyed since 1937.

Time passed and gradually we began crowding in with her—my brother, his wife and small daughter. Later they left for their own place, and I moved in with my family. Then for many years it was the four of us: Mother, myself, Tanya, and Alexei. Both children finished school and went to college. Tanya brought my son-in-law, Efrem, here. I brought Academician Sakharov. We celebrated three weddings in this house—Tanya's, mine with Andrei, and Alexei's. My first grandson, Matvei, came here from the maternity ward. These walls had seen so much joy. Our work, our crowding—no one had enough space—our friends. Home! Mother's house! Chkalov Street, 48-B, apartment 68. Tanya and Efrem and their small children left here on September 5, 1977. Before that, Tanya was expelled from the university, we received a menacing visit by Arabs from the

*Elena (Lena) Kopelev (1939–   ). Editorial assistant and friend of Elena Bonner.

†Tsitsilia (Tsilya) Dmitrieva (1899–1981). Friend of the Bonner family.

PLO, there were threats against Matvei, his mysterious convulsions, threats against Efrem, and the case against Tanya.

Soon after their departure Alexei, an excellent student, was expelled from the institute, for not completing his military service. On a gray morning, March 1, we drove to Sheremetyevo Airport. Liza was as black as her hair. Alexei had three carnations in his hand. I thought he had bought them for her. He asked the driver to stop in front of the Pushkin monument, so beloved by the poet Tsvetaeva. If I shut my eyes, I can still see the crimson of the carnations against the wet granite of the pedestal.

On the morning of January 22, 1980, Andryusha, as usual, stared out the window. We have an extensive view from there, all the sky and half of Moscow. Then he left for a seminar. Later he telephoned, and that evening a plane carrying us and eight guards brought us to Gorky. We were fed unusually well on the plane and people calling themselves doctors carried on about our health.

In May 1980 Mother left this house for Sheremetyevo, going to visit her grandchildren in the United States. As I stood with her near passport control (everyone was so considerate—I handled customs and brought her as far as the passport booth), I hugged her and held her close, and could feel her heart pounding like a sparrow's. Alexei had left Liza in our care, and even though one person isn't a family, the house remained a home.

We fasted for Liza in November and December 1981. On December 19 at the airport, leaving for the States, she said, "Elena Georgievna, I want to go back home; I'm afraid."

And now I was back, I even lived there for five days. Strange. It wasn't a home—it was walls. Within them my friends arranged a bon-voyage party. There were lots of people. I had not expected to see them and I hadn't expected that their presence that evening would turn the walls back into a home—I had not expected that at all.

XIV

I am sitting on a veranda. The sky surrounds me on all sides and I am in the center of the bowl. Its sides rise like slopes. They are fuzzy green. Groves of low, wide-branching pines. The pines are quite different. The air is like our Karelian air, but the pines don't grow straight upward; they live expansively. Maybe it's the proximity of the ocean that does that to them. But what has done this to me? As I look up at the clouds floating in the sky, these words from Galich's song run through my head:

> Clouds float, clouds,
> and they don't need a——

I've forgotten how it goes and yet I can't get rid of the lines. I do remember the third line: "And they don't need an amnesty."

Why does that line keep running through my head when I'm seven leagues and kingdoms (both geographically and otherwise) away from home? I wait for Tanya and the kids to come back from the woods to tell me the missing word.

Well, I've described my workplace. I am in Truro, Cape Cod, Massachusetts. And now the kids are back. Tanya replies instantly:

> And they don't need a lawyer,
> And they don't need an amnesty.

This morning I spoke with Andrei. That's just an expression—actually I shouted and heard nothing because we were constantly cut off. That's what we pay for, being cut off. Still, as a conclusion to the saga of our car, Andrei told me he tried to give a lift to a gypsy woman who was hitchhiking. He received an official warning that he would lose his license for using private transport for profit. An official warning not in the Aesopic language I've already written about, not cockroaches scattering from packages and not four tires going flat at one time.

Andrei also asked me what he should do about planting flowers on the balcony. I tried to shout (apparently this topic is also forbidden) that he should wait until June, when I would be home. This year I would plant seedlings and not seeds, and it wouldn't be too late for seedlings. But I don't know if he understood me, if he heard me at all.

Apparently they don't want Andrei to know when I'm returning. What trick are they planning now?

But let me go back to December 1985. I was afraid of the trip—that long voyage from Gorky to Newton, and to the doctors. Never letting go of my nitroglycerine for a second, under the glare of spotlights and the eyes of friends and enemies, I went through customs. I was sorry that I had taken so few books—they let me take everything out. I went through passport control and ended up—here. At any rate, on the other side of the border.

I was recognized in the waiting room. There were familiar journalists, too. And strangest of all, no one was afraid of me. I had to get used to that again—which I did very quickly. I don't remember anything about the flight, I wasn't even sure where I was headed until the plane landed. The engines died down, and a small airport service car drove up—I was watching rather aloofly through the porthole against which I had huddled from the moment of takeoff. (But perhaps you don't call them portholes in an airplane?) I was still in Gorky, or at least in Moscow.

And then I saw Alexei, and after him Efrem, getting out of the car. I think that was the moment when I realized that my trip had actually, truly, taken place.

But I didn't get to see Italy. I didn't see it, but I felt a warmth as I had never felt it—from people I knew and didn't know, with flowers and welcomes. I have this great mutual love affair with Italy; I can't explain it. But this time it was all in a rush, all done to police sirens; we were in such a rush in both Florence and Siena that I didn't have time to look at anything. I'm even amazed that the four of us (Irina* joined us in Rome) survived the rushing.

I think we were only in two places where I did not rush, where I could catch my breath and think a bit: the Vatican and the Prime Minister's living room. In both cases I left comforted, knowing that my husband was respected and loved here and that his well-being was a real consideration, not just empty words. I could also sit down with my legs stretched out—they hurt no less than my heart—in the homes of three friends, Nina Harkevich, Maria Olsufieva, and Lia Wainstein.†

I left Europe on December 7 in the morning, and I arrived in the States the same day, in the daytime. Ah, the twentieth century, you don't have time to prepare for anything, to prepare yourself spiritually. Everything happens at such speeds. I really longed to have Andrei with me on the plane. God knows, I always miss him, but this was a special case. As a VIP, I was invited into the captain's cockpit. Now that's a sight for modern man. I wanted to fly by myself. A Natasha Rostova,‡ but with nitroglycerine. I remembered a sentiment once expressed by Victor Shklovsky.** "Age does not differ greatly from youth—you want to do the same things, you just can't."

I don't remember a thing about being met, greeted, photographed. I only remember Mother and the little ones—I saw them all and that new, funny, sturdy, and totally unknown little girl.

My medical care began on December 9. Andrei had told me not to hide anything from the doctors, to tell them everything. The first operation was to remove a small tumor from my lip. A Dr. Nathanson did the surgery so fast that I hadn't time to feel it, or even to get frightened. The papilloma turned out to be benign, so Andrei had worried for nothing. The worst part is the fear you feel beforehand.

---

*Irene Ilovaiskaya-Alberti. Editor of the Paris Russian-language weekly *Russkaya mysl'*.

†Lia Wainstein. Italian journalist.

‡Natasha Rostova. Character in *War and Peace*, a dreamy and romantic adolescent.

**Victor Shklovsky (1893–1985). Literary critic.

Back in Florence I had seen my faithful eye physician Dr. Frezzotti. He said it wasn't urgent, that I shouldn't deal with my eyes until after I had taken care of my heart. Another eye man, Dr. Charles Schepens, said the same thing. They said the same thing about my legs. And the scariest of them all, the dentist, said the same about my teeth. So it all came down to my heart. And my heart hurt unbearably. I would have cursed it, but they say you shouldn't curse your heart; it's an evil omen. Besides, I hadn't come to curse it, but to cure it.

The first cardiologist I saw, Dr. Adolph Hutter, apparently didn't believe I was so ill. I guess my personality let me down again. In one film about us, the announcer said that I led an active life. What would they have me do? You can lie down and die, just say: I'm sick and that's it. Period. Or you can try. There's a famous story of two frogs that fell into a pitcher of milk. One said, "That's it; I'm drowning." And quickly drowned. The other got so mad that it began beating its front legs against the milk. It beat and beat and whipped up butter, and even though it was slippery, the frog climbed up the butter and out of the pitcher.

The American press took the cardiologists' comments to mean that I wasn't really ill. What reached Andrei was that I was simply malingering. I had just wanted to go for a trip abroad!

I was examined, and conservative treatment prescribed. The medication did not differ significantly from what I was taking at home. The medicines are not made in the Soviet Union but are available sometimes in Soviet pharmacies. Of course, they did add a few things, but I knew we wouldn't get very far with just those, and that the miracle Andrei was hoping for was not going to happen.

Incidentally (I'm writing this in a friendly spirit and hope that he will not be offended—at least, I don't want to offend anyone), the doctor was not particularly informed about Andrei or me. Of course he had heard of us and even knew that the climate in Gorky was not ideal for my heart, but, for instance, he had not read Andrei's letter in *U.S. News and World Report* (I am writing this in late March) nor had he seen the film about us with Jason Robards and Glenda Jackson. I would call his level of information average, assuming that the average person is one who has heard of us but doesn't know much.

I am well disposed to people like that, or at least better disposed to them than to those who know everything but out of some sort of principle refuse to see things from a human point of view. The average ones are capable of understanding and of helping if possible, once you explain things to them.

While Dr. Hutter was in no hurry to put me under the knife, he did catheterize my heart and even draw a picture of everything they saw.

A look at his drawing made clear to me what was blocked—and where. Andrei now had an idea too, because I sent him a copy of the drawing by mail. It did not look so horrible, but my heart ached even more, I think, after the catheterization than it had before.

The catheterization deserves being described a bit. They do not hospitalize you for long. In the evening you check in, early the next morning everything is done, and by evening, if everything has gone well, you can go home. Time expended—twenty-four hours. The procedure itself takes about two hours. What makes it frightening are the preliminary conversations with the doctors about possible complications and the consent form you sign. It is tiring to lie on your back in an uncomfortable position both during the whole procedure and thereafter, but it's bearable.

There is only one brief moment that is difficult, no more than an instant, when the dye is injected. You've gotten used to the nauseated feeling inside, you no longer consider the long lying-down as something terrible, merely something bad but which has an end. You think it will be over soon. And then . . .

Do you know the story of Ivanushka, who had to be boiled alive and come out of it handsome, so that the tsar's daughter would fall in love with him? Well, just think that you're not in a hospital, but in that fairy tale. I know for a fact that the procedure was like being boiled, and if I didn't come out beautiful, it's due to some medical error. At least I'm still loved. I hope.

Sometime before Christmas, my doctor began doubting that conservative treatment would give positive results and said he would take me to a surgeon after the New Year.

In the meantime we got ready for the holidays.

XV

Since time immemorial the genre of the Christmas tale has existed
in Russia. It continues to exist at a time when literature tries to use
the word "Christmas" as little as possible and the main holiday is
New Year's. But still the genre—the Christmas tale—remains.
Those of us who were brought up more on literature than on material things will always have a tender affection for it. But if we find
ourselves in a world where things are available, they also become
attractive. We stop feeling ashamed of a love for possessions and
don't tiptoe fawningly around literature. Our unbalanced love for
literature in Russia gradually evens itself out in America as other
things complement it; we become (at least in that regard) more
harmonious personalities.

I came (I flew; no one walks over the ocean) to the United States
in December, just when the all-American shopping spree begins. If
literature is stronger where I came from, it's just the opposite here.
Above everything in the weeks before the holidays stood the object,
the Christmas thing (also a genre). It defined the holiday and perhaps
the whole coming year.

Christmas shopping involved everyone; people talked about it at
home, in coffee shops, at the hospital (in every country, the hospital
is a world that gives a mass of new knowledge). And it looked as if
everyone were shopping—poor and rich and those in between. It
was a form of release. A person has at least once, somewhere, somehow, to feel satisfied (I'm not talking about being utterly sated). You
can't always "want."

It's not good on a personal level—with time it will change your
outlook, the colors, tastes, sounds, and smells of the living world.

The whole world will seem bitter. Of course, some have less and they must deal with that; others have more; and still others have dangerously much. The same thing is true with respect to entire societies. I think this is well understood by those who work with Third World countries, in Latin America, Asia, and Africa. And it is important for our leaders to understand this phenomenon.

I can understand that an immigrant wants to buy as much as possible. He's a neophyte, and his faith is at a high pitch. But I was amazed that Americans are just as passionate about shopping as the new arrivals. I liked the shopping public of America in the weeks and days before Christmas—lively and interested.

A huge department store—not for the rich, but for ordinary people. Incidentally, in general Americans are careful with their money and prefer to spend their hard-earned cash in places that don't overcharge. A middle-aged couple, not émigrés (I watched them for over an hour, perhaps violating their privacy a little). How carefully they select, look, discuss, buy—they take many things, in two large carts. They must have children and grandchildren and many friends.

That's all understandable. But the concentration during all of this, especially on the part of the man, was something unusual for me. There aren't many Russian men who would consider shopping for presents so important; even men who care about appearances and prestige leave shopping to their wives. Maybe it was a question of family closeness, manifested in a common concern for gifts, even in a place where there is a sea of products.

People filled the stores throughout the preholiday period. I went with my family and was amazed by the number of shoppers and the amount of time they gave to the stores. And the last day or two before Christmas the stores were almost empty. Everyone had finished shopping, everyone was happy, and in all the stores, cafés, streets, everywhere across America: "Have a nice holiday."

How many presents do you think we wrapped (pretty paper, ribbons, name cards)? Over a hundred. How many robes did our family buy or receive as presents? Eight. A friend of my children (not the grandchildren), who was visiting while the presents were being given out, asked, "Why so many robes?"

By that time the living room in my daughter's house looked like a small department store. And a ditty kept going through my mind: "In this small basket I have lipstick and perfume, ribbons, laces, shoes, whatever you may choose."

"Why so many robes?" There weren't many robes, it was we who were many. A robe for Mother, a robe for Natasha, a robe for Tanya, a robe for Liza, and for me—even three robes! (One from the children and two from friends.) I was from the USSR, where robes are hard to come by.

I did not see or talk to people here who oppose consumerism, who berate America's consumer spirit. Not Americans, but people who came and did not want to join the consumer society. I know such people exist, and I would be curious to find out if they follow through on their intentions, or if they buy gifts for Christmas, if they give presents to their wives, husbands, children, parents, and friends. Maybe they are staunch nonconsumers. I don't know whether their slogans apply only to others or whether they practice what they preach. If they do, then I fear for the harmony of their personalities. Nonconsumerism can unbalance them much faster than consumerism. I sometimes have the sneaky thought that the consumer society and its flaws are not as bad as they are depicted. We start to worry ourselves into insomnia and might even (it's doubtful, but we might) stop buying. While those who lecture us on the evils of materialism sleep well and buy things. And trick us.

Christmas with its present-giving spree passed. New Year's was just like in Russia—the only ones in the house were people who could not be President, except for Sasha, who was born here.

On January 6 I went to see the surgeon, Dr. Austin. This is a man born to make decisions. After one session with him I saw myself lying under his scalpel and knew that no amount of explanations about the percentage of complications or unexpected results would change that. He and his colleague Dr. Akins were already cutting into me mentally. And with them, action followed thought.

For some reason I remember the sensation the catheterization had given me—as if I were being boiled alive. The doctor somehow reminded me of my old friends from the First Medical Institute. And I thought: At least that procedure had been bearable, despite the pain, but what was awaiting me now?

On January 12 I went into the hospital. The surgeon would

operate the next day. Still, I have this thing about omens. As I was signing the release forms for the anesthesiologist, the cardiologist, and the surgeon, I remembered Seva's "Let's throw ourselves into the swim, boys." (If after this someone finds and reads Vsevolod Bagritsky's book—this is the third time I mention it in these notes —I will feel that I have achieved something.) As Dr. Cary Akins, my heart surgeon, put it: just consider that you will lose one day out of your life. He may have phrased it more gently, but that's how I understood it too. Who was translating for me—Tanya or Alexei? I don't remember.

The children left. Evening in the hospital. I took a shower. Two nurses came and tossed a towel on the floor, as blue as the ocean that existed before anything else in this world did. They stood me on the towel and stripped me naked. I suddenly grew afraid. Something inside ached and tugged at me. I wanted to cry and to say, "Farewell, beloved friends, farewell, blue sky . . ." I had goose bumps from the cold and from my terror. The nurses laughed softly and talked about something. They began shaving me—not just my armpits and chest (I knew that my chest would be cut open and that the surgical field had to be shaved). They shaved every inch of me—from my neck down: chest, sides, back, stomach, legs, tops of my feet, shoulders, forearms, hands. I was turning into a solid surgical field, or a sacrificial victim for a ritual.

My goose bumps got in the way, but the nurses managed and then began dousing me generously with an iodine solution from large bottles, rubbing it in with towels.

It must have stung my skin; they fanned me with the towels, but I didn't feel it too much. I was still in panic. They stuffed me into something sterile blue, put me to bed, and gave me something to drink. I asked the time. "Twenty to eleven" sank into my consciousness. I was amazed by my voice as I asked the question. I was going off into oblivion, and my voice was like an old story. . . .

I was filling up the primus stove under the autoclave. Does anyone know nowadays that bandages used to be sterilized that way? Through the narrow crack of the door I could see the low October sky. I heard them flying. It was strange, in such bad weather. There were two of them. They were flying low, and out of my field of vision. And I saw it, it was falling, and I could see that it was coming toward me. It was big. I no longer heard anything—not it, not the planes—but I felt moisture on my face, it was snowing, and the snow fell on me. There was nothing else. For a long time? I don't know. Right above me were stars and the sky. It was frosty, the color of blue frost, and I did not know whether I was alive or dead.

Then I felt my arms, especially my left arm, which hurt. But I couldn't feel my legs at all, and I thought: "How will I dance?" And I heard a voice: "Please don't die." Who said that? Me? Could that be my voice?

The rest I know from what people told me. They heard me, found me, dug me out. That means that I had died once already. Almost for twenty-four hours. At Valya station, not far from Efimovskaya station. From the morning of the twenty-sixth until dawn on October 27, 1941.

Coming back to life was very hard. I think that I vaguely heard Tanya's voice, and then Efrem's and Liza's. Maybe that did not happen? Maybe it's just a layering of their stories. It happened. But the feeling that I was alive and not in some other world came later.

Alexei's voice. Alexei's "Mama." Then oblivion. Then once again, "Mama, do you hear me? Mama, squeeze my hand." I heard him, I thought I was squeezing, but I had no sensation of his hand.

Then I heard his voice again and even smelled an odor, as if he had just been smoking. Then emptiness again, and a stranger's voice —in English. I understand that the operation is over, that there were six bypasses. (Why six—we had spoken about three, well, maybe four.)

I heard my own breathing—or wasn't it mine? A machine forced air into me, breathed for me. Another machine beat for my heart.

I felt the warmth of Alexei's hand and the difference between my temperature and his. I was afraid—he was sick, he was little and sick and his hand was hot. But why was there the smell of tobacco?—I didn't smoke then. What a mix-up. Maybe it was a dream or it wasn't happening at all. And once again, "Mama, squeeze my hand." I squeezed. Alexei said in English, "She hears me."

"I hear you, I hear you," I wanted to say, I wanted to shout—but I couldn't. That's how I returned to life. Once again in early morning, once again at dawn. This time on January 14, 1986. A strange repetition. As if the return to life in 1941 had been nothing but a rehearsal.

Later I was unplugged from the machines and I said my first words. Then they unplugged me from the monitor, and took me to my room—this was medicine, good medicine, but medicine. Before that it was something else. I know that it was beyond the limits, "existing" or "not," being between "here" and "there." I left that, and the post-operative routine took over. Nights and days of pain, when after the first improvement I developed pericarditis and pleurisy, constant pain. Lord, all my bones were cut or broken. I couldn't lie down or sit or walk and my leg hurt and my left arm hurt. The shoulder was so bad I wanted to scream. And this and that and on and on. I don't think I was ever so sick, so unable to cope with it all in my life.

And maybe it wasn't worth doing all this, maybe it would have been better not to undergo such radical treatment. Even now I still wonder—do we have the right to intervene in our own lives that way? And after all I have lived through now, I have another question: "What if it's not me?" (Anna Akhmatova). I still have not resolved my doubts about the rightness of such an operation, such treatment, even after finding myself able to sit down to work. This only happened after they let me into the operating theater at Massachusetts General Hospital to observe open heart surgery. I would never have been allowed to see this, like never seeing my own ears, if I weren't a doctor and hadn't been predisposed, and if the main anesthesiologist hadn't agreed, and if Dr. Hutter hadn't brought me in. It's like a fortress or the Pentagon—very hard to get into. I had to sign in. Where was I from? they asked. (They wrote "Russia.") Then I was admitted. Only into the dressing room so far. I changed and went on.

All my concerns of many weeks about whether man has the right to do such operations had made me nervous from early morning, and by then I was feeling a slight chill. I remembered that when we were making plans for my visit, a few days earlier, Dr. Hutter asked, "You won't faint, will you?"

I was insulted. "Who, me?" After all, before I became a doctor

I had been a nurse for many years. But now I asked myself the same question. And answered it myself: "Hold on."

What had I expected? I looked for an embodiment of my doubts, my questions—but instead I came into a normal workplace, where people were working. Of course the work was high-class, but it was work, and not a Question, especially with a capital Q. It was very interesting and I had no emotional responses except—what fine work!

Of course they do fine work. Just look at the schedule—sixty operations today, Thursday, May 6, 1986. They work in forty rooms. Some surgeons have two or even three operations a day. Dr. Akins has three today. Now he was standing over an open chest cavity— cut down the middle, edges spread open and clamped, the heart open to everything, eyes, hands, breeze.

Such a precise name for the operation—"open heart" surgery. There's nothing to add or subtract from that.

It beat steadily, the heart I was watching and on which the surgeon was performing his miraculous and monstrous work. With every beat the blood level in the heart rose and fell. Then clear plastic tubes were attached to the large blood vessels; they filled with blood, even looking heavier, and across half the room a machine began pumping blood through the tubes. The large circulatory pathway and the small one left the confines of the body but went on function- ing the way they were supposed to, and the heart grew lighter and stopped.

I remembered how terrifying it used to be in the operating room when we lost the pulse on the patient or could no longer hear the heartbeat. But here, nothing of the kind. The heart was unplugged for the sake of convenience, to make it easier to operate on it. The fine, lacelike work continued. The surgeon sewed bypasses, one, another. Everything was quiet, calm, habitual—habitual for them.

Once he asked the body temperature. "Twenty-three point nine," replied one of the people who was watching the apparatus and from time to time injecting something into the marble-white arm. Two bypasses in thirty minutes. Then the circulation of blood was restored to its normal route. The heart shuddered, once, twice, grew pink and with the color life returned to the heart. For now only to the heart, not to the patient. Several hours would pass, the body temperature had to rise from 24° C to at least 32° or 33° C before he could return to our world. The patient would return. And the doctor had two more operations to do today.

In another operating room a small body lies on top of light blue sheets, a child of two. The chest is also open and it's another "open heart." Just like in an adult, but smaller, and there isn't a speck of fat on the organ. In order to live, however, the child has to go through this. The heart is open. While the blood flows through the small and large circles of plastic and the stopped heart waits, the doctor, like a child making a dragon, is cutting an oval patch a bit larger than a thumbnail and trying it on for size on the part of the heart that needs to be repaired. The child has an opening in the interventricular septum. The doctor sews it on, neatly, slowly, calmly. He asks about the temperature, too. 21.9° C. He continues his work with concentration, creating a miracle.

In the waiting room, the mother of that little boy suffers, waits, hopes, doubts. Doubt is essential; it makes us more responsible. But how good it is that the doctor who is sewing the patch right now has golden hands, and doubt, and responsibility.

After open heart surgery, any other operation is simply not an event. So I took the second angiography and angioplasty on my right leg without excessive emotion. Of course, it was like being back in boiling water and the pain in my leg was persistent and strong. For some reason I had expected no pain this time. To tell the truth, I am tired of pain and have not yet recovered from my major surgery; my chest still hurts, and it's still hard to take a deep breath. And God forbid if I lean my chest against something or if a friend embraces me. The pain pierces through me—I want to scream. It hurts to sit at the typewriter.

But I am free of the anticipation of further surgical interventions. That is very pleasant, knowing that the knife no longer threatens, or awaits (that's nicer). I am supposed to rest and I want to observe my children calmly. But the devil made me do it, so I sat down at the typewriter.

It would be great if instead of all the robes, the new suit, the piles of blouses, shirts, and presents for my friends and the children's friends, I could pack up these pages and take them to Andrei. That would be a present for him. He would sit and read them. And I would bake a raspberry or apple pie.

I hope there will be a pie. But he won't read the pages. I'm so sorry, it's almost unbearable. But it was because of these pages that I wrote to him less frequently, and in the last few days I have been in a real rush and not writing at all to him, hurrying to finish, to get it done in time—no longer about Gorky, but about my American holiday.

XVI

During my visit to America, there were many receptions, lunches, dinners, and serious conversations about Andrei and his fate. The questions vary, but sometimes it is abundantly clear that the questioner knows nothing about him. You don't even know why you came here to ask. Everyone was coming, so you came, too. It's that way back home in Russia, when you see a line in the street. That means something has been "put out," so you get in line, too. ("Put out" is a synonym for "on sale." The items are not always cheap—for instance, fur hats are now put out at three hundred fifty rubles each, and some people buy two at a time.) You don't know what they're selling. And the people ahead of you don't either. It doesn't matter; you'll figure it out later. But even friends who know quite a lot about Andrei ask: "Who takes care of Andrei while you are here?"

No one. He is alone. *Alone.* He cleans up, mops the floor in the kitchen, does the laundry. He goes to the store, buys food, brings it home and cooks it. He eats alone, then washes the dishes.

"Does he really know how to manage?"

Yes, he knows. And it does not bother him. He does not think that household chores divert him from "eternal" and "immortal" matters. He respects such tasks and is willing to help even when I am home, sometimes snatching work right out of my hands. It is important to understand his attitude toward such things. It resembles his attitude toward people. Just as there are no little people or unimportant lives, there is no insignificant work.

He gets annoyed when someone asks: "Andrei Dmitrievich, you are such a great man, you need peace and quiet. Why should you risk your health going on hunger strikes for Liza and Elena and Vladimir Bukovsky and Igor Ogurtsov and Valentin Moroz?" He finds it difficult to reply to people who do not understand the roots of his behavior.

Sometimes people have asked him: "Why bother writing about some Jew who would like to emigrate?" Such questions he finds offensive, and he is puzzled that people who have met him do not know him at all.

He approaches household matters and everyday life with the same simplicity and respect he does people. But it is difficult for him to be alone. He does not have time for everything he wants to do. Things require much more effort than they do in America. Sometimes he lacks the physical strength to cope.

"And when you were living alone, was your life like that too?"

It was.

"How did you manage if you needed six cardiac bypasses?"

I managed. I did what I could. Two years ago I could not wash the windows before I sealed them for the winter. I washed them last summer, but I was feeling worse again in the fall, so over the winter they were dirty. I have money to pay a window cleaner, but I am forbidden to have contacts with people.

One day my television broke down. I found the telephone number of a repair shop in the phone book and went outside to call. I did not have to look too far for a pay phone; the first two were out of order, but the third was working. I was still dialing the number when my secret service escort (or KGB agent—I don't know what to call him in order to avoid being accused of slander) pulled open the door and held down the button. He berated me, saying I knew very well that I was not allowed to use the telephone. Then he agreed to tell his boss that I needed a television repairman. Two days later the policeman who stands guard at our door politely told me: "The repairman is coming tomorrow."

"Why did you have to go to a pay phone? Can't you call from your house?"

We have no phone in our apartment. Academician Sakharov has been living in Gorky for six years without a telephone. There have been times when I needed urgent medical assistance, not a television repairman. Andrei would have to run outside, even in freezing weather, to look for a phone booth. In winter, still fewer work properly. But now he is alone, and I don't know what would happen in case of a medical emergency.

In Soviet-made films shown in the West, Andrei speaks quite a bit on the phone. It is a deliberate attempt to convince the audience that he has a telephone. While I have been in America, they allow us the luxury of speaking to each other. Andrei is summoned to a telephone center, but not the usual one for international calls. Post Office 107 is specially equipped with a hidden camera, and the films have demonstrated how easily, with no regard for the law, they listen to and record conversations between a husband and wife. I don't know who makes the movies, but I think the sequences exposing our family affairs to the whole world are anti-Soviet. In any democratic country, where the law protects the individual and not the state, Andrei and I would win a court case against the anonymous Peeping Toms who direct the films and the government officials who authorize them. Remember Watergate. A President was forced to resign because of wiretapping.

"Do you listen to the radio?"

Yes, we do. In order to tune in, we travel to the extreme edge of town, to the racetrack or to the cemetery. There we can pick up some Western stations. It isn't bad in spring and summer, but it is cold and windy in winter. The days are short; we don't like to drive at night because the roads are often not clear—you can see that in one of the films—and they are slippery. So we seldom listen to the radio in winter.

"Why don't you listen at home?"

Because the reception there is jammed. In our house, or at least in our apartment, since I don't know about the rest of our ten-story building, some device has been installed which prevents us from listening to the radio, which interferes with our television reception and also with our phonograph. The jamming occurs around the clock. We have tested it morning, afternoon, evening, and night.

"Is it harmful for your health?"

Andrei has thought about this and doesn't know. I don't understand such things at all.

"Can you read newspapers and magazines?"

All the Soviet ones we want. The Western magazines which we had managed to collect over four years, among them issues of *Newsweek, Time, Paris-Match, U.S. News and World Report,* were all taken during the search of May 8, 1984. They have not been returned, nor have our clippings from Western newspapers. Even our Soviet press clippings were confiscated.

"What else do you read?"

Andrei does not read a lot—I am speaking about belles-lettres, where he usually follows my recommendations. He spends more time on scientific journals and reprints. I read a great deal, mostly Soviet intellectual magazines, both fiction and nonfiction; they contain a good deal that is interesting. I also read books. While I was able to go back and forth between Moscow and Gorky, I would get English and American detective stories. My English is not up to more serious reading, but I'm quite able to understand my favorite heroes, Nero Wolfe and his sidekick Archie, the ladies' man. I also read Agatha Christie and John le Carré (difficult for me), among others. Occasionally, Andrei also reads English mysteries.

"Where do you get Russian books and magazines? Do you buy them?"

Some newspapers we simply buy. We have yearly subscriptions for most of the literary journals and the newspapers. Subscribing is rather complicated in the Soviet Union, because many publications are "limited." That means there is a ceiling on subscriptions and very few copies ever appear on sale. This may seem astonishing to people in the West—there are willing customers who cannot buy what they want—but that's the way it is. I don't know if there is any other explanation for the limits besides the paper shortage, but often they are on the most popular publications. There is also a shortage of books that people would want to buy.

Andrei Dmitrievich and I have no problem getting subscriptions, and we can order practically anything we want, with the exception of the magazines *America* and *England.** That is because I am a war

---

*Magazines published in the Russian language by the government information services of the U.S. and England respectively.

veteran, and war veterans may subscribe to whatever they desire without worrying about limits. All I have to do is show my papers and pay for the entire year. For 1986 I spent nearly five hundred rubles on subscriptions—and by Soviet standards, taking into account the low prices of our publications, that is a lot of money. As the saying goes, "Read until you can't stand it."

We have no problems with obtaining books, either. As long as Andrei Dmitrievich is an Academician, he may order any book published in the USSR from the Academy Bookstore in Moscow. In the past, we used to go there every month, and the two of us are with Karl Marx, who when asked, "What is your favorite pastime?" replied, "Digging around in books."

Now we order books from the Academy catalogue and receive them by mail. That's less exciting. And for some reason, the best books often don't reach us. On the average, we order twenty-five to thirty rubles' worth of books a month. Books and magazines are the luxury of our life, just as they had been in my life before I met Sakharov.

Besides the things necessary for everyday living, we have made few purchases in our years together. In Moscow we did not buy any furniture except for some things for the kitchen and the bed we slept in. In Gorky, I bought a desk, a bookcase, a table, and a few table lamps. We have not purchased a single carpet or crystal *objet d'art* (material, albeit superficial, indicators of life-style in our society). And we're not overly extravagant in terms of clothing, either. (Look how far the question of reading material has taken me. However, I think that the reader, interested in much or even in everything about Andrei Dmitrievich, will forgive me.)

"What is the food situation in Gorky?"

It's not catastrophic and probably very much the way it is in any Soviet city other than Moscow or Leningrad. I will simply list what there is in the stores—not even in stores in general, but in the one where we market. It is located two or three blocks from us, perhaps a bit more. The return trip is uphill, and carrying groceries is too much for me since my heart attack. So I drive to the store. Andrei usually walks.

The grocery store always has sugar, tea (very poor quality), salt, some sort of cookies, rice, vegetable oil, several types of candy, semolina, and sometimes other grains and macaroni, but there hasn't been any buckwheat in the last six years. There is no butter, but it does have margarine, sometimes cheese, almost always eggs. As for other food products—meat, chicken, sausage, fish—when they appear, so do long lines.

The dairy store almost always has milk and yogurt in the mornings, and often has cottage cheese and sour cream, and sometimes regular cheese. The vegetable store sells potatoes, cabbage, carrots, and beets, and, very rarely, squash or cauliflower. Apples, grapes, and other fruits create very long lines—especially bananas or oranges. There are always juices.

The bakery has bread, black and white, during the day, but runs out in the evening, especially on Fridays, when people shop for their weekend trips to the country.

There is also a wine and vodka shop. They don't always have vodka, and long lines form when it's on sale. As a war veteran, I can shop without standing in line, simply by showing my papers. I sometimes use that right, especially to buy cottage cheese or fruit. Once I used it to purchase vodka. In the summer of 1985 I had lost weight drastically and developed abscesses under my arm. Concerned that the infection might spread, I decided to disinfect the skin thoroughly. Neither alcohol-saturated pads nor alcohol is available, so I went to buy some vodka. I picked the wrong day, a Friday, and the line was long. I took out my papers and people let me through to the front of the line. I asked for a bottle and then for two—it would save me a trip if the infection spread. When I came out of the store, a bottle of vodka in each hand, my KGB escort said, "Elena Georgievna, you didn't use to drink, did you?"

"You'd drive anyone to drink."

I don't know whether he believed I had taken to drink or not. But this was during the gloomiest days of June 1985.

Gorky has several outdoor farmers' markets. On the average, the prices are three times what they are in the stores, and for some items, even higher. For instance, meat in the store costs two rubles a kilogram and between six and eight rubles at the market. Potatoes in the store are ten kopeks a kilogram and thirty to fifty kopeks in the market. Cottage cheese is one ruble at the store and four to five rubles in the market. To all intents and purposes, berries and certain fruits and vegetables exist only at the markets.

In the winter, the selection is very poor, and in order to get anything at all, you must arrive before eight in the morning. I always oversleep. In the summer, the market is much more festive. There are flowers, berries, and colorful fruits, primarily from the southern republics.

But the prices are horrifying. On a television program for New Year's Eve 1984, one of our comics joked that the Division for Combatting Embezzlement of Socialist Property would do well by arresting anyone shopping for melons or pears at the market; they would never go wrong, because no one can afford them on his salary alone. That's an exaggeration, of course, but there is a grain of truth in it, even though I see many shoppers at the markets.

Once again, my status as a disabled veteran of the Great Patriotic War (World War II) allows us not to worry too much about groceries. Every city has special stores for this category of people. When I was exiled, I requested that I be put on the eligibility list of one of these stores. Before that, I used to bring almost all of our groceries from Moscow. Once I was assigned, we visited the special store twice a month to pick up our allotments.

Each allotment includes one and a half kilograms of meat, one chicken, one kilogram of fish, buckwheat groats, peas, mayonnaise, six hundred grams of butter, canned goods, and a half kilogram of cheese. That food order really helps us out, especially in winter.

As I said, we used to go twice a month. But it was a form of social contact—with other customers, with the salespeople—and so we were forbidden to visit the store. Now the order is delivered to our apartment. Unfortunately, the privileges accorded disabled veterans of the Great Patriotic War are not extended to other handicapped persons, who could use this sort of help to alleviate the hardships of their life.

One of the most frequent questions: "In the past, Andrei Dmitrievich did not want to emigrate. What is his attitude now?"

It seems to me that as soon as Andrei began to have contacts with journalists in 1972, they started asking this question. We were living

on Chkalov Street, never suspecting we would wind up in Gorky.
Andrei would reply in a few words, most often in one brief sentence:
"I don't discuss hypothetical situations."

In 1973 he received his first invitation, to spend a year at Princeton University as a visiting professor. He accepted with thanks, but
said he was not ready to emigrate and he was not preparing to do
so. He added that he did not consider emigration possible for himself
and gave several reasons why. This conversation was not reported
accurately by the correspondent who discussed the invitation with
him; the second half of Andrei's response was simply omitted. To
the best of my recollection, Andrei did not make any official attempt
to go to Princeton.

When he received the Nobel Prize, he applied to OVIR for a visa
and was refused.

In 1977 he accepted an invitation to attend the AFL-CIO conven-
tion in America, although he did not reach OVIR in the application
process. The Academy of Sciences refused to issue one of the documents needed to proceed.

In early 1983 Andrei received an invitation from the Norwegian
government to take up permanent residence in Norway. The invitation was sent at the behest of the Norwegian Storting, and all the
political parties voted for it. Andrei replied to the invitation with the
following letter:

To: The Norwegian Government

I accept with gratitude the invitation of the Norwegian
government to move with my family to Norway for permanent residence. Any possibility for my departure from the
USSR depends on the decision of the Soviet authorities. I
was earlier (1975 and 1977) denied permission to take trips
abroad and reference was made to the secret character of my
work until July 1968. I hope you will ask the authorities about
the possibility of my departure at this time.

In the case of a refusal, I hope the Norwegian government will support the following request, which is of vital
importance for our family. In September 1982, my wife, Elena

Bonner, submitted an application to travel to Italy for ophthalmological treatment, including possible eye surgery. Her eye disease is the result of a concussion she suffered at the front during World War II. Because of the special conditions under which we live, medical treatment in the USSR is not possible.

We received permission for her treatment in Italy in 1975. She has traveled to Italy on three occasions for medical care, the last time in 1979. Now she needs to go again. But we have received no reply after six months. Your support could be decisive in this matter.

Respectfully,

February 24, 1983
Gorky   Andrei Sakharov

P.S. Please find some way to let me know the results of your conversations on both the first and second points.

XVII

I've seen many films about our life in Gorky sold through the West German newspaper *Bild*—six, I think.* I can take them apart individually, or I can deal with them as a whole; it doesn't matter, because they're full of lies made to look like half-truths passed off as the truth. It is very difficult to explain even to myself and to figure it all out episode by episode, and I can't imagine how to do it for others, but I must. No one but I can explain it at all. Andrei knows how to do things without getting emotional and he speaks precisely, without my superfluous words and my impure language. It would be easier if, besides understanding the general line of disinformation made to create the impression of our well-being, I could also understand the reasons for issuing the films, why each was released at a particular time and for what reason.

The general impression given is that the KGB has been filming us constantly, and for a long time—even before Gorky. And since we moved to Gorky, it seems almost as if every one of our outings has been filmed for the files. All the films are narrated by the same familiar voice. Who is it? An actor? A professional announcer from the KGB?

Each begins with traditional shots of Gorky. Whether it's winter, summer, spring, or fall, it's a tourist city, with views of the Oka River, the Kremlin fort, the two or three cathedrals still standing, a fountain, the main street (Sverdlov), but never our end of Gagarin Avenue, since in fall and spring there is a puddle about three blocks long in front of our building. In summer it turns to dried mud,

*See Appendix IX.

which the wind raises into a sandstorm of dust. In winter the street is full of snow or ice; the last film shows Andrei pushing our car down the street through the snow.

And then we see the park with the tomb of the unknown soldier, beaches, riverbanks, people strolling, children playing, the Volga, the Oka, a steamboat, a hydrofoil flying past. An unsophisticated viewer might think that all this has something to do with our real life. But in our six years in Gorky we have never been able to get close to the dock. Once in the summer of 1984, on my mother's birthday, I tried, but my guards did not allow such independence and asked me not to approach the river. No thoughts of ships and excursions. What if we were to sail away?

The first film offered to the world through *Bild* appeared in August 1984. It begins with that festive city I've already described. The narrator's voice speaks of a metropolis of auto plants, cathedrals, and churches, monuments of old Russia, and over 1,300,000 inhabitants. "By decision of the authorities Academician Sakharov has lived here since 1980." The narration doesn't even hint at legality: it says "decision of the authorities," but it's really "whatever my left leg feels like doing," as they say in Russian. Then we see the building where we are quartered, and the interior of the apartment. It was taken in our absence, so the filmmakers have shown the world the "inviolability of one's home" in action.

After that come scenes from the summer of 1981, of spring 1980, planting trees. "They live in isolation but readily receive company" —what does that mean? Logic demands "live in isolation and don't receive guests." Do they mean we "have been put in isolation"? A winter walk with Andrei's son, Dima, is from the fall of 1981. His daughter Tanya and granddaughter Marina—that's a visit on May 21, 1981. "The academician does not leave Gorky, but Bonner until recently enjoyed that right" is constructed in a way that might make one think that the right to move around the country is something exceptional—and perhaps it is? Next comes a sequence from 1975, when I was traveling to Italy. That's not Gorky; it's Moscow, the Belorussian train station. And yet the film's purpose was to show, as the narration puts it, that in the summer of 1984 Andrei Dmitrievich Sakharov was alive, well, and free.

What do scenes from 1975 have to do with the situation? If memory does not fail me, I left Moscow on August 16, 1975, and arrived in Paris on August 18, and it was then that a photograph of me boarding that train appeared in many Western newspapers.

Then come pictures that actually were taken in the summer of 1984. I am going to the procurator's office for yet another interrogation. One of our guards manipulates a copy of *Ogonyok* magazine in order to show the date. The shots of me walking around Gorky freely in the company of a person described as my friend were taken on July 25, 26, and 27, 1984. They were photographing my lawyer Elena Reznikova and me discussing my case during the breaks when we went out to eat.

Then we see Sakharov with the commentary: "The Academician has gained six pounds. He is watching his health. He is punctilious in that regard and prefers to eat alone." Those are false assertions. Andrei may have gained six pounds then—this was after the hunger strike, which he interrupted on May 29, 1984. But he never preferred eating alone. His postcard to Newton, Massachusetts, dated March 4, 1986, reads in part: "I'll calm down (or not calm down) only when I see you opposite me at the kitchen table (I felt the same way in the hospital)."

The word "hospital" does not appear in the film at all. Everyone is carefully shown not wearing a hospital gown. And the narration remarks: "The Academician is resting." "What could be more pleasant than a walk in the fresh air?" "What could be more pleasant than a good chat?" Andrei is "chatting" in all the films either with chief physician Obukhov or with someone (from the KGB?) off camera. As he "chats," Obukhov displays a magazine, to show the date. The *Ogonyok* in the guard's hands was for Soviet viewers, if there ever will be any. For Western audiences, there is a *Paris-Match* being shown by a more important personage—the chief physician of the regional hospital. But perhaps the guard is higher in rank. After all, he is in the KGB, while Obukhov serves merely as an occasional collaborator.

This film had been sent out of the USSR to prove that Sakharov was alive in the summer of 1984—but the editing and text mean something else to me. A film like that can easily be produced and distributed when both or one of us is no longer alive. The KGB has everything it needs for that, plenty of different shots. I can only warn my friends: films can be forged, just like letters and telegrams and the many other things that they have contrived up till now.

The second film was offered by *Bild* on June 29, 1985. This film is medical, in that the doctor does most of the talking. It begins, however, with the announcer. He informs the audience that Efrem Yankelevich, "who is portrayed in the West as Sakarov's official representative," and the International League for Human Rights have termed Sakharov a "disappeared person." Then there are once again tourist shots of Gorky. In this film, "by decision of the authorities" has been dropped, and it has become simply "Academician Sakharov has been living in Gorky together with his wife since 1980." Apparently I am an ordinary resident instead of an exile. And then the doctor continues: "Sakharov has been under observation by the staff of the regional hospital since 1981. He is a disciplined patient, who regularly comes for check-ups and punctually takes his medicine . . . diagnosis: hypertension, ischemia of the heart, atherosclerosis of brain vessels." In the second part of this film, the doctor says: "Under observation since 1980 . . . diagnosis: atherosclerosis of the brain vessels with circulatory encephalopathy and symptoms of Parkinson's disease; atherosclerosis of the aorta, postinfarctal cardiosclerosis, ischemic disease of the heart with arrhythmia."

This movie gives two different dates for the start of his care, 1980 and 1981—which is correct? Andrei was first forcibly hospitalized on December 4, 1981, and he was hospitalized of his own volition only once (April 1984), when he had an abscess on his leg; he was also taken in by force on May 7, 1984, and on April 21 and July 27, 1985. Under duress he spent the following time in the hospital: in 1981 from December 4 to December 25—twenty-one days; in 1984 from May 7 to September 7—one hundred twenty-three days; and in 1985 from April 21 to July 11 and from July 27 to September 23—one hundred seventy-one days.

Thus this hospital was a place for isolating Sakharov from the rest of the world and even from his wife for a total of two hundred ninety-four days. I am not counting the days in 1981 as we spent many of them together. The only voluntary hospitalization lasted from April 12 to April 21, 1984—just ten days: even that's a lot for a lanced carbuncle, but that could be put down to excessive concern for the "Academician." (The narrator in the films always calls him that: "the Academician likes . . . ," "the Academician rests," "the Academician prefers . . .") But it was during those days that the medicine prescribed by Dr. Evdokimova (incidentally, she told us and repeats in the film that she is a hematologist—why is she Sakharov's treating physician then?) caused grave disruptions in his heart rhythm.

Apparently Sakharov has always had extra heartbeats, one or two per minute. I have myself observed them since 1971. They have appeared on all his EKGs at least since that year. They did not cause him any discomfort; he simply was not aware of them. It can be assumed that he has had them all his life and they must have kept him from being admitted to the military academy in 1941. Such extra beats do not respond to treatment, especially by digitalis or drugs that normalize the rhythm of the heart. In April 1984 Dr. Evdokimova prescribed digitalis and Isoptin for Andrei, and the number of heartbeats increased sharply—in some periods to two or three times the normal rate. There was a spell when this turned Andrei from "in effect a healthy man" (as the Soviet press wrote about him) to "in effect a sick" one.

But of course the most terrible result of Sakharov's stay in the hospital was the spasm or stroke he experienced during force-feeding in 1984. As now seems clear, permission for the force-feeding was given by his KGB case officer, Sokolov, and an unknown doctor who visited Sakharov in the hospital around 10 P.M. on May 10.

The next day, May 11, the first force-feeding began. Andrei describes it in his 1984 letter to Alexandrov, president of the Academy of Sciences: he was pushed down and tied up; he lost consciousness and control of his bladder; and when he awakened, there were changes in his vision, his handwriting, and his speech. After Andrei came home almost three months later, I could detect a loss of work capability, a slight tremor of his hands, and persistent involuntary movements of the lower jaw—the jaw movements continue in a much lesser form to this day. There are oblique references to these conditions in the film. In a conversation with Dr. Troshin, a neuropathologist, Andrei responds to a question about his tremor by saying that it was evident in June and July, but most pronounced in May 1984, after May 11. And Troshin immediately changes the subject.

For almost half the film, Sakharov eats. Those clips are supposed to demonstrate that there was no hunger strike. But even the way he is eating shows that he is coming off a hunger strike. I know he stopped the strike on May 27, 1984, and he was kept in the hospital not because he still had symptoms from the vascular spasm or even stroke during the first force-feeding, but only to prevent him from attending my trial, as a witness or as my next of kin.

Scenes from 1984 are passed off as scenes from 1985. Andrei has told me that in 1985 he did not accept any medication in the hospital, refusing it outright, but suspected they were adding something to the food they were forcing into him. Yet he is shown taking pills from a nurse, confirming that the film dates from 1984.

Dr. Evdokimova speaks of a consultation with Gorky cardiologists Vagralik and Saltseva. But Andrei told me he had declined their help and even in April 1984 did not wish to have anything to do with those doctors. He never saw them again.

The film describes a consultation by a cardiologist from the Moscow Cardiology Institute, but he did not see any such physician. Even in the film of March 1986, Dr. Obukhova (the wife of Dr. Obukhov) is pleased and satisfied with the improvement in Sakharov's EKG. She assumes it is the result of her treatment. But from our telephone conversation of April 3 this year, I know that since Andrei left the hospital last October 23, he has not taken a single pill she prescribed. And it was the absence of treatment that actually reduced his extra heartbeats to their previous rate.

For me this is direct proof that all throughout Andrei's stay in the hospital some medication was mixed into his food (I am not speaking of psychotropic drugs, but of cardiac medication). Otherwise his heart would have returned to normal much more quickly.

The second part of the film is almost entirely a medical examination dating back to April or late March 1985—before Andrei began the hunger strike of April 16. Here there is nothing for me to explain because Dr. Evdokimova describes and shows everything. She says that people in the West claim that Sakharov is not receiving necessary treatment and is even starving and that this is painful for "us" (Soviet doctors, apparently) to hear, and so "we" are showing a film that was made during an examination. Thus Evdokimova has demonstrated to the world that Soviet doctors either do not know that they have no right to film an examination without the patient's permission or else do it anyway.

The patient unbuttons his trousers, stands there half naked and pulls up his trousers with one hand, because they are slipping, with the belt unbuckled and the suspenders off his shoulders. The doctor feel the glands under his arm; Andrei is asked about his sleep and his stool. He replies, thinking he is speaking with his doctor. He adjusts his socks and lies down, and the doctor stands with her side to him, so the viewers can get a better view of the patient.

No sooner had I arrived in Newton than another film from Moscow caught up with me. It said, in effect: "So, she wanted to go abroad? Go ahead." "Wanted to see her children? That's easy." "Get treatment? Why not?"

And in a way, it is true: I went, I saw, I'm being treated. But for that to become the truth, one little thing must be added: I left on December 2, 1985, but it was on September 25, 1982, that I applied to travel for medical treatment. You can die in three years. By the time I was granted a visa, I was suffering other ailments besides my eye problems. The authorities had made me a criminal and my husband had to go on two hunger strikes—a total of one hundred ninety-seven days of hunger, the torture of force-feeding, and nine months of incarceration in a hospital. Without that addendum, nothing in the film even approaches the truth.

In that film we see Andrei's conversation with the chief physician of the hospital, a serious discussion about the problems of disarmament. The actual circumstances were this: I was at the dentist's, getting a bridge. I was kept in the chair a long time—over two hours. When we were going home, Andrei told me he was surprised that Obukhov had nothing better to do than spend all that time with him, feeding him tea and carrying on serious conversations.

"What about?" I asked.

"About disarmament and Gorbachev's new proposals."

And in the film we witness a nice chat, Andrei drinking tea, still very emaciated. He states: "We say that they have surrounded us with bases." I don't know how that was translated for television, but in *Bild* Sakharov is saying: "They have surrounded us with bases."

The next film contains important conversation—once again about disarmament. The questioner is not seen (judging by the voice, I'd say it's Obukhov again), the subject is Gorbachev's March arms control proposal, while the responding Sakharov still looks the same —emaciated, after his hunger strike of October 1985. Any expert who placed two television monitors next to each other and compared the two shots would know that this is not the Sakharov of March 1986. And since it is an old conversation, with only the question being new, they do not show the other party.

In the same film Sakharov walks into an entryway carrying a bouquet of flowers. The impression is that he lives a normal life and is probably going to visit someone. But actually he is entering the apartment where he resides alone while I'm away; he bought the flowers for himself. The entryway is filmed from an unusual angle, so it doesn't resemble the building where we live only because it is shot from the roof of a nearby one-story post office.

I was sure that was the explanation of the flower scene as I watched on TV in Newton, and later I received confirmation. A postcard from Andrei dated February 15: "I celebrated your birthday. Earlier I bought a jewelry box and the traditional perfume 'Elena.' Today I bought carnations—six red and three pink."

I can see through those tricks, but what about a stranger? He'll say: "What do you mean Sakharov is not allowed to go anywhere? I saw him myself, going to visit friends—and bringing flowers."

There is a sequence of Sakharov freely speaking to a man on the street. I know he is no friend but the head mechanic of the car repair shop. By phone Andrei told me in astonishment that he had been summoned to the repair station (via a policeman)—allegedly they had made a repair incorrectly. The head mechanic himself came out to see Andrei and shook his hand warmly. And they did the repair for free! But my husband, amazed by this, does not know he is being filmed to be displayed to the entire world.

The viewer may believe we aren't telling the truth when we say we are forbidden all contacts, even chance encounters in the store or on the street. After all, Sakharov is shown strolling with a man I know to be the physicist D. A. Kirzhnits from the Lebedev Institute. And then comes a postcard from January 28, and I quote: "On Mon. Kirzhnits and Linde came (the physicists are coming more frequently)." And during our telephone conversation of April 13, speaking of another visit, he said: "Purely formal, tiring." And from a postcard of December 17: "A woman from Dr. Obukhov came telling me to go to the dentist." In the film you see him getting out of a car with a woman near the main entrance of the hospital. I know what it is, but the viewer does not.

From a postcard dated March 18: "Today a nurse from Dr. Obukhov came, and asked me to return the newspapers he so kindly lent me last week as he needs them for my case history. Rather funny." Andrei does not know he is being filmed by a hidden camera and apparently is surprised that he is given newspapers and then asked to return them—and what does his case history have to do with it? In our conversation on April 14 I learned that the newspapers were copies of the London *Observer* and that Obukhov had been trying to get Sakharov to discuss his letter to Alexandrov published there, maintaining that the letter contained inaccuracies. Just imagine the situation: the chief physician, the boss of those who tortured Sakharov, trying to convince Sakharov that it wasn't true.

According to a postcard of February 11, after seeing Andrei, "Obukhov unexpectedly proposed a sanitorium: 'to strengthen the effects of the treatment' (what treatment? ha, ha)." It means we can expect a conversation on that topic in the next film. It doesn't matter that Obukhov knows Sakharov was not treated in his hospital. He will say those words in a future film.

In the most recent film, Andrei is in a telephone booth, talking to me, and I ask him if he knows about Gorbachev's interview in *L'Humanité*, where the general secretary mentions him. The film does not include my question; there is only Sakharov's answer, and the impression given is that he considers himself justly sent to Gorky and isolated from the world.

There are an endless number of distorted scenes, but I do not have the strength to go on listing them. I can only ask people not to believe such films, now or in the future. I dread the thought that when I return to Gorky, I will be subjected along with Andrei to constant camera surveillance.

It is horrible to live under the all-seeing eye of the telescreen (as in *Nineteen Eighty-four*). These films come out of Orwell's Ministry of Truth. Each of them is designed to show and prove to the viewer something concrete, whatever it is that the government needs at a given moment. First Sakharov is well, then he's sick, then he's not on a hunger strike, then he's resting, then he's freely receiving treatment, then he's driving around somewhere, then his wife is free to go abroad, and so on. The truth of individual scenes is made to support the lie required at that moment. The films do not differ from the announcements of TASS and Novosti Press Agency.

While I was in the United States, TASS and Novosti claimed that I was healthy and had come here not for treatment but just to see the world and show myself, as they say, and that the authorities had not asked me to remain silent. Fine. That means no one can say anything about my writing this book; after all, that would make TASS (or perhaps it was the film—I don't remember) a liar. Later —after the announcement of my surgery and the necessity of performing six bypasses—they stopped saying that I was healthy. But they did assert that these operations are a snap in Moscow and that I could have had it done at home, and for free.

I can understand that position—after all, it's risky writing about someone who's undergone such surgery. It might give the impression that they put healthy people under the knife at Massachusetts General Hospital. That wouldn't look nice. The Moscow commentator said (Andrei told me this by telephone) that I can go back for further treatment whenever the need arises, and that in actual fact no one had stopped me in the first place.

At the same time the Western press reported that on May 18 my husband would be exchanged for a multitude of spies. A rumor that I do not intend to return to the Soviet Union also appeared. And our friends began saying: "Well, why don't they exchange Sakharov? They made an exchange for Shcharansky." (They did it with Bukovsky, Ginzburg, Moroz, Vins, Dymshits, and Kuznetsov, too.) Really—"Why not Sakharov?"

People said things like this: "After all, she didn't come here in order to go back." (The six bypasses were forgotten.) "Sakharov didn't go on a hunger strike just for her to go back, did he?" That was said in 1977 and in 1979 and now again. Among the many things my interrogator Kolesnikov lectured me about, there was this: "How can we let you go to the West for treatment? You'll just stay there, and Andrei Dmitrievich will suffer, and his health is so bad."

I've been flooded with questions about how I feel toward the reports that Sakharov will be exchanged and that I will not return. I don't have any feelings about the reports at all—they have no relation to me. What does relate to me is that I came to see my mother, children, and grandchildren and to receive the medical treatment I needed. Sakharov went on a hunger strike for that. I consider reports of an exchange a provocation. The aim was to spoil or to forestall preparations for Andrei's sixty-fifth birthday made by many people and organizations and governments. That is why the date for the alleged exchange on May 18 was so close to his birthday on May 21; the idea must have been to make people wait, so they wouldn't have time to make arrangements in just three days.

The films are immoral and violate ethical norms—medical, professional, and human. And that holds most of all for the "medical" films. All over the world people deal with medicine, perhaps in its essence the most human and moral activity. Among the audiences for the films there must have been many physicians; moreover, each of us has at some time been a patient. So I want to pose a question. Would you agree to be a patient of Dr. Evdokimova or Dr. Obukhov if one of them said: "We are filming you during this examination." What does "we" mean? "We doctors?" "We, the KGB?" "We, Victor Louis, the journalist, and I?" Who would agree to be filmed with his trousers dropped; opening his mouth; having the glands under his arms felt; or discussing his sleep and stool?

The humiliation of these scenes is so overwhelming that I want to pull my head into my shoulders, cover my eyes with my hands, and see nothing, hear nothing. Who gave a doctor the right to debase a patient? For twenty minutes a physician shows his patient coming off a hunger strike, chewing. He chews his breakfast and a persistent voice babbles about calories. He chews lunch, and the same voice talks about calories again; he chews dinner, and there's that voice about calories. The days on the calendar change, and once again we witness breakfast, lunch, and dinner; yet again, breakfast, lunch, and dinner. And they've turned this man into a chewing machine. Who did this? People did. (I recall my grandson's question when he saw a crucifix in the Uffizi Gallery: "Mama, who hammered nails into his hands and feet?" "People did that." "Were they really people who did that?") People (nonhumans in my book) made these films. Andrei remains himself, older, exhausted, but he has overcome all the torture, the threats that "we won't let you die but we will make you an invalid." He began a hunger strike and won, calling his doctors "the Mengeles of today."

How can it be that so many in the West who saw this film do not understand all this, do not recognize its astonishing immorality? How can they watch doctors discuss a patient's diagnosis or how he has aged in appearance (an article in *Bild*) and not realize what is most important—that the doctors' actions are incompatible with humanity and medical ethics.

I wish that all the doctors who saw these films could express their attitude toward them from a professional point of view, and answer one question: may a doctor exhibit a patient in this way without his knowledge or consent? It is a question that should be posed to Soviet physicians, scientists, administrators, and politicians. Which of them would face the eyes of the world as a chewing machine or with his trousers falling down?

Such questions and answers will defend not only my husband and myself, but public confidence in the medical profession. No one should be displayed to the world like a guinea pig or a bacillus on a slide under a microscope. And Sakharov should not be presented that way.

Perhaps this is all clear. But I know that many people do not understand how monstrous these films are, and think that I am simply talking about abstractions. That is not so. For me this is all very personal and intimate: this is my husband and me. I think we are both mentally stable, but I am afraid of living under the eye of a camera. I will not go to doctors in Gorky under any circumstances, because I know they will record me on film. I am frightened about being on camera as I go outside, or to the store, the market, adjusting my stocking, talking to my husband, or taking him by the arm. No one, no matter how strong, is safe in these circumstances from a breakdown, depression, or suicide.

On May 2 American newspapers published photographs of the May Day parade in Kiev, full of joyous faces on a day when the people of the world were reading their papers with anxiety. It's possible that the photograph is from last year—the way they use old footage in the films about Sakharov. It's also possible that people unaware of the real situation actually did go out onto the street. In either case, this is not the truth of their life. The truth is a fire raging in Chernobyl and a nuclear cloud over the Ukraine and over the entire world.

XVIII

I am convinced that Americans want peace. I'm as quick to form opinions as an American tourist who spends a week in the USSR. However, I feel I have more of a basis for my conclusion. I have spent more time here, and my children and grandchildren live here.

Everything for the American tourist in Russia (in dollars) is very cheap. Nothing is as bad as American right-wingers say. Public transportation is marvelous. The Metro is just like the Metropolitan Museum (some even think that there is a direct connection between the names, the subway being named for the museum, or vice versa). The food is plentiful, the people are well dressed. And whomever he might ask, "Do the Russians want war?" the answer is always "No." And based on that no, the American will create his theory, in which some Russian Dr. Spock will appear and tell the Russians, "Don't go to war, boys." Maybe it'll be Dr. Chazov of the International Physicians for the Prevention of Nuclear War. And the boys won't go. Anyway, a war would turn into a Vietnam for the Soviets, the American thinks. It's all so simple, and almost any unprejudiced tourist who is well served in his hotel and shown Moscow, Leningrad, and, quite daringly, even Bukhara and Samarkand, will come home and say: "The Russians don't want war. Everything's okay. We don't need rockets and all that."

I don't know about America. I'm not a specialist, like the schoolchildren who travel around the world on peace missions and can explain everything about rockets and so on. So while I'm not as competent to judge as that tourist, I maintain that Americans do not want war. What Americans want is a house. No matter their place on the social ladder, their salary, capital, inheritance, winnings in the lottery or on the stock market (for me with my lack of education in these matters it is almost one and the same thing, even though I do know that people win more frequently—and lose more frequently! —playing the stock market than the lottery), they want a house of their own. (Perhaps it is only in New York that an apartment will do—elsewhere it's a stopgap. But New York is practically another country.)

Dear Mayor Koch, you wonderful kind man. Your cheerfulness is a mark of your goodness. Don't be insulted that I am excluding your city from the United States, but it is really another country, in a class by itself. And New Yorkers are a nation apart, a separate community. "I Love New York" is knitted into the scarf Mayor Ed Koch gave me, and that motto expresses my sentiments perfectly. I truly Love New York.

But we were talking about Americans and houses. They want a house and the ground it stands on, and a surrounding bit of land. That's all. Some own a tiny house, like a toy cottage, and only the soil in their flowerboxes; others have lots of bedrooms, baths, and extensive lawns. The desire to own a house is not a class ambition; it encompasses upper-, middle-, and lower-income groups.

Even one of New York's homeless, huddling in a blanket over a grating, will be insulted if you invade his privacy. A house is a symbol of independence, not merely a material one, but some sort of combined spiritual and physical independence. The American's feeling about his House (it should be capitalized) expresses the main traits of Americans—the desires for privacy and for independence. But that attitude gives rise to a third trait, "My house is my pride and joy." The balance between this last trait and the other two creates harmony between the individual and the nation. It defines the Americans' attitude toward their country and the world in general.

Please, do not laugh at me—that's how I see it. I will speak of this third trait the way it appears to me. The English say, "A man's home is his castle." While castle is not a peaceful concept, it is not an aggressive one either.

I don't know what other Europeans say about their homes. I have heard of the French reaction to unexpected visitors (and I did see it once, though only once): "We're not expecting anyone; we won't open the door." This is a form of privacy too, but with a total absence of the American "Can I help you?"—an attitude typical of a large, strong adolescent. His physical well-being saves him from all sorts of complexes, which does not mean at all that he is stupid. He is always ready to help and often his help is accepted, but for that reason he is not overly loved.

So let us return to the third trait of the American attitude toward his House, "My house is my pride and joy." And from that comes "My city, my state, my country is my pride and joy." There is no aggression or parochialism in that attitude. It is open and kind and caring both toward the house and toward everything that it stands for, the soil in the flowerboxes and the lovingly tended lawn, even if it's only three yards square. And, I say, this shows that Americans care about land in general and about the whole world. Only the other day my son told me that according to a poll, 43 percent of all Americans prefer growing flowers to any other pastime.

Americans do not want war. They want a house. The First Lady says that when the President retires, they will sell the house in which they lived before the presidency. The children are grown and the place is too big for them, so they will buy a smaller house. A wonderful plan! And it's wonderful that the whole country knows it. The President doesn't want war, he wants a new house.

I also want a house. As I write, I am leaving an island. My time here has been a highlight of my entire life. I had never been in a climate like this, near palm trees—coconuts really do fall—my bare feet had never felt sand like this; the warm and quiet sea splashed just twenty steps away from me. I would call it paradise, but paradise is not simply a question of climate, or sand, or sea, or even apples (or pears—that historical argument from the Garden of Eden has yet to be resolved). Paradise is being with people you love and treasure and not worrying about them. I wish Andrei were here. I wish my mother could sit in a rocker in the shade near those sweet, sleep-inducing oleanders, and I wish I could pick up the phone once a week and hear the calm voices of my children. Paradise, it turns out, is so simple and, it turns out, unattainable for me.

Well, here it is, the last sunset by the sea. I have spent five days here, days that passed in a flash. And yet they were long days of writing—six pages a day. Long, hot hours on the white, hot sand; the sea—light blue, dark blue, turquoise. The bay is small; even with my ailing legs I managed to wander all the way to its left point one day, and to its right on another. I will always remember that arc, a smooth edge of sand, and the sea, which doesn't roar, but whispers, babbles. I'm afraid of lapsing into sentimentality (I think I already have, in fact). But I've never seen such a sea . . . it has such tranquillity. Perhaps I have grown more tranquil here. I am grateful that I was invited to the island and that it was so simple to give me five days to catch my breath, to work, and to have peace. Maybe these days will let me regain my senses—to stop losing my temper with my family; to understand that I can change nothing or correct nothing; to cease tormenting my heart (the six bypasses may not be able to take it) and the hearts of others, hearts I love.

Here is an old and almost forgotten story. We are students in our first year of college. A group of us are sitting around a marble table. This is how we work: first we read a section in the textbook, then we prepare it. The instructor (only now do I remember that she was young and pretty, at the time she seemed very severe) said, "Open your books; today we study the heart."

"The heart?" I asked. "The organ of feelings?"

"For you, Bonner, it may be the organ of feelings, but for everyone else it's the organ of circulation."

So now with my surgically repaired organ of feelings/circulation I have a desire for a house in addition to my usual wants that everyone be together and healthy and that there be no war. With enough land around it, and no more, for me to plant flowers. For the sake of nostalgia I could grow an ordinary Russian cornflower and an ordinary Russian daisy and a single birch tree. But to tell the truth, these grow everywhere I've been. I find nostalgia a form of playacting.

I don't need a lot of bedrooms, just one for us and one for Mother, a guest room and one more so that I'm always ready for our grandchildren. And I'd like a room where I could at last spread out my books and where Andrei could make a mess. What nonsense I'm writing! I want a house! This is me, who should be counting the days —no, the hours—of my freedom to do what I want, even to type away this freely, to type all my unattainable nonsense, such as "I want a house."

But you know, I'm sixty-three, and I've never had a house; not only that, I've never had a corner I could call my own. I started out like everyone else: a normal childhood. But then came a strange orphanhood—father and mother arrested and no one knowing whether they were alive or not. I lived in a single room with my grandmother, brother, and sister. On the other side of the wall (we could hear everything) lived a man named Fyodorov with his wife and four children. When he got drunk he beat them. If they managed to get away, they would spend the night with us, sitting on the old trunk. That trunk is in my mother's room on Chkalov Street in Moscow, and our visitors (correspondents, scientists, congressmen, and senators) also sat on it. Fyodorov never broke into our room. He was afraid of Grandmother—everyone was afraid of her except me. I had my own fears, of course, but ever since my parents' arrest, I have never allowed myself to show my dread of anything.

Then there was the army. I guess there was a time when my "house" was a compartment in the hospital train, where I was head nurse. The war ended, and many people shared my room with me —girlfriends in Leningrad after the evacuation was over. Later, we had a room in a communal apartment—my first husband, two children, my mother, and I; often we had friends staying the night. There were forty-eight people in the apartment, and one toilet; often there was a line to use it, so I made my children bring their own potty—I was afraid of germs—and that upset them because I was invading their privacy.

Later in Moscow, we had two rooms in the apartment where my mother lived, the children and I, and then we were joined by my son-in-law, and then by Sakharov. I think that the first time I was mistress of my own place was—it's hard to believe—in Gorky, in exile.

I do not want that. I want a house. My daughter has a house in Newton, Massachusetts. It makes me so happy to think that she has a house. Her family is caught up in our affairs, in our Gorky horrors and suffering, and our cares. They have forgotten the pleasure of their house. I want them to go back to caring about it. It has done so much for them. My daughter and her husband and their two children have been living in the house since their arrival in 1977; my son came there, followed by his wife, and their daughter was born there. Two families shared the house in a most un-American way. It was almost a communal apartment and it had almost a third family: my mother arrived, and the impossibility of going back to Russia has kept her there close to six years. Where else could she go—to live in exile in Gorky? I would be depriving her of freedom with my own hands.

And this house has been the first home on American soil for so many émigrés. My dream, my own house, is unattainable for me and my family—that is, for my husband and myself—as unattainable as heaven on earth. But I want a house. If not for me, then for my son and his family. We plan to buy one. And I am learning many new things. The house should be near good schools—my granddaughter is three and schooling is not far off in the future. It should be in the suburbs; vacations are short, and a child should not have to grow up in a polluted city. It should be close to their work; both parents have jobs and there is only one car. It should have a full foundation and basement (I had never known such considerations to exist). It should have three bedrooms, so that my mother can be with them, or at least visit. It should have a room and bath in the basement for guests. It should have a studio: Alexei wants more than a house; he needs a workroom for his mathematics. It should not cost anything, or very little. But the cost is . . . oh! I want, I want, I want. More than children do, I want. But it's time for me to pack my bags. Not tomorrow, but very soon. The children live here; I live over there. I want a house. I don't want war. But Americans want a house, too. Americans don't want war.

I am now writing in a hotel in New York, which is simultaneously a city and a country and a world. I am on the eighth floor in a corner room. One window opens on Sixty-first Street, the other on Central Park. In two directions, unfolding from an angle, stretches a panorama that needs nothing added to it. Against the blue of the sky are the gray silhouettes of buildings that pierce it (light gray in the sun, darker in shadow), lines, lines, lines. How can anyone say that New York is not beautiful? For me it is the city of cities, ready for the future.

The future will come and naturally we humans will find cars inadequate, and all sorts of red, yellow, blue, and green helicopters, delta planes, and other individual aircraft will take off from these flat roofs, and each one will send out a friendly "Have a good day today" or "Have a nice day" to passing craft.

What difference does it make if Gorbachev and Reagan meet in June or some other month? What difference does it make which of them is being cranky? First Gorbachev plays hard to get, like a girl invited for a date, pouting, considering: "I don't know, I have to think about it, probably not," clearly indicating that someone better might ask. Then Reagan sounds like a jealous girl, "It's her or me. Now or never." But perhaps they're both men, admirers, husbands? In that case, the date—lunch, dinner—and the mutual smiles are not so important. A recent newspaper article set me thinking along these lines. Actually, all three are alien to me—the newspaper and the two heads of state. I must be one of the world's least interested people in the problems that Reagan and Gorbachev are threatening to discuss or not discuss, when and if they meet or don't meet.

My husband told me just five months ago (God, I haven't seen him in five months and want to be with him so much!), "The world is further away from war than it has been in a long time." I believe him, and on that score, I live calmly. Especially since I have more than enough worries, cares, and misfortunes of my own. It would be better for me, during the days remaining to me, to remember that today I saw something amazing from the windows of this room.

I got up early, a bit after six. The haze of burgeoning buds barely showed over the trees, and the grass had not yet taken on a greenish hue. It was still yellow, the color of grass shoots. And now it's noon, and there is a delicate green smoke over the trees and the grass has turned green, a tender, tender green. So quickly, spring came in six hours. Lord, I want the whole world to feel this good. They say New York is at its best in springtime. And now I'm going downstairs into the city.

XIX

The time has come to make the most important and most difficult decision in the five months of my life here in the West. Mother and all of us must decide: Mother about herself, I about her, and all of us about her. She had come to visit her grandchildren. We had hoped that my husband's situation would improve somehow and that she would be able to return. I now understand the unreality of that, at least for the near future.

Taking her back with me now to the USSR would mean that she would have to live all alone in Moscow without the help of her children—that is, us—or to live with us in our incarceration, our isolation, our illegal situation. She has already been through the Soviet camps and exile. I cannot personally send her back into exile.

But it is very difficult being a guest for six years, without her own apartment, her own Social Security, and her own health benefits. The status of permanent resident would give her a sense of freedom and independence.

But there is a complication in her situation. She joined the Communist Party in 1924. Her membership was suspended, naturally, while she was in prison, camp, and exile, but after her rehabilitation in 1954, she was reinstated in the Party. If she had refused that, she would have lost the right to her pension of eighty rubles a month. She has been in the United States since May 1980, and her membership in the CPSU was automatically terminated. For all practical purposes, she severed her ties with the Party when she allowed Academician Sakharov to live in her apartment.

She will probably be given permanent resident status. This country flings open wide the doors of its house and I am not worried in the least that things will be bad for my mother. But why does my heart ache, and why was this decision so hard to make, and why, like a child, do I keep thinking that perhaps we haven't made it yet? Have we decided? We have.

I had not noticed how my manuscript was growing thicker and my pile of blank paper growing thinner. But I have not said everything I wanted to say. That is still to come—today or tomorrow, but in any case, very soon. I cannot put it off for long, because everything I want to say I must say before June 2. That is the term of my freedom to speak. Is it only freedom to speak?

I am returning. Why? It's not that I miss the birches, the *beryozkas*—not the trees, not the stores, not the café of that name. Incidentally, here in Boston, two sweet people from Kiev, Misha and Valya, have opened their own Beryozka. It's a nice little place with tasty food. It meets the gastronomic demands of people who left the USSR (here they all say "Russia") and their not very savage nostalgia. It didn't quite satisfy me. If their object is to make all the cakes baked in Soviet Russia, then why don't they have the best of my youth—the Leningrad, Mordovian, northern cake called Ideal? Maybe they'll have it another time. But will I have "another time"? I doubt it.

About émigrés. You see many living in difficult circumstances. Our close friends, almost total strangers, and many elderly émigrés —all sometimes speak of their hardships. But there wasn't one among them who wanted to go back. This does not mean that I doubt reports in the Soviet press about the people who find life in the West unbearably hard and who ask for permission to return. Of course there are people like that, but I haven't met them. Friends say there is an émigré dream, the nightmare of being back, from which you awaken in a cold sweat. I haven't had dreams like that yet. But the sensation of the ever-contracting shagreen leather, the tick of the clock counting off my time, I feel these more and more strongly inside me.

In the evening my son and daughter-in-law go back to their place, and my youngest grandchild, born here, says: "Let's kiss." And I think, "How many more evenings like this do I have?" In the morning the older children go off to school, talking about what they'll do during the day: basketball, Russian lessons. "How many more mornings will I see them off to school?" The question throbs within me. And as usual, when you are afraid, that vague and anxious chill goes up your spine. Soon. I have already spent five times more days and nights here than I have left. We know that May 23 is set aside for all those who might want to come and say goodbye. I'm making up my shopping list.

Andrei's already written his request to me in a postcard dated March 25. In a takeoff of the folktale, he writes: "Dear Golden Fish, take pity! Buy me a pair of jeans, my old ones have fallen apart. And a roomy jacket; I wear nothing but my red one. And whatever else God prompts you to get; He won't suggest anything useless."

I'm already thinking about when I'll be in New York for the last time, when in Washington. Already! Already! Already! There are almost no "mores" and "agains" left.

A few days ago in New York, we were in a taxi and the driver said, "I'm from Minsk." I latched onto him and began asking him questions, so persistently that at first he asked, "You wouldn't happen to be in the KGB, would you?" Then he believed me that I wasn't, and toward the end of our talk, he suddenly asked, "Aren't you Sakharov's wife?" It had taken him a half-hour ride to recognize me, but he told me a lot about himself.

He's been here close to five years. He bought his taxi medallion, borrowing at a bank, and it's almost paid off. He had come here not knowing English, and now he manages to get along (and he is over fifty). He's spent his life—both here and there—behind the wheel. He says, "The Russians are a good people, what fine people!" (Incidentally, he is a Jew.) But "America is the best country in the world. It's not true that there is no work; you just have to want to find it, and they'll help you and there will be work. And there's such an abundance of things, and there's freedom." At the end of his speech, he said, "Now how could I, an old Jew from Minsk, ever think that I would see Canada, and Florida, and Spain, and Israel?"

There, that's freedom. We said goodbye. I had arrived at the *New York Times* office, where the publisher had invited me to lunch. It was all very beautiful. A beautiful room, a beautiful table, set with flowers. Now I can confess: when I saw all that beauty, I was afraid that that would be it—beauty and food. But I was wrong. There was beauty and the food was good, but most important, the talk was serious. This was a rare occurrence in my American life: I was not annoyed at making serious conversation over food.

They knew about Andrei, and there were no empty, foolish questions. Everything was full of meaning and sense. But even as we talked, I was enjoying a private joke. Secretly—I kept my expression quite serious. But here is what I was thinking. There were twelve of us at the table—all gentlemen; I was the only lady. I kept wanting to make the joke that I felt like Furtseva* at a Politburo meeting. To complete the resemblance (which was apparent to me alone), I recalled how I had once seen Furtseva up close. She was at the Writers' Union Club, at a reception for the first exhibit of works by Rockwell Kent in the USSR. She was wearing a bluish gray suit. I immediately felt a deadly desire for one just like it. But there was neither the time nor the occasion for a suit like that in all those years. Then here in America, the children, Alexei and Liza, gave me a suit for my birthday—bluish gray, just like the one the Politburo member wore to the reception. No, even better.

Memories of that cab driver ate away at me. "Freedom," the freedom to go wherever you want. I am always free to think what I want, but to go? Or not to go. Yes, it's just like "to be or not to be." After all, I know what's awaiting me there—I'm not talking about external things. Not about checking in and the eight P.M. curfew, not about the fact that I can't talk to anyone but Andrei, that that strange and alien city makes me ill. That two great Russian rivers meet in Gorky doesn't make it any better for me. Maybe if I were there without exile and without humiliations, without cockroaches scurrying from packages of books, I might come to like it, but "you can't force love," and I don't love it; I don't love it at all.

And now I have the freedom to go there or not to go there—the freedom of choice. I realize this is a unique experience in freedom of choice for a dissident; I've been abroad so many times and I never chose to stay. Each time it was very difficult to return. For truly,

*Ekaterina Furtseva (1910–1974). Member of the Presidium (1957–1961), the only woman to hold that position in Soviet history.

things are backward: abroad, beyond the border, isn't out here, it's there, in the Soviet Union, and from there you can't call out, you can't shout loud enough to be heard.

All the times that I returned (beginning in 1960), as soon as I crossed the border, such a heavy fog, such darkness befell my soul that it is impossible to describe. In the past I had gone back to a complete, large family: husband, mother, children; I had returned to my own house, my home, and even then it had been hard, indescribably difficult. It is an indescribable sensation, not having the freedom "to go wherever you want." It constrains and shackles you both spiritually and physically.

It takes incredible willpower to force yourself to learn once again how to breathe without air, swim without water, walk without ground. You force yourself to live, to do your routine, daily chores. Gradually, everyday duties bring you back to life; they heal you. But it is a difficult healing process. It is hard to undergo the cure.

Each time, it was harder for me to go "abroad," beyond that border. My family grew smaller. My daughter was here in America, with her children, and then with my son, his older daughter, and my mother. My family here grew—Liza came and the youngest grandchild was born. It got emptier there. Now I do not have a home there —just walls blocking out what we had once loved. All that is left is a strange city, a strange apartment filled with strange government-issue furniture, countless guards, like dogs on a single leash. And cameras constantly pointed at us.

And beyond all that, there is Andrei—alone, sad without me, happy and calm with me. All right. Somehow we'll get over yet another depression, we'll manage somehow.

Remember what I wrote about the Christmas tale? Everything in my life is like that. I was sick; I was dying; Andryusha suffered so much and underwent torture. And everything passed. I came here; I was treated; it was very bad, but it passed. A miracle occurred. I used to carry nitroglycerine constantly, taking as many as twenty-five pills a day, and now there are days when I simply forget that nitroglycerine exists. I saw my mother. I embraced her. My grandchildren are charming. The children—well, there are a thousand problems there, as in any family. "Small children keep you awake, and worries about your big children don't let you sleep, either." But that's normal and usual; you have a free choice: either a calm life or children.

Yes, I have most of the ingredients for a Christmas tale. Now all I need is the happy ending, but I can't make one up. Until this point, the writing has come easily, simply, like family conversation around the kitchen table. (I see that Americans are gradually moving out of their living rooms and into their kitchens, too. Aren't they? Why the big kitchens, if not?) This book wrote itself, without resistance, so easily that these pages probably should not be called a book. I regret having to put the final period and regret even more not having the time to clean it up, to finish it properly. I must beg the reader's forgiveness. And also beg forgiveness for the fact that it's not a dissident book in any way. I've always told everyone, "I'm not a dissident; I'm simply me." I hope you're convinced now.

But where do I get a happy ending? Maybe it's in the fact that Andryusha and I remain together. And in the fact that there, beyond the border which separates us from the world and from all of you, dear family and friends, we are still free to be ourselves.

> *Thanks to God, you are free*
> *In Russia, in Boldino, in quarantine.*
>
> —*David Samoilov**

Yes, that must be it, the happy ending.

---

*David Samoilov (Kaufman) (1920–   ). Poet. An epidemic forced Pushkin to remain some time at his estate, Boldino, which is not far from Gorky.

APPENDIXES
AND INDEX

I

Death Certificate of Elena Bonner's Father

РСФСР

СВИДЕТЕЛЬСТВО О СМЕРТИ

II-А № 803960

Гр. *Алиханов*
Геворк Саркисович
(фамилия, отчество)
умер (ла) *11/XI 1939, тысяча девятьсот*
тридцать девятого года.
(цифрами год, месяц и число)
возраст *42 года*
Причина смерти *Воспаление Легких*
о чём в книге записей актов гражданского состояния о смерти
19 *54* года *Декабря* месяца *2* числа
произведена соответствующая запись за № *660*
Место смерти: город, селение _____
район _____ область, край,
республика _____ *Москва*
(наименование)
Гр. Куйбышевск. р-за ЗАГС.
(местонахождение органа ЗАГС)
1 Декабря 19 *54* г.
Заведующий бюро записей актов
гражданского состояния *подпись*

Гознак. 1946.

The death certificate for Citizen Alikhanov, Gevork Sarkhisovich, states that he died on November 11, 1939, at the age of 42. The stated cause of death is pneumonia. There is no indication of the place of death, which was not registered until December 1954.

II

TASS on the Sakharovs

Over the period from May 4 to June 4, 1984, TASS issued four statements on Sakharov and Bonner, an unprecedented amount of attention given to a dissident issue.

The following is an excerpt from the first TASS statement, released on May 4, 1984.

BEHIND THE SCENES OF A PROVOCATION

. . . Our foes have assigned a special place in these sordid gambits to the notorious anti-Sovieteer Sakharov, whose anti-Soviet conduct has long been condemned by the Soviet people.

Sakharov's wife, E. G. Bonner, also ought to be mentioned, she has not only constantly prodded her husband into undertaking actions hostile to the Soviet state, which has been the subject of repeated press reports, she has also acted as liaison-person between the reactionary circles in the West and Sakharov. For a number of years, Bonner has supplied Western anti-Soviet centers, and not at all for a song, with blatant calumnies and malicious libels defaming our country, our system, and the Soviet people.

In this activity it has been proved irrefutably that she has used the services of staff members of the American Embassy in Moscow, who have sent the material received from Bonner abroad via diplomatic channels. This kind of assistance has been given to her of late, in particular by First Secretary Edmund McWilliams and Second Secretaries George Glass and Jon Purnell.

It recently became known to competent Soviet agencies that a far-reaching operation had been masterminded with the involvement of American diplomats, in accordance with whose thoroughly detailed scenario Sakharov was to call another "hunger strike", with Bonner in the meantime getting "asylum" in the U.S. Embassy in Moscow. The plan provided for exploiting Bonner's stay in the Embassy to organize meetings with foreign correspondents and send abroad mendacious allegations about the Soviet Union and all kind of falsehoods about the position of her husband Sakharov.

These coordinated actions were to signal the start of an anti-Soviet campaign, first of all in the United States.

It was planned at the same time to try and organize under a far-fetched pretext, namely her state of health, Bonner's departure abroad, where she was to become a leader of the anti-Soviet scum on the payroll of Western special services.

As a result of timely measures adopted by Soviet law-enforcement agencies, the operation has been foiled. An official representation, listing facts of direct involvement by staffers of the U.S. Embassy in Moscow in this provocation and demanding an end to such inadmissible actions, has been made to the American side . . .

Although the statement did not directly acknowledge either Sakharov's hunger strike or Bonner's detention (the hunger strike was never officially acknowledged), it was the first indication, after Elena Bonner failed to come to Moscow on May 2, as had been expected, that something was happening in Gorky. The statement, published in *Izvestia*, prompted the Sakharovs' friend, the mathematician Irina Kristi, to undertake a trip to Gorky. After being detained overnight by police, Irina Kristi returned to Moscow on May 8 and broke the news of Sakharov's hunger strike and the criminal charges brought against Bonner.

The subsequent, largely repetitive, TASS statements were made, apparently, in response to a strong Western reaction to news of the hunger strike. The Soviet position, repeatedly expressed in TASS statements and elsewhere, was essentially as follows:

1. Bonner is in good health and does not need special treatment abroad.

2. Should she require medical treatment, she can get it in the Soviet Union, the best available anywhere, and free of charge.

3. While in the past she has been allowed to travel abroad, under the pretext of obtaining medical help, she has used these opportunities to engage in anti-Soviet activities.

4. The so-called "hunger strike" declared by Sakharov is a part of an anti-Soviet campaign, masterminded and coordinated by "U.S. special services," with the Sakharovs as willing participants.

The first two points were elaborated upon in the TASS statement of May 18, entitled "The Sickly Imagination of Provocateurs":

The state of health of Yelena Bonner, the wife of Academician Sakharov, has been discussed in great detail in the West lately. Western propaganda is raising a clamour about the supposedly "dramatic" condition of Bonner who is in a "hopeless" state and for this reason must immediately leave for treatment abroad.

At the same time in the press and also from very high official rostrums, in particular in the United States, contentions are being made that Bonner supposedly is under arrest and is being denied the necessary medical treatment.

All this is nothing but the sickly imagination of the organisers of a new anti-Soviet propaganda campaign. To begin with, until recently the "gravely ill" Bonner made regular shuttle trips between Gorky and Moscow and led a very active way of life, this boiling down mostly to professional exercises in anti-Sovietism. . . .

. . . Bonner, just as her husband, is being treated free of charge (attention: Messrs Propagandists) at the best clinics of the city of Gorky and the central clinical hospital of the USSR Academy of Sciences, when it was necessary. These clinics use the services of most authoritative medical consultants. Thus, the physicians treating Bonner in the Gorky Regional Clinical Hospital named after N. A. Semashko reported that Bonner's medical examination was carried out in the third week of last April.

For precision's sake, we will use medical terminology in quoting the medical conclusion: "No dynamic change on the cardiogram as compared with the preceding one has been found. No deviation from the norm has been found in echocardioscopy in the aorta and the mitral valve. The patient is in a satisfactory condition." Bonner, who was, incidentally, a physician herself, checked the diagnosis at Outpatient Clinic 7 of the Administration of the Self-Sustained Medical Institutions of the Moscow City Soviet. The diagnosis was fully confirmed there.

At Bonner's request she was examined also by Dr. Sc. (Medicine) G. G. Gelshtein, head of the Functional Diagnosis Department of the Institute of Cardio-vascular Surgery of the Academy of Medical Sciences of the USSR. Our correspondent interviewed Professor Gelshtein. This is what he had to say: "As a result of age factors, the patient suffers from a degree of coronary insufficiency. More than a year ago she had a local myocardial infarction.

The condition has stabilised since that time, and I did not notice any worsening. Bonner's state of health is satisfactory. She is recommended prophylactic treatment, customary in our country, which takes into account all the latest achievements in cardiology."

Bonner thus receives the necessary treatment. But Bonner claims that her eye ailment can only be cured in Italy. Bonner was indeed operated on in the past at a private Italian ophthalmological clinic. Here is what a recent medical checkup of Bonner showed. According to Soviet specialists, the operation was made at a very low level, with a crude scar being left in the patient's eyeball. Our correspondent learnt this from a major authority on eye ailments, Candidate of Medical Sciences E. F. Pristauko who consulted Bonner at her request. By the way, the doctor told us that operations, similar to the one Bonner had had in Italy, are carried out here at ordinary eye clinics, and at a higher level at that. There is hardly any need to tell competent people in the West that many Soviet experts on eye surgery enjoy world-wide renown and, in accordance with Soviet laws, render any aid to our citizens in clinics free of charge. . . .

The *Izvestia* article of May 21, "Renegades and Their Obliging Friends" (translation courtesy of David Levy), however, acknowledged that "Sakharov and Bonner do not shine in excellent health," which the article attributed to their age and "certain habits and inclinations [?]." The article, for the first time, hinted at criminal charges brought against Bonner, while suggesting that Sakharov has been already punished in accordance with the law:

. . . As is well known, Sakharov has been punished for his anti-social activity. At present, the organs of law and order have taken measures, flowing from the law, with regard to Bonner also.

Unlike the TASS statements, the *Izvestia* article portrayed Elena Bonner as the main culprit, rather than "U.S. special services," and seemed to be directed specifically against her:

. . . One should not ignore the fact that recently, amid the provocations organized in the West by using Sakharov's name, increasingly more odious has become the role of his wife, E. G. Bonner. She clearly wants to promote herself to the forefront, to become some sort of chief executive of the anti-Soviet escapades and slanderous statements in respect of the Soviet people.

Bonner has long taken upon herself the function of link with Western reactionary circles, not worrying about engaging in shady dealings in the process. She does all this by no means without self-interest. Several times Bonner traveled to Italy, referring to the necessity of undergoing medical treatment. She was given permission for that. Finding herself there in 1975, she contracted to sell, for a solid sum, Sakharov's provocation, his book, *My Country and the World,* to one of the publishing houses.

Arriving once more in Italy in September 1977, Bonner, in the course of her almost three-month stay, forgetting about "medical treatment," immersed herself up to her head in the dirty swamp of the so-called "Sakharov Hearings" from which thus wafted the stench of out-and-out anti-Sovietism. In 1979, finding herself yet again in Italy, she secretly flew to the United States. . . .

. . . There Bonner was brought together with little groups of anti-Sovietchiks with the job of trying to unite the various stripes of renegades squabbling among themselves. It was then that she tossed the Americans the idea of her staying in America for good. However, she was talked out of that, and it was suggested that she return to the USSR and try to squeeze out of Sakharov everything that he was capable of in subservience to the anti-Communists. . . .

. . . Bonner, as NATO-ized provocateur, looked after the surfeit of sensation over Sakharov abroad. When this raucous sensation subsided, she prodded her husband on to a real caper. It was Bonner who planted the idea of Sakharov going on a "hunger strike" in order to feed the propaganda organs of the U.S.A. About the health of her spouse she worried least of all, acting on the principle: the worse the better. The worse it is for the academician, the better it is for her. . . .

. . . The basic thing for her was to slip out to the West, as before, so to say, even over her husband's dead body. . . .

Although the article ascribed to Sakharov a relatively passive role, he was accused of "hatred toward his country and his people," as allegedly expressed in his 1983 article in *Foreign Affairs,* "The Danger of Thermonuclear War." *Izvestia* accused Sakharov of expressing in this article the view that

. . . the capitalist countries must find in themselves "a readiness for economic sacrifice" in order to achieve superiority and "to settle accounts with socialism".

On May 30, two days after Sakharov abandoned his hunger strike, TASS issued a new statement, where under the headline "Healers from the CIA" it recounted the earlier accusations. It also read:

What about the "hunger strike"? Let us cite exact medical facts: Sakharov feels well, takes regular meals and lives an active way of life.

"Once Again About Sakharov's and Bonner's Health" was the title of TASS's statement of June 4, issued following the TASS announcement of the forthcoming visit to Moscow by French President Mitterrand. The statement—apparently intended to quiet critics of Mitterrand's decision to visit Moscow despite continuous uncertainty about the Sakharovs' welfare and whereabouts—ridiculed widespread rumors of Sakharov's death:

The U.S. special services and their sponsors would not reconcile themselves to the fact that their act of provocation with Sakharov and Bonner has been a flop. They continue to spread, again and again, slanderous reports based on fantasies and on nothing else. . . . some gullible people have joined in the anti-Soviet campaign instigated in the West from the White House. Regrettably, they believe lies rather than facts. But the facts are, we repeat: Sakharov and Bonner are in good health. Perhaps, in the Western centres of psychological warfare they would like to hear different news, but we cannot tell them anything different.

III

Elena Bonner's Service Record

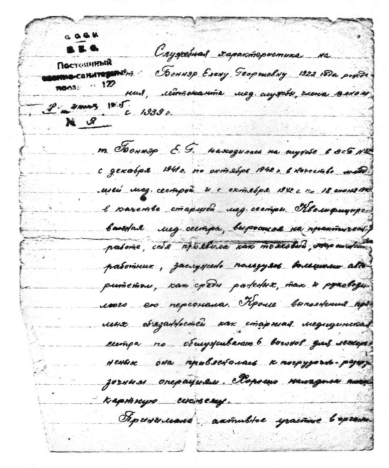

Service record for Bonner, Elena Georgievna, born 1922, lieutenant in the Medical Corps, and member of the Komsomol since 1939.

The certificate describes Bonner's work as a nurse on hospital train 122: "She is a qualified nurse, whose skills grew through experience, and she has shown herself to be a responsible and self-sacrificing worker, who has deservedly a great reputation among the wounded and the personnel under her. . . . For her exemplary performance of her duties she has received numerous expressions of gratitude and has been listed on the honor board of hospital train 122."

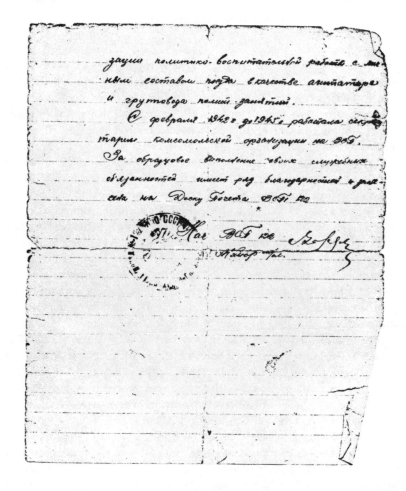

IV

The Hunger Strike Appeal

TO FRIENDS THE WORLD OVER

I am appealing to my scientific colleagues, to public and government figures, to all those who have ever come to my defense or who are prepared to do so now at this tragic moment of our life.

I am beginning a hunger strike with the demand that my wife Elena Bonner be allowed to travel abroad for medical treatment and for a meeting with her mother, children, and grandchildren.

On April 25, 1983, she suffered an extensive miocardial infarction. Her condition has not yet returned to normal and has become worse in some respects. It is life threatening. She suffered new heart attacks in October 1983 and January 1984. Throughout this period she has been denied any real medical care. My wife cannot receive effective treatment in the USSR while she is subject to an organized campaign of persecution and constant KGB interference. Moreover, I am convinced such treatment might be extremely dangerous. In the press the responsibility for my public statements is shifted onto her. She is branded an agent of the CIA and Zionist organizations.

In my opinion this is not merely provocative slander, but part of a considered plan for the "solution of the Sakharov problem." There are serious grounds for concern that another part of this plan is the physical destruction of my wife. KGB actions which justify such fears include: a search aboard a train following a heart attack; the constant police guard at her apartment door in Moscow (the guard was posted just after she had suffered a heart problem and it prevented visits to her home by doctors other than Academy doctors); disconnecting her home telephone; slanderous articles and books published in 1983 in editions totaling eleven million copies; the refusal of a judge to accept her slander suit; a pogrom on a train in September 1983; the refusal to hospitalize us together in the Academy Hospital in June-July 1983; forbidding Academician N. living in Gorky to buy her train tickets; and the failure to answer appeals by my wife and myself to allow her travel.

Elena Bonner submitted her application in September 1982 to travel abroad for urgently needed medical treatment—follow-up care for her eye disease including another operation. On November 10, 1983, I wrote to Yury

Andropov requesting permission for her to travel. On February 21, 1984, I sent to Communist Party General Secretary Konstantin Chernenko a request for permission for her travel. On March 30 I was summoned to the Gorky Visa Office where I was told: "Your application is under consideration. But the answer will come after May 1." This vague and empty formula is simply a KGB effort to seize the initiative.

In 1981 we were forced to resort to a hunger strike to obtain permission for my daughter-in-law to join her husband abroad. Now, once again, in view of the facts I have described concerning my wife's application to travel, I see no alternative to a hunger strike. I made a decision in principle regarding a hunger strike in September 1983. I have postponed it for some months at my wife's insistent request. But it is impossible to delay any longer!

My wife's health prevents her participation in the hunger strike. The irreparable damage which a hunger strike could cause would only assist the plans of the KGB. Therefore I ask her not to undertake a hunger strike.

I have asked the U.S. Department of State and the American Ambassador in the USSR to grant Elena Bonner temporary refuge in the Embassy during the hunger strike. I fear that if my wife cannot remain beyond the reach of the KGB during my hunger strike, she will become a victim of their hatred and might disappear without a trace. We saw how this can happen during our 1981 hunger strike. They dragged us out of our apartment after breaking down the door, separated us by force and put us in different hospitals. We had no news about each other until our hunger strike ended. Now our situation is incomparably more precarious.

My hunger strike is of indefinite duration. I will end it only when my wife receives permission to go abroad. Her death will be mine as well. Once again, as I did two years ago, I ask for your help. Save us!

V

Letter to American Ambassador Arthur Hartman
and the State Department

I am asking you to offer my wife, E. G. Bonner, temporary asylum in the embassy of the United States of America during my hunger strike to secure permission for her to travel abroad for medical treatment and to see her mother, children, and grandchildren. I am not asking for political asylum for my wife and am not placing responsibility for obtaining permission on you, even though I will be grateful if you deem it possible to support our demands.

Two years ago, during our joint hunger strike for an exit visa for our daughter-in-law so that she could join her husband, we were separated, and taken by force to different hospitals. We knew nothing about each other until the last day of the hunger strike. Now the situation is much more difficult and dangerous. During my hunger strike, E. G. Bonner, if she is accessible to the KGB, might become a victim of the KGB's hatred, so strongly manifested in recent years. I am afraid that she will be subjected to enforced isolation and will vanish without a trace, perhaps even die. That is why I am appealing to you to grant her temporary asylum. The choice of the American embassy is not related to any political considerations; one of the reasons is the availability of a physician in the embassy.

I am asking the State Department and the ambassador of the United States, if you deem it possible, to make an attempt to settle the question of my wife's trip abroad through the Ministry of Foreign Affairs during the first few days of my wife's stay in the embassy. Having no other possibilities, I am appealing through you to the ministries of foreign affairs and the ambassadors of other Western states. The authorities of the USSR may be interested in avoiding publicity in this affair, and may respond positively. If you have not received a satisfactory reply, five days after I begin the hunger strike, I ask that you give my wife the opportunity to appeal through foreign correspondents in Moscow for support from world opinion. Confined to Gorky in the most strict isolation, I cannot do it myself.

I am writing this letter in a tragic moment of our life. I am hoping for your cooperation.

6 April 1984   With profound respect,
    Gorky   Andrei Sakharov

VI

A Letter to the Family

Dear Ruth Grigorievna, Tanya, Alyosha, Liza, and Efrem.

I kiss you all. Two years of such harsh trials and anxiety for Lusia and me and for you are now behind us. And during all this time direct communication has been impossible. But you managed better than anyone to understand what was happening, and your intuition and your wise actions saved us. Here is a short account of some of the things you may still not know.

In 1984 Lusia and I were afraid that during my hunger strike she would fall into the hands of the KGB. I came up with a plan according to which she would ask for temporary asylum at the embassy of the United States of America. Lusia hesitated greatly and put off the start of the action, even when we set the date for March. Finally, we decided to begin on April 13. On April 7 she left Gorky.

But back in March I had cut my leg on a garbage can and developed an abscess on the knee. While Lusia was away they lanced it at the polyclinic, but apparently it did not drain completely. On April 12 doctors came to see me and on April 13 they hospitalized me to lance the abscess again. Lusia flew back on the thirteenth (without her things, without warm clothing) after my telegram of the twelfth, which she received two hours before they came for her from the embassy. . . .

While I was being taken from doctor to doctor at the hospital, I carelessly gave up . . . my bag with documents, which I always carried with me. . . . I had forgotten that I had not destroyed the draft of my letter to the American ambassador. So the KGB learned of my plan. Lusia and I understood that. But we could not retreat. On May 2 when Lusia tried to fly out to Moscow, she was detained at the airport and searched. More documents fell into KGB hands, including her letter to you. Lusia was charged under Article 190-1, you know her case very well (even though the final text of my administrative complaint did not reach you).

Before she got home, I had begun a hunger strike, after taking a laxative. The chief of the Regional KGB came into the house with Lusia. He intoned a "threatening" monologue, in which he called Lusia "Elena Bonner, CIA agent."

The rest you basically know. On May 7 I was forcibly hospitalized. On

May 11 I was force-fed (with intravenous injections). That day I had a small stroke (or a spasm). On May 15 Lusia received a telegram:

"Elena Georgievna, we, the children of Andrei Dmitrievich, ask and implore you to do everything you can to save our father from this mad undertaking, which could lead to his death. We know that only one person can save him from death—that is you. You are the mother of children and you should understand us. Otherwise we will be forced to turn to the procurator's office, because you are inciting our father to commit suicide. We see no other way out. Understand us correctly—Tanya, Lyuba, Dima." . . .

This cruel and unfair telegram caused Lusia additional suffering and anxiety in her already horrible and almost unbearable situation. The telegram gave the KGB the "green light" for any action against us. . . . It was the reason that I did not write to my children for the next year and a half, until November 1985.

Lusia will tell you about subsequent events, about our unheard of, unprecedented isolation for that entire year and a half.

In November 1984 I sent a letter (I won't tell you how) to Alexandrov and to the presidium of the Academy of Sciences, in which I asked for help in obtaining permission for Lusia's trip. I described what I experienced during force-feeding. In conclusion I wrote that I was the only academician whose wife has been subjected to shameless slander in the press, illegal sentencing as a criminal for actions she performed at my behest, and for actions which she never performed, and has been deprived of the opportunity to see her family and to have medical care. I wrote that I did not want to participate in a worldwide hoax and asked that my letter be considered as my resignation from the Academy of Sciences if my request was not satisfied (at first I gave them until March 1, and then extended the deadline to May 10).

. . . I started a new hunger strike on April 16, 1985, and was forcibly hospitalized—again taken to the Semashko hospital—on April 21. From that day (April 21) right up to July 11, I was subjected to forcible feeding. During this period and the one that followed, my resistance was sometimes, though not always, of a merely symbolic type.

The feeding was sometimes extremely painful. I was tied up and held down against the bed so violently that my face became badly bruised. A spoon was used to open my mouth and another spoon to pour in the food. My nose was held tight by hand or with a clamp. I resigned myself to eating only when the "feeding team" was present in full strength and only when I was actually in the ward. Twice, they dragged me into the ward with the help of KGB men.

I had no idea whether or not anyone outside Russia knew about my hunger strike.

On July 11, not being able to bear my separation from Elena any longer and not knowing anything about her, I wrote a statement that my hunger strike was at an end. The same day, I was discharged from the hospital. The KGB, clearly, badly wanted me discharged before the Helsinki meeting started.

Lusia and I were together for two weeks. It was a good time to be alive, and it gave us strength to go on. On July 25, I resumed my hunger strike and was hospitalized on July 27. During our short period of freedom, the film known to you was taken by a hidden camera. I ceased my hunger strike and was discharged on October 23. On October 25, the permission for Elena's travel was received.

. . . My weight declined constantly during the period of forcible feeding. My normal weight is 170 to 176 pounds. When I was discharged on July 11, it was 145 pounds. My lowest weight during the second round was 138 pounds on August 13.

Beginning that day, they administered subcutaneous (into both thighs) and intravenous drips containing glucose and protein preparations—15 subcutaneous and 10 intravenous. The sheer quantity of the drip was enormous. My legs blew up like pillows and were painful.

The most cruel measure used against us was a 10-month separation—isolation from each other. It was especially difficult for Elena in her solitude and isolation. In 1985, she did not go on any hunger strike but lost more weight than I did.

These 10 months were as though they had never existed, a period of time deleted from our lives.

In March 1985 Lusia appealed to the Presidium of the Supreme Soviet of the USSR for a pardon and with a request to be allowed to travel. In 1984 and in 1985, I wrote many letters to the leaders of the country and to the KGB, including letters on May 21, 1985, to Chebrikov and on July 29, 1985, to Gorbachev. I stated why Lusia's trip was vitally important, her right to see her mother, children, and grandchildren. I stressed that she was a disabled veteran of the Great Patriotic War, having served four years, and a seriously ill person, I explained the illegality of her conviction. Later I wrote, "My wife has influenced me to place greater stress in my public activity on the fate of specific individuals and on humanitarian concerns, she has not influenced my ideas on general issues. . . . I am prepared to bear the responsibility for my actions—even though I consider the measures directed against me to be unfair and illegal. But a situation in which responsibility for my actions is transferred to my wife is totally intolerable for me." I wrote, "I want to end my public activity and statements (except, of course, for extraordinary situations) and to concentrate on my work. If there is a positive decision on my wife's trip, I am prepared to ask Western scientists, and everyone who acted in my defense, to halt their efforts on my behalf."

Twice (May 31, 1985, and Sept. 5, 1985) I was visited in the hospital by a representative of the KGB of the U.S.S.R., S. I. Sokolov, evidently a big chief. In May, he also talked to Elena.

He conversed with me in a harsh manner. He stressed the reasons why my request for Elena's travel—and also for the children's travel to the U.S.S.R.—could not be granted. He also led me to understand that I must disavow certain previous statements. In particular, my letter to Drell, my statements on the Moscow subway explosion, and my ideas on convergence. I was on a full hunger strike—there was no force feeding. Thus, they "prepared" me for the conversation [with Sokolov in May].

In September, Sokolov informed me that Gorbachev had familiarized himself with my letter and had assigned a group of people to prepare an answer. Sokolov asked me to write a statement on the question of my knowledge of secrets and to convey to my wife a request that she write a statement obliging her not to meet representatives of the mass media while abroad or to take part in any press conference.

I was then allowed 3 hours with Lusia, and we carried out Sokolov's requests. I wrote that I accept the Soviet authorities' right to refuse me permission to travel beyond the country's borders, since I did in the past have access to especially important secret material of a military nature, some of which might still be of significance even now.

(I wish to call attention to the fact that the formulation I used and the similar formulation in my letter to Gorbachev do not justify my deportation to Gorky, which I consider unjust and illegal.)

... I have the feeling that I am going with Lusia to visit you, plunging into your colorful, event-filled life. I hope that it will now go into a more peaceful, more "family-like" track. I hope that Lusia has everything necessary done, including her heart, eyes, teeth, and papilloma, and that she will return in better health and less worried about you. I kiss you, be healthy and happy. Kiss the children. . . .

November 24, 1985. Andrei.

P.S. Alexei, in the reprint of my article, "Cosmic Transitions with Changes in the Metrics Signature," the dedication to Lusia was omitted. How did that happen? Can the dedication be reinstated in some of the preprints sent out? It's very important to me.

November, 1985

VII

To the Procurator of the RSFSR
From SAKHAROV, Andrei Dmitrievich,
Academician; Gorky-137, Gagarin Avenue,
214, apt. 3

ADMINISTRATIVE COMPLAINT

In the case of Elena Georgievna BONNER, my wife, sentenced under article 190-1 of the Criminal Code of the RSFSR with the application of article 43 of the Criminal Code of the RSFSR* to five years of exile by the Gorky Regional Court on 10 August 1984, and affirmed without change by the Judicial Collegium on Criminal Cases of the Supreme Court of the RSFSR on 7 September.

On 1 August, 1984, I sent a statement to the investigator and the chairman of the court in the case of my wife, a copy is attached. I stand by the assertions and requests contained in that statement. I received a reply from the investigator, senior assistant of the procurator of Gorky Oblast, G. P. Kolesnikov, according to which my statement was passed on to the Judicial Collegium on Criminal Cases of the Gorky Regional Court. However, my statement was not appended to the case file for E. G. Bonner, and the requests contained therein were not examined by the court. This is a serious procedural violation. I was not called to testify in my wife's trial as a witness, nor was I notified of the date of the trial. Thus, none of my wife's relatives (or friends) had the opportunity to be present in the courtroom, which is a gross violation of the principle of access and openness. Another procedural violation is having the trial and (in my opinion) the investigation in the city of Gorky, because before my wife was charged and not allowed to leave Gorky, she lived in Moscow at Chkalov Street, no. 48B, apt. 68, and because not a single incriminating charge had anything to do with Gorky.

The indictment, the verdict, and the decision of the appeals court are not, in my opinion, well founded, they contain factual and conceptually incorrect statements and opinions, and are prejudiced and nonobjective.

---

*Article 43 permits the court to set a milder punishment than the minimum specified for a particular crime when mitigating circumstances exist.

One of the central charges, as I maintain, is based on perjured testimony.

I will begin with a discussion of an episode which was not shown to be a crime either in the indictment or during the trial or during the appeal hearing. There was no discussion of the arguments of the defense attorney and the defendant.

My wife was charged with participating in the writing and distribution of a document by the Moscow Helsinki Group titled "Summary Document for the Belgrade Conference." The indictment, verdict, and decision of the appeals court assert that her participation in the writing and distribution is corroborated by the testimony of Felix Serebrov, and that her participation in writing it is also corroborated by my wife's signature in the text of the document published by Khronika Press in New York. No other proof of my wife's participation in the writing and distribution was produced. The court was not given an original of the document with my wife's signature in her own hand. It was not proved that the document was written before her trip to Italy (the published text does not give the date the document was written, which in itself deprives it of any juridical meaning). At the trial she stated that she learned of the existence of the document when she was in Italy, by telephone, and it was by telephone that she gave permission to sign her name to the document. The verdict and the appeal ruling do not offer any arguments to refute my wife's testimony and do not even mention it except to say that she corroborated her signature.

The flimsiness of the references to Serebrov's testimony is particularly significant, because it is the only attempt to prove Bonner's participation in distributing the document and in general it is the only testimony mentioned in the verdict and the decision of the appeals court in the entire case against my wife. Witness Serebrov maintained in court that P. G. Grigorenko (one of the members of the Moscow Helsinki Group) told him that Bonner brought the documents for the Belgrade conference to Italy and had participated in writing it. But this is *obvious* perjury, in any case, as relates to the distribution. My wife left for Italy for treatment on 5 September 1977. Serebrov was arrested on 16 August 1977, twenty days before my wife left, which is confirmed by documents in the case. After his arrest, Serebrov never saw Grigorenko, who left the USSR in November of that year. This chronological discrepancy was discussed in great detail by the court of the first instance. In direct questioning by defense attorney Elena Reznikova on how he explained this discrepancy, Serebrov could not give an answer and was silent. The attorney's argument at the appeal hearing and the written appeal stressed once again that Grigorenko could not have spoken before

August 15 about my wife's bringing out any document on September 5. But this entire discussion (written and oral) was completely ignored in the verdict and the decision of the Judicial Collegium on Criminal Cases of the Supreme Court of the RSFSR. The decision does not even mention that Reznikova disputed Serebrov's testimony dealing with the distribution of the document for the Belgrade conference. I view the above as evidence of the nonobjectivity and prejudice of both courts and as a basis for protesting the sentence.

Article 190-1 of the Criminal Code of the RSFSR deals with "dissemination of deliberately false fabrications slandering the Soviet social and state system." The law does not specify whether the defendant must know that the statements ("fabrications") are false at the time they are disseminated, or whether it is sufficient for their falsehood to be evident only to the members of the court. Since the views and opinions of the members of the court might differ substantially from the views of the defendant by virtue of differing information accessible to them and for ideological reasons, this question is very important for the practical application of article 190-1. If article 190-1 does not envisage criminal prosecution for beliefs, then undoubtedly the first interpretation is correct and the court *must* prove that the accused consciously spread lies, that is, not simply false opinions but statements whose falseness was known to her. This interpretation is reflected in the *Commentary to the Criminal Code of the RSFSR* (Yuridicheskaya Literatura Publishing House, 1971, edited by Professor Anashkin, Professor Karpets, Professor Nikoforov, pp. 403–404, paragraphs 2 and 9a). But the decision of the appeals court, of the second instance in the case of my wife, on the contrary, reads: "Familiarization with the *content* (italics mine—A.S.) of the interviews given by the defendant, and the documents she signed is evidence of the fact that they contain deliberately false opinions slandering the Soviet state and social system." That is, the Judicial Collegium on Criminal Cases of the Supreme Court of the RSFSR (just as the trial court) simply does not consider it necessary to prove that my wife consciously spread lies; thereby these courts are in fact supporting the position of *persecution for beliefs.*

I ask the procurator of the RSFSR to direct particular attention to this circumstance. I feel that such an incorrect interpretation of article 190-1 is a definite basis for reversing the conviction.

The appellate ruling on my wife's case states that "the violation of the human rights of the particular individuals mentioned by Bonner did not take place, the individuals were convicted in conformity with established legal procedures for crimes they had committed." But, according to the beliefs of my wife (and my own beliefs), based on information on the trials of many individuals, they were convicted illegally, that is, for their beliefs, and are prisoners of conscience (they did not use or advocate violence). For my wife, and for myself, the fact of a sentencing does not by itself constitute proof of the rightness of a conviction; a concrete evaluation is necessary, in particular taking into account the fact that the courts systematically use the above-mentioned incorrect interpretation of the concept of deliberate falsehood in charging people under article 190-1 of the Criminal Code of the RSFSR and systematically violate the principle of access and openness in relation to defendants under political articles.

As I indicated in my statement of 1 August 1984, the majority of the statements incriminating my wife were either statements of my own ideas or word-for-word citations (at press conferences in Italy in 1975 and at the Nobel ceremony and the Nobel press conference that same year, and also a press conference in January 1980, after my illegal deportation to Gorky). My wife in accordance with her beliefs appeared on those occasions as my fully empowered representative. She always noted that this was my point of view.

It is perfectly obvious that trying her for these statements without charging me or even calling me as a witness is absolutely illegal. I am prepared to answer for these statements, which correspond with my beliefs. But my wife must be freed of responsibility for them!

The indictment, the verdict of the trial court, and the decision of the appeals court are characterized by inaccurate and prejudiced quotations taken out of context and distortions of my wife's statements. Here is a typical example: My wife is charged with stating that "Soviet newspapers print total lies." But the only evidence given is a citation from an article in the newspaper *Russkaya mysl'* (Russian Thought), which is a free rendition of an interview with my wife in a double translation. And the rest of this long article on my life in Gorky is not mentioned in the summation or by the court. In actual fact my wife never uses such sweeping generalizations as "total lies." I call the prosecutor's attention to the illegality of using an unauthorized text as evidence of guilt.

I find particularly outrageous from a moral point of view the use in the summation and sentence of my wife's emotional response during an unexpected meeting with a French correspondent only three days after she had been diagnosed as having had a heart attack. In the indictment, the decision of the appeals court, and (apparently) in the verdict, it is maintained that my wife allegedly said that "the Soviet government has created conditions to kill the academician and her." However, if you study the text of the television interview, you will be convinced that those words are not in there. Actually, when asked "What will happen to you then?" my wife replied, "I don't know, I think they're simply killing us." She was not talking about being shot with a gun. But obliquely we are being killed, especially my wife—we are convinced of that—she is being killed with persecution and slander in the press (in the year 1983 alone, she was attacked by publications with a circulation of over ten million),* by the actual deprivation of effective medical care, searches, exhausting interrogations and a trial of a seriously ill person, deprivation of normal contact with her mother, children, and grandchildren. And they are killing me by slowly killing her!

An important basis for protesting the sentence is the incorrect application by the court of article 43 of the Criminal Code of the RSFSR. The sentence does not mention that *my wife is a group 2 invalid of the Great Patriotic War and that she had a myocardial infarct* (there are affidavits to that effect in her case file), does not mention that she suffers from chronic uveitis and irreversible glaucoma, that she has had three eye operations and major surgery for thyreotoxicosis, and also it does not mention that my wife has an impeccable work record of thirty-two years. All it mentions is my wife's age and the fact that she has no prior convictions. According to the code (article 43 of the Criminal Code of the RSFSR), listing mitigating circumstances in the verdict is mandatory. In using article 43, the court should have given a sentence that was lower than the minimum possible under article 190-1 of the Criminal Code of the RSFSR, that is, a sentence of less than a fine. Exile is not such a sentence.

I summarize: The basis for annulling the verdict of the trial court and protesting the decision of the appeals court is the absence of any crime in the actions of E. G. Bonner, in particular, the absence of *deliberate* falsehood in the statements of Bonner, which were made in accordance with her beliefs. Other important reasons for reversing the sentence are the reliance of the indictment, verdict, and decision on the clearly perjured testimony of F. Serebrov—the only witness mentioned in the verdict, the violation of the principle of access and openness, and the improper application by the court of article 43 of the Criminal Code of the RSFSR.

Based on the above, I ask the procurator of the RSFSR to make use of his right of administrative supervision in order to review this case and annul

---

*Yakovlev's book *CIA Target—The USSR* (circulation 200,000); *Smena*, 1983, no. 14 (circulation 1,170,000); *Man and the Law*, 1983, no. 10 (circulation 8,700,000).

the verdict of the Gorky Regional Court and the decision of the Judicial Collegium on Criminal Cases of the Supreme Court of the RSFSR.

29 November 1984   A. Sakharov
Gorky

EDITOR'S NOTE

Sakharov included two appendices with his administrative complaint (they are not included here):

1. A copy of the decision of the Judicial Collegium on Criminal Cases of the Supreme Court of the RSFSR.

2. A copy of A. D. Sakharov's statement to the assistant procurator of the Gorky Oblast, G. P. Kolesnikov, and to Judge V. N. Vorobyov, who had presided at Elena Bonner's trial.

Sakharov did not send a copy of the verdict, since it was stolen from the Sakharovs' apartment in August 1984, and Judge Vorobyov refused to supply another copy.

The administrative complaint was sent by registered mail on 11 December 1984, and the return receipt was dated 17 December 1984.

On 6 February 1985 Sakharov received a reply from the Procurator's Office of the RSFSR dated 31 January 1985, No. 13-108-84, signed by a procurator of the department supervising KGB investigations, V. M. Yakovlev. The reply did not address any of Sakharov's arguments and his complaint was rejected.

VIII

Anatoly Alexandrov, President,
U.S.S.R. Academy of Sciences
Members of the Presidium,
U.S.S.R. Academy of Sciences

Dear Anatoly Petrovich:

I appeal to you at the most tragic moment of my life. I ask you to support my wife Elena Bonner's request for permission to travel abroad to visit her mother, her children and her grandchildren and to receive medical treatment for her eyes and her heart. I shall explain why this trip has become an absolute necessity for us. Our unprecedented situation, our isolation, the lies and slander regarding us compel me to write in detail. Please forgive me for the length of this letter.

The authorities have been greatly annoyed by my public activities—my defense of prisoners of conscience and my articles and books on peace, the open society and human rights. (My fundamental ideas are contained in *Progress, Coexistence and Intellectual Freedom*, 1968; *My Country and the World*, 1975, and "The Danger of Thermonuclear War," 1983.)

I do not intend to defend or explain my position here. What I wish to make clear is that I alone am responsible for all my actions, which are the result of convictions formed over a lifetime. As soon as Yelena Bonner married me in 1971, the KGB adopted a sly and cruel plan to solve the "Sakharov problem." They have tried to shift responsibility for my actions onto her, to destroy her morally and physically. They hope to break and bridle me, while portraying me as the innocent victim of the intrigues of my wife—a "CIA agent," a "Zionist," a "mercenary adventuress," etc. Any remaining doubts about this have been dispelled by the mass campaign of slander mounted against my wife in 1983 (attacks against her were printed in publications with a circulation of 11 million copies); by the two 1984 articles about her in *Izvestia*, and especially by the KGB's treatment of us in 1984, which I describe below.

My wife, Elena Bonner, was born in 1923. Her parents, who were active participants in the Revolution and the civil war, became victims of repression in 1937. Her father, the first secretary of the Armenian Bolshevik Party's central committee and a member of the Comintern's executive committee, perished. Her mother spent many years in labor camps and in exile as a "relative of a traitor to the motherland."

My wife served in the armed forces from the outbreak of World War II until August, 1945. She began as a first-aid instructor. After she was wounded and suffered a concussion, she became the head nurse on a hospital train. The concussion severely damaged her eyes. My wife is classified as a disabled veteran because of her loss of vision. She has been seriously ill ever since the war, but she has managed to lead a productive life—first studying, then working as a physician and teacher, raising a family, helping friends and strangers in need, sustaining her associates with respect and affection.

Her situation changed drastically after our paths merged. Tatyana and Alexei, my wife's children—whom I consider my own—and our grandchildren were forced to emigrate to the United States in 1977 and 1978 after five years of harassment and death threats. They had in fact become hostages. The pain of this tragic separation has been compounded by the absence of normal mail, cable and phone communications. My wife's 84-year-old mother has been living in the United States since 1980. It is the inalienable right of all human beings to see their families—and that includes my wife!

As long ago as 1974 many events convinced us that no effective medical treatment was possible for my wife in the U.S.S.R. and, moreover, that such treatment would be *dangerous* because of inevitable KGB interference. Now the organized campaign of slander against her is an added complication. These misgivings relate to my wife's medical treatment and not to my own, but they were reinforced by what physicians under KGB command did to me during my four-month confinement in a Gorky hospital. More about this later.

In 1975, with the support of world public opinion (and I assume on Brezhnev's order), my wife was allowed to travel to Italy to receive treatment for her eyes. My wife visited Italy in 1975, 1977 and 1979 for eye care. In Siena, Dr. Frezzotti twice operated on her for glaucoma, which could not be controlled by medication. Naturally, the same doctor should continue to treat her. Another visit became necessary in 1982. She submitted her application in September, 1982. Such applications are reviewed within five months—and usually within a few weeks. Two years have passed, and my wife is still waiting for a reply.

In April, 1983, my wife Elena Bonner suffered a massive heart attack, as confirmed by a report of the academy's medical department issued in response to an inquiry from the procurator's office. Her condition has not yet returned to normal. She has had recurrent attacks. (Some of these attacks have been confirmed by academy physicians who have examined her; one examination took place in March, 1984.) Her most recent major attack occurred in August, 1984.

In November, 1983, I addressed an appeal to Comrade Yuri Andropov [General Secretary, 1982 to Feb. 9, 1984], and I addressed a similar appeal to Comrade Konstantin Chernenko [General Secretary at the time this letter was written] in February, 1984. I asked them to issue instructions permitting my wife to travel. I wrote: "A trip . . . to see her mother, children and grandchildren and . . . to receive medical treatment has become a matter of life and death for us. The trip has no other purpose. I assure you of that."

By September, 1983, I realized that the question of my wife's trip would be resolved only if I conducted a hunger strike (as in the earlier case of our daughter-in-law Liza Alexeyeva's departure to join Alexei). My wife understood how difficult it was for me to do nothing. Nevertheless, she kept putting off the hunger strike. And, in point of fact, I began the hunger strike only in direct response to actions of the authorities.

On March 30, 1984, I was summoned to the Gorky province visa office. A representative there announced: "On behalf of the visa department of the U.S.S.R., I inform you that your statement is under consideration. The reply will be communicated to you after May 1."

My wife was to fly to Moscow on May 2. I watched through the airport window as she was detained by the aircraft and taken away in a police car. I immediately returned to the apartment and took a laxative, thereby beginning my hunger strike for my wife to be allowed to travel.

Two hours later my wife returned, accompanied by the KGB province chief, who delivered a threatening speech in the course of which he called my wife a CIA agent. My wife had been subjected to a body search at the airport and charged under Article 190-1 [of the Russian Socialist Federal Soviet Republic (RSFSR) Criminal Code]. They also made her sign a promise not to leave the city. So this was my promised reply to my declaration about my wife's trip abroad.

During the months that followed, my wife was called in for interrogation three or four times a week. She was tried on August 9–10 and sentenced to five years' exile. On September 7 a picked group from the RSFSR Supreme Court made a special trip to Gorky to hear her appeal. They confirmed the sentence. Gorky was designated her place of exile so that she could remain with me, thereby creating a semblance of humanity. In fact, however, it was camouflaged murder.

The KGB managed the whole enterprise—from the charges to the sentence—in order to block my wife's travel abroad. The indictment and the verdict are typical for Article 190-1 cases, although particularly flagrant examples of the arbitrariness and injustice involved. Article 190-1 makes it a crime to disseminate slanderous fabrications known to be false that defame the Soviet state and social system. (Article 190-1 refers to statements that the defendant knows are *false*. In my experience, and that includes my wife's case, the defendants believed their statements to be *true* beyond a doubt. The real issue was their *opinions*.)

Most of the eight counts in my wife's indictment involve her repetition of statements made by me. (To make matters worse, they have been taken out of context.) All the statements concern secondary issues. For example, in *My Country and the World*, I explain what "certificates" are, noting that two or more types of money exist in the U.S.S.R. My wife repeated this indisputable statement at a press conference in Italy in 1975, and she was charged with slander because of it. I—and not my wife—should be charged with statements made by me. My wife acted as my representative in keeping with her own beliefs.

One charge in the indictment exploits an emotional outburst of my wife during the unexpected visit of a French correspondent on May 18, 1983, *three days after her massive myocardial infarct had been diagnosed*. (As you know, in 1983 we requested, without success, that we be admitted together to the academy's hospital.) The correspondent asked, "What will happen to you?" My wife exclaimed: "I don't know. I think they are trying to kill us." She was clearly not referring to being killed by a pistol or knife. But she had more than enough grounds to speak of indirect murder (at least of herself).

My wife's alleged drafting and circulation of a Moscow Helsinki Group document was a key point in the indictment. It was based on patently false testimony and was completely refuted by defense counsel's examination of the chronology of events. A witness testified at the trial that he had been told by a member of the Helsinki Group that my wife had taken one of the group's documents with her when she left the country in 1977. But the witness had been arrested on Aug. 16, 1977, and my wife left for Italy on September 5. Thus he could not have met anyone "from outside" after my wife's departure. Under questioning, the witness replied that he had learned of the document's being carried out of the country in July or August—that is, before my wife's trip.

Moreover, no proof that the document had been written prior to my wife's departure was presented in the indictment or during the trial. (The document was undated. That alone was enough to deprive it of any juridical significance.)

The only "evidence" corroborating the witness's unsubstantiated allegation was the statement of a person who had emigrated in 1977. In defiance of logic this count was included in the verdict and in the decision of the appellate proceeding. If the appellate court had eliminated that count, it would have had to annul the verdict—in part because the only directly incriminating testimony would be lost, in part because of the dated and inconsequential nature of the 1975 episode. Most important of all, none of the charges bore the slightest juridical relation to Article 190-1, which presupposes intentional slander.

In practice my wife's exile has led to restrictions much more severe than those stipulated in the law: The loss of all communication with her mother and children; complete isolation from her friends; still less opportunity for medical care; the virtual confiscation of property left in our Moscow apartment—which is now inaccessible to us—and the potential loss of the apartment itself. (The apartment was given to my wife's mother in 1956 after she was rehabilitated and after her husband was rehabilitated posthumously.)

There was no mention during my wife's trial of the accusations made in the press—her alleged past crimes, her "immoral character," her "links" with foreign intelligence agencies. That is all simply slander for public consumption—for the "sheep" held in such contempt by the KGB directors of the campaign. The most recent article of this sort appeared in *Izvestia* on May 21. The article pushes the idea that my wife has always wanted to leave the U.S.S.R., "even over her husband's dead body." The article claims that as long ago as 1979 she wanted to remain in the United States but had been persuaded to leave. (The context implies that American intelligence agents did the persuading.)

My wife's tragic and heroic life with me, which has brought her so much suffering, refutes this insinuation. Before marrying me, my wife made several trips abroad. She worked for a year in Iraq on a vaccination project. She visited Poland and France. The idea of defecting never entered her mind. It is the KGB that wants my wife to abandon me: It would provide the best demonstration that their slander had been true. But they were hardly hoping for that. They are "psychologists." They carefully hid the May 21 [*Izvestia*] article from me. They did not want to strengthen my resolve to win my goal before seeing my wife. I wanted to protect her from responsibility for my hunger strike.

For four months—from May 7 to September 8—my wife and I were separated from each other and completely isolated from the outside world. My wife was alone in our apartment. Her "guards" were increased. Apart from the usual policeman at the entrance to our apartment, observation posts operated around the clock, and a van with KGB agents on duty was parked beneath our terrace. Outside the house she was followed by two cars of KGB agents who prevented the most innocent contact with anyone. She was not allowed into the regional hospital when I was confined there.

On May 7, while accompanying my wife to the prosecutor's office for her next bout of questioning, I was seized by KGB men disguised in doctors' white coats. They took me by force to Gorky Regional Hospital, kept me there by force and tormented me for four months. My attempts to flee the hospital were always blocked by KGB men, who were on duty round-the-clock to bar all means of escape.

From May 11 to May 27 I was subjected to the excruciating and degrading process of force-feeding. The doctors hypocritically called it "saving my life," but in fact they were acting under orders from the KGB to create conditions in which my demand for my wife to be allowed to travel would not have to be fulfilled. They kept changing the method of force-feeding. They wanted to maximize my distress in order to make me give up the hunger strike.

From May 11 to May 15 intravenous feeding was tried. Orderlies would throw me onto the bed, tie my hands and feet and then hold my shoulders down while the needle was inserted into a vein. On May 11, the first day this was attempted, one of the hospital aides sat on my legs while some substance was injected with a small syringe. I passed out and involuntarily urinated. When I came to, the orderlies had left my bedside. Their bodies seemed strangely distorted as on a television screen affected by strong interference. I found out later that this sort of optical illusion is symptomatic of a cerebral spasm or stroke.

I have retained drafts of the letters I wrote to my wife from the hospital. (Hardly any of the letters, apart from those that were quite empty of information, were actually delivered to my wife. The same is true with respect to the notes and books she sent me.)

In my first letter written (May 20) after force-feeding began and in another draft written at that time, my writing wavers and is remarkably deformed. Letters are repeated two or three times in many words (mainly vowels, as in "haaand"). This is another typical symptom of a cerebral spasm or stroke and can be used as objective, documentary evidence in attempting a diagnosis. The repetition of letters does not occur in later drafts, but the symptoms of trembling persist. My letter of May 10 (the ninth day of my hunger strike but prior to force-feeding) is entirely normal. My recollections from the period of force-feeding are confused, in contrast to my memory of events from May 2 to May 10. My letter dated May 20 states: "I can barely walk. I am trying to learn." The spasm or stroke I suffered on May 11 was not an accident; it was a direct result of the medical measures taken in my case on orders from the KGB.

From May 16 to May 24 a new means of force-feeding was employed: A tube was inserted through my nose. This was discontinued on May 25, supposedly because sores were developing along the nasal passages and esophagus. I believe it was stopped because this method is bearable, if painful. In labor camps it is used for months—even years—at a time.

From May 25 to May 27 the most excruciating, degrading and barbarous method was used. I was again pushed down onto the bed without a pillow and my hands and feet were tied. A tight clamp was placed on my nose so that I could breathe only through my mouth. Whenever I opened my mouth to take a breath, a spoonful of nutriment or a broth containing strained meat would be poured into my mouth. Sometimes my jaws were pried open by a lever. They would hold my mouth shut until I swallowed so that I could not spit out the food. When I managed to do so, it only prolonged the agony. I experienced a continuing feeling of suffocation, aggravated by the position of my body and head. I had to gasp for breath. I could feel the veins bulging on my forehead. They seemed on the verge of bursting.

On May 27 I asked that the clamp be removed. I promised to swallow voluntarily. Unfortunately this meant that my hunger strike was over, although I did not realize it at the time. I intended to resume my hunger strike some time later—in July or August—but kept postponing it. It was psychologically difficult to condemn myself to another indefinite period of torture by suffocation. It is easier to continue the struggle than to resume it.

Much of my strength that summer was dissipated in tedious and futile "discussions" with other patients in the semiprivate room where I was never left alone. This, too, was part of the KGB's elaborate tactics. Different patients occupied the other bed, but each of them tried to convince me what a naïve fool I am—a political ignoramus—although they flattered my scientific ability.

I suffered terrible insomnia from the overstimulation of these conversations, from my realization of our tragic situation, from self-reproach for my mistakes and weakness and from anxiety for my seriously ill wife, who was alone and, by ordinary standards, bedridden or almost bedridden much of the time. In June and July, after the spasm or stroke, I experienced severe headaches.

I could not bring myself to resume the hunger strike, partly from fear that I would be unable to bring it to a victorious conclusion and would only delay seeing my wife again. I never would have believed that our separation would last four months, in any case.

In June I noticed that my hands were trembling severely. A neurologist told me that it was Parkinson's disease. The doctors tried to convince me that if I resumed my hunger strike there would be a rapid and catastrophic development of Parkinson's disease. A doctor gave me a book containing a clinical description of the disease's final stages. This, too, was a method of exerting psychological pressure on me. The head doctor, O. A. Obukhov, explained: "We won't allow you to die. I'll get the women's team out again to feed you with the clamp. We've got another method up our sleeve as well. However, you *will* become a helpless invalid." Another doctor added by way of explanation, "You'll be incapable of putting on your own trousers." Obukhov intimated that this would suit the KGB, since it would escape all blame: Parkinson's disease cannot be artificially induced.

What happened to me in a Gorky hospital in the summer of 1984 is strikingly reminiscent of Orwell's famous anti-Utopian novel, even down to the remarkable coincidence of the book's title—*1984*. In the novel and in real life the torturers sought to make a man betray the woman he loves. The part played by the threat of the cage full of rats in Orwell's book was played for me in real life by Parkinson's disease.

I was able to bring myself to resume the hunger strike only on September 7. On September 8 I was hastily discharged from the hospital. I was faced with a difficult choice: End the hunger strike in order to see my wife after a four-month separation or continue for as long as my strength held out, thereby indefinitely prolonging our separation and our complete ignorance of each other's fate. I could not continue.

Now, however, I am tormented by the thought that I may have lost a chance to save my wife. It was only after our reunion that I first learned about her trial and she learned about my painful force-feeding.

I am very concerned about my wife's health. I believe that a timely trip abroad is the only chance of saving her life. Her death would be mine as well.

I hope for your help, for your appeal to the highest levels seeking permission for my wife's trip. I am asking for help from the presidium of the U.S.S.R. Academy of Sciences and from you personally, as president of the Academy and as a man who has known me for many years.

Since my wife has been sentenced to exile, her trip will probably require a decree of the Supreme Soviet's Presidium suspending her sentence for the period of her travel. (Precedents for this exist both in Poland and, quite recently, in the U.S.S.R.) The Supreme Soviet's Presidium or another body could repeal her sentence altogether on the grounds that my wife is a disabled veteran of World War II, that she recently suffered a massive myocardial infarct, that she has no prior convictions and that she has an irreproachable work record of 32 years. Those arguments should suffice for the Presidium of the Supreme Soviet. I will add, for your information, that my wife was unjustly and illegally convicted even from a purely formal point of view. In reality she was convicted for being my wife and to prevent her from traveling abroad.

I repeat my assurance that her trip has no purpose other than to seek medical treatment and to visit her mother, children and grandchildren; it is not intended to effect any change in my situation. My wife can supply the appropriate pledges herself. She may also pledge not to disclose the details of my confinement in the hospital if that is made a condition for her departure.

I am the only Academician in the history of the Academy of Sciences of the U.S.S.R. and Russia whose wife has been convicted as a criminal, subjected to a malicious, vile campaign of public slander and deprived of all communication with her mother, children and grandchildren. I am the only academician whose responsibility for his actions and opinions has been shifted onto his wife. That is my situation, and it is unbearable for me. I hope you will help.

If you and the Academy's presidium do not find it possible to support me in this tragic matter, which is so vital for me, or if your intervention and other efforts do not lead to resolution of the problem before March 1, 1985, *I ask that this letter be regarded as my resignation from the U.S.S.R. Academy of Sciences.* I will renounce my title of full member of the Academy—a proud title for me in other circumstances. I will renounce all my rights and privileges connected with that title, including my salary as an academician —a significant step since I have no savings.

If my wife is not allowed to travel abroad, I cannot remain a member of the Academy of Sciences. I will not and should not participate in a great international deceit in which my academy membership would play a part.

I repeat: I am counting on your help.

Oct. 15, 1984   Respectfully,

Gorky   A. Sakharov

P.S. If this letter is intercepted by the KGB, *I will still resign from the Academy* and the KGB will be responsible. I should mention that I sent you four telegrams and a letter during my hunger strike.

P.P.S. This letter is handwritten because my typewriter (together with books, diaries, manuscripts, cameras, a tape recorder, and a radio) was seized during a search.

P.P.P.S. I ask you to confirm receipt of this letter.

Translated by Nicholas Bethell and Richard Lourie

IX

The Gorky Tapes

The cooperation between the West German mass-circulation newspaper *Bild* and Soviet "journalist" Victor Louis apparently began in June 1984, when *Bild* published, on June 19, two pictures of the Sakharovs, as proof that they were alive. Separate photos of Elena Bonner and Andrei Sakharov, taken allegedly on May 12 and 15 were, said *Bild*, provided by Louis, who has been widely regarded for many years as an unofficial channel to the Western media for the Soviet government, and particularly for the KGB. In the last three years he has become a major authority on the Sakharovs' case, providing reports and commentaries, denying or confirming rumors. For example, on May 29, 1986, on the eve of Bonner's meeting with British Prime Minister Margaret Thatcher, Louis for the first time praised Sakharov, who is, he declared, "on our side of the barricades" and "is respected by the overwhelming majority of the Russian people." However, according to Louis, Sakharov's return to Moscow had been jeopardized by Bonner's misbehavior abroad.

The first videotape—showing Sakharov in a hospital and Bonner on the streets of Gorky in June and July 1984, and also containing some earlier footage—was released by *Bild* on August 24, 1984. *Bild* implied that it came from Victor Louis, the "same source" as had the two photographs published in June. As of the summer of 1986, seven more videotapes of a similar nature, ranging from 10 to 40 minutes in length, have been released by *Bild*. Most of these have been purchased and run, in full or in excerpts, by European TV stations and by ABC News in the United States.

The following is a brief chronology of subsequent *Bild* releases:

December 15, 1984. Photographs of the Sakharovs in a park and at the entrance to a movie theatre, taken presumably in October. Release of the pictures concided with Mikhail Gorbachev's arrival in London.

June 28, 1985. Two videotapes: Sakharov undergoing a medical checkup, apparently in the spring of 1985; and Sakharov in a hospital room, mostly eating in bed, allegedly in early June. The tapes also featured Dr. Natalia Evdokimova, who denied that Sakharov was on a hunger strike or that he was being treated with psychotropic drugs. She presented a list of the medical problems which were supposedly keeping him in the Semashko hospital.

July 29, 1985. The videotape showing Sakharov being discharged from the hospital July 11 and reunited with Elena Bonner, the Sakharovs walking the streets of Gorky, etc. Released by *Bild* on the eve of a high-level meeting in Helsinki commemorating the tenth anniversary of the Helsinki Accords. By that time Sakharov was again in the hospital on a hunger strike.

December 9, 1985. Bonner is shown in a local OVIR office discussing her travel plans, then in a dentist's chair. Sakharov, answering questions posed by chief physician Dr. Oleg Obukhov, explains the Soviet position on arms control, and his own views on this subject and on the Star Wars program. Sakharov sees Bonner off at the Gorky train station. Bonner is pictured in front of her Moscow apartment and then at Sheremetyevo Airport, surrounded by friends and the Moscow foreign press corps.

March 24, 1986. Sakharov in a telephone booth at a local post office gets an overseas call from Elena Bonner. The recording of the conversation is then superimposed on shots of Sakharov walking, visiting a garage, pushing his car in the snow. Sakharov visits a physician, Dr. Ariadna Obukhova, then is again shown engaged with her husband, Dr. Oleg Obukhov, in a heavily edited discussion of arms control issues. In both videotapes, those of December 1985 and March 1986, Sakharov appears to be supportive of the Soviet position on arms control.

May 30, 1986. Sakharov discusses the Chernobyl accident with a young man who introduces himself as a correspondent from a local newspaper, and with passers-by. His views on the accident are contrasted with Bonner's interpretation of Sakharov's views on nuclear energy, as presented in the Italian weekly *Il Sabato.*

June 18, 1986. A tape recording of a conversation between Elena Bonner and Andrei Sakharov, apparently obtained by bugging their apartment, is superimposed on footage of the Sakharovs walking the streets of Gorky. On the tape, Bonner reproaches Sakharov for being provoked into conversations for the benefit of KGB cameras.

Efrem Yankelevich

Index

269

A Note on the Type

This book was set in a digitized version of Janson. The hot-metal version of Janson was a recutting made direct from type cast from matrices long thought to have been made by the Dutchman Anton Janson, who was a practicing type founder in Leipzig during the years 1668–1687. However, it has been conclusively demonstrated that these types are actually the work of Nicholas Kis (1650–1702), a Hungarian, who most probably learned his trade from the master Dutch type founder Dirk Voskens. The type is an excellent example of the influential and sturdy Dutch types that prevailed in England up to the time William Caslon (1692–1766) developed his own incomparable designs from them.

Composed by ComCom, Allentown, Pennsylvania

Printed and bound by the Haddon Craftsmen, Inc.
Scranton, Pennsylvania

Designed by Virginia Tan